THRILLERS

Martin Rubin

CAMBRIDGE
UNIVERSITY PRESS

PUBLISHED BY THE PRESS SYNDICATE OF THE UNIVERSITY OF CAMBRIDGE
The Pitt Building, Trumpington Street, Cambridge, United Kingdom

CAMBRIDGE UNIVERSITY PRESS
The Edinburgh Building, Cambridge CB2 2RU, UK   http://www.cup.cam.ac.uk
40 West 20th Street, New York, NY 10011-4211, USA   http://www.cup.org
10 Stamford Road, Oakleigh, Melbourne 3166, Australia

First published 1999

Printed in the United States of America

Typeface Cheltenham 9.5/13 pt.   *System* QuarkXpress® [MG]

A catalog record for this book is available from the British Library

Library of Congress Cataloging-in-Publication Data
Rubin, Martin, 1947–
    Thrillers / Martin Rubin.
        p.   cm. – (Genres in American cinema)
    Filmography: p.
    Includes bibliographical references.
    ISBN 0-521-58183-4 (hb.) – ISBN 0-521-58839-1 (pbk.)
        1. Suspense in motion pictures.   2. Detective and mystery films –
    History and criticism.   3. Spy films – History and criticism.   4. Police films –
    History and criticism.   I. Title.   II. Series.
    PN1995.9.S87R83   1999
    791.43´6 – dc21   98–38139
                                                                        CIP

ISBN 0 521 58183 4 hardback
ISBN 0 521 58839 1 paperback

THRILLERS

The thriller is perhaps the most popular and widespread movie genre – and the most difficult to define. Thrillers can contain gangsters or ghosts, space helmets or fedoras. They charge our familiar modern world with a spirit of exotic, old-fashioned adventure. They give us pleasure by making us uncomfortable: Anxiety, vulnerability, and fright are all part of the thrill.

Thrillers provides the first comprehensive, in-depth treatment of the movie thriller, from silent serials to stalker films, from Alfred Hitchcock to Quentin Tarantino, from *The Great Train Robbery* to *L.A. Confidential*. Martin Rubin's accessible, wide-ranging volume – designed to appeal to students and general filmgoers alike – shows how this visceral, supercharged genre has employed suspense, speed, and sensation to keep us on the edge of our seats throughout a century of American cinema.

Martin Rubin was the Film Program Director of the New York Cultural Center and an Associate Director of the San Francisco Film Festival. He has taught film courses at various institutions, and his publications include the book *Showstoppers: Busby Berkeley and the Tradition of Spectacle.*

GENRES IN AMERICAN CINEMA

General Editor
Barry Keith Grant, *Brock University, Ontario, Canada*

Genres in American Cinema examines the significance of American films in a series of single-authored volumes, each dedicated to a different genre. Each volume will provide a comprehensive account of its genre, from enduring classics to contemporary revisions, from marginal appropriations to international inflections, emphasizing its distinctive qualities as well as its cultural, historical, and critical contexts. Their approach will be methodologically broad, balancing theoretical and historical discussion with close readings of representative films. Designed for use as classroom texts, the books will be intellectually rigorous, yet written in a style that is lively and accessible to students and general audiences alike.

To Penney
You thrill me . . .

Contents

Illustrations

Acknowledgments

For generous assistance:
Fred Camper, Adrian Curry, Charles Derry, Terry Geesken, Michael Gnat, Chris Hart, Ron Magliozzi, Gelah Penn, Anne Sanow, and Charles Silver.

For finding a message in a bottle:
Barry Grant.

Stills are courtesy of Academy of Motion Picture Arts and Sciences, Larry Edmunds Bookshop, the Museum of Modern Art Film Stills Archive, Jerry Ohlinger's Movie Material Store, and the author's personal collection.

PART ONE

Approaches

1

Introduction

The label *thriller* is widely used but highly problematic. To the foolhardy writer setting out to define the subject, it might seem impossibly broad and vague.

The American mass-circulation magazine *TV Guide* includes "Thriller" as one of the categories used to describe the movies in its weekly listings. However, the way this label is applied seems more arbitrary than illuminating. In one randomly selected week, the tongue-in-cheek horror film *Basket Case* (1982) was listed as a Thriller, while its sequel *Basket Case 2* (1990) was deemed a Comedy. *Black Widow* (1987), in which a policewoman sets out to snare a psychotic femme fatale who targets wealthy businessmen, was designated a Thriller, whereas *The Banker* (1989), in which a policeman sets out to snare a psychotic businessman who targets prostitutes, was considered a Crime Drama. Michael Crichton's *Looker* (1981), mixing speculative technology with murder investigation, was listed as a Thriller, yet the similarly themed *Coma* (1978, directed by Crichton) and *The Terminal Man* (1974, based on a Crichton novel) came under the headings of Mystery and Science Fiction, respectively.

An anthology series entitled *Thriller,* hosted by horror icon Boris Karloff, ran on the NBC network from 1960 to 1962, during which time it presented a wide-ranging variety of ghost, horror, mystery, spy, gangster, and crime stories – backed by the host's authoritative assertion, "Let me assure you, my friends, *this* is a thriller!" Lawrence Hammond's 1974 book *Thriller Movies* and John McCarty's 1992 book *Thrillers* both specifically exclude horror films from their surveys; but the lyrics of pop singer Michael Jackson's 1982 hit "Thriller" (as well as the visuals of its music video) concentrate exclusively on horror-film imagery.

A *genre* is a set of conventions and shared characteristics that have historically evolved into a distinct, widely recognized type of composition within an art form. The pastoral poem, the Christmas carol, and the still-life painting are examples of genres within their respective art forms. In terms of the forms of fictional film and literature covered in this book, *genre* refers to a certain conventionalized category of story, such as detective, western, science fiction, and horror.

One cannot consider the thriller a genre in the same way that one considers, say, the western or science fiction a genre. The range of stories that have been called thrillers is simply too broad. Films as diverse as the stalker horror movie *Halloween* (1978), the hard-boiled detective film *The Big Sleep* (1946), the Harold Lloyd comedy *Safety Last* (1923), the grim police drama *Seven* (1995), the colorful Hitchcock spy film *North by Northwest* (1959), the seaborne disaster film *The Poseidon Adventure* (1972), the science-fiction monster movie *Alien* (1979), and the early serial *The Perils of Pauline* (1914) can all be considered thrillers.

The concept of "thriller" falls somewhere between a genre proper and a descriptive quality that is attached to other, more clearly defined genres – such as spy thriller, detective thriller, horror thriller. There is possibly no such thing as a pure, freestanding "thriller thriller." The thriller can be conceptualized as a "metagenre" that gathers several other genres under its umbrella, and as a band in the spectrum that colors each of those particular genres.

Because of the amorphous boundaries of the thriller, this book has a multichanneled focus. It deals with several genres to which the concept of thriller can be applied and extracts the overarching, "thrilleresque" common denominators that link them. This thrilleresque quality is more compatible with some genres than with others. It attaches itself easily to such genres as spy, horror, and various subsets of the crime film; other genres, such as westerns, musicals, and war films, are less receptive. On the other hand, within a single genre – for example, science fiction – there may be some films that are clearly thrillers (e.g., the 1956 alien-invasion drama *Invasion of the Body Snatchers*) and others that do not fit the label so well (e.g., the 1971 satiric fable *A Clockwork Orange*). To help clarify this issue, Chapter 6 compares two detective films, one a thriller, the other not – or much less so.

Genre analysts such as Tzvetan Todorov, Fredric Jameson, and Rick Altman have proposed that a genre comprises two types of element: *semantic* (i.e., related to the specific signs used to produce meaning) and *syntactic* (i.e., related to the general relationships between those signs).[1] Another way of stating this concept is that a genre operates on two interrelated levels: a level of specific themes and iconography (e.g., cowboys, saloons, six-shooters, Southwestern landscapes, revenge themes in the western) and a level of general relationships, patterns, and structural elements (e.g., again in the western: the opposition between wilderness and civilization, the fraternal relationship between hero and villain, the hero's movement between social rejection and acceptance). In thrillers, because of the widely varying forms they can take, the presence of iconographic elements that conventionally connote "thriller" is weak or nonexistent. (A thriller might contain gangsters or ghosts, fedoras or space helmets.) Although some of the iconographic and thematic elements of individual thriller-related genres are mentioned when those genres are covered in this book, its attempt to define the thriller necessarily concentrates on conceptual, relational, and structural elements.

The remainder of this introductory chapter deals with concepts that are applicable to the thriller itself rather than to its position amid the constellation of genres. These are basic, general concepts; more advanced and specific concepts are covered mainly in Chapter 2, as well as in some of the film-analysis chapters (Part III).

The thriller is a *quantitative* as well as a qualitative concept. It involves not just the presence of certain qualities but also the extent to which they are present. Virtually all narrative films could be considered thrilling to some degree, because they contain suspense and action and a sense of departure from the routine world into a realm that is more marvelous and exciting. At a certain hazy point, however, they become thrilling enough to be considered thrillers. The thriller is by nature an imprecise concept, loosely and at times arbitrarily applied – as indicated by the above citations of the *TV Guide* movie listings and the *Thriller* television series.

In relation to the issue of quantity, the thriller often involves an *excess* of certain qualities and feelings beyond the necessity of the narrative: too much atmosphere, action, suspense – too much, that is, in terms of what is strictly necessary to tell the story – so that these thrilling elements, to a certain extent, become an end in themselves.

Important to the concept of thriller is not just an excess of feelings but the question of *which* feelings are emphasized. The thriller works primarily to evoke such feelings as suspense, fright, mystery, exhilaration, excitement, speed, movement. In other words, it emphasizes visceral, gut-level feelings rather than more sensitive, cerebral, or emotionally heavy feelings, such as tragedy, pathos, pity, love, nostalgia. In a 1963 essay entitled "How to Write a Thriller," Ian Fleming, creator of the superspy James Bond, stated that his books were aimed "some-where between the solar plexus and, well, the upper thigh."[2] The thrill-er stresses *sensations* more than sensitivity. It is a sensational form. This property links the thriller to the sensation-oriented "cinema of at-tractions" prominent in early film history (see Chapter 3). It also links the thriller to such popular amusements as the carnival, fun house, Fer-ris wheel, merry-go-round, and roller coaster – a link that is sometimes literalized by having these devices conspicuously featured in the films themselves. Examples include the baroque fun house that climaxes Orson Welles's topsy-turvy film noir *The Lady from Shanghai* (1948), the Viennese Ferris wheel on which the disoriented hero meets the enig-matic Harry Lime in Carol Reed's postwar thriller *The Third Man* (1949), the merry-go-round that goes berserk at the end of Alfred Hitchcock's *Strangers on a Train* (1951) [Fig. 1], the title attraction wherein several foolish teenagers tempt fate in Tobe Hooper's horror film *The Funhouse* (1981), and the various rides and attractions through which the police-men scramble in John Landis's comedy-thriller *Beverly Hills Cop III* (1994), much of which is set in a Disneyland-like amusement park.

The thriller involves not just the presence of certain feelings in ex-cess but also a *combination* of those feelings. Just as a roller coaster makes us laugh *and* scream, the thriller often works to double emo-tions, feelings, sensations: humor *and* suspense, fear *and* excitement, pleasure *and* pain. Harold Lloyd, in his silent-comedy "thrill pictures," sought to combine laughter and fright in a way that sharpened both responses; Alfred Hitchcock, in such classic thrillers as *The 39 Steps* (1935) and *North by Northwest,* joined comedy and suspense in a mu-tually reinforcing manner.

These doubled emotional responses also involve *ambivalence.* The viewer is pulled in opposite directions – between anxiety and pleasure, masochism and sadism, identification and detachment – and this ten-sion is a great part of what gives thrillers their kick. A thriller works to undermine our emotional stability (in contrast to the whodunit, a very stable form, as discussed in Chapter 6). It creates an off-balance ef-fect. The viewer is suspended between conflicting feelings – and this suspension is related to the concept of suspense, one of the primary ingredients of the thriller (see Chapters 2 and 7).

The overload and combination and ambivalence of feelings that the thriller creates, with a resultant lack of stability, produce a strong sen-sation of *vulnerability.* As on a roller coaster or in a fun house, there is a certain loss of control that constitutes an important part of the thrill.

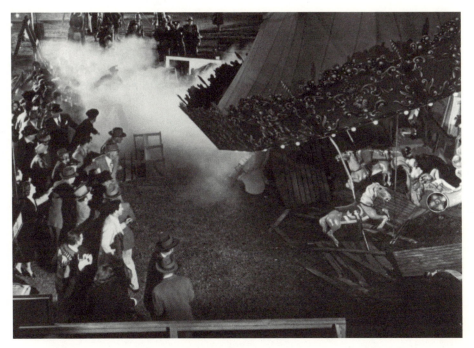

Figure 1. *Strangers on a Train:* End of the ride on a berserk merry-go-round. (The Museum of Modern Art Film Stills Archive)

Thrillers characteristically feature a remarkable degree of passivity on the part of the heroes with whom we as spectators identify. These heroes are often acted upon more than they act; they are swept up in a rush of events over which they have little control. The thriller creates, in both hero and spectator, a strong sense of being carried away, of surrendering oneself. Control–vulnerability is a central dialectic of the thriller, closely related to sadism–masochism. The thriller is a form with strong sadomasochistic appeal: We derive pleasure from watching characters suffer (e.g., Cary Grant hanging from the edge of a cliff in *North by Northwest*), but we ourselves also suffer by virtue of identifying with those characters. The thriller puts both hero and audience through the wringer.

Of possible relevance to these issues is the etymology of the word *thrill,* which comes from a Middle English root meaning "to pierce." This association relates to the aggressive, sadomasochistic nature of the thriller, and also to its visceral, sensational side: A thrill is a sharp sensation, as if one had been pierced or pricked by a sharp instrument.

Also intriguing is the similarity between the words *thrill* and *thrall* (slave, captive). These meanings come together in the word *enthrall,* which carries connotations both of being enslaved, captured, and of being thrilled, spellbound. Similarly, in a thriller, it is as if we give our-selves up to be captured, carried away, in order to be thrilled, to re-ceive a series of sharp sensations.

2

Critical Overview

The existence of critical and theoretical writings that deal explicitly with the thriller as a general category (rather than with one particular thriller-related genre, such as detective or horror) is limited. The majority of the few books that have been written on the general subject of the movie thriller – such as Brian Davis's *The Thriller* (1973), Lawrence Hammond's *Thriller Movies* (1974), and John McCarty's *Thrillers* (1992) – are primarily picture books that provide descriptions of several thrillers, with a minimal effort to define the underlying concepts that distinguish the thriller from other types of movies. More substantial approaches have been offered by academics Ralph Harper, Jerry Palmer, and, especially, Charles Derry.

Charles Derry, Ralph Harper, Jerry Palmer: Thrillers in General

In *The Suspense Thriller* (1988), Charles Derry, a genre-studies specialist who has also written books on the horror film and on the TV series *thirtysomething,* takes a taxonomic approach to the movie thriller: He is primarily concerned with classifying different categories of thriller rather than with tracing the historical evolution of the form. Derry limits his discussion of the "suspense thriller" to crime films that lack a central, traditional detective figure and that feature a protagonist who is either an innocent victim or a nonprofessional criminal (e.g., the scheming lovers of many a film noir). He excludes from his defined area several types of film to which the loose label of thriller has been frequently applied, including detective films (hard-boiled as well as whodunit – see Chapter 6), police films, heist films, horror films, and spy films whose hero is a professional spy. Derry finds nonprofessional and/or victim protagonists essential to the suspense thriller, because these characters are placed in unfamiliar situations that enhance their vulnerability and thereby produce greater suspense.[1] The present book also notes the special advantages of the amateur-protagonist case but allows that other varieties can provide sufficient suspense, vulnerability, and mystification to qualify fully as thrillers.

Similarly to myself, Derry sees the suspense thriller as a broad "umbrella genre" that cuts across several more clearly defined genres.[2] However, rather than classifying different types of thriller according to traditional, widely recognized generic categories, such as spy, detective, and film noir, Derry proposes fresh categories based upon the films' thematic and plot content (e.g., the thriller of acquired identity, the thriller of moral confrontation, the innocent-on-the-run thriller).

Derry also introduces concepts drawn from two books written by specialists in the field of psychology: Michael Balint's *Thrills and Regressions* (1959), which discusses thrills in terms of the subject's attraction or aversion to dangerous situations, and Altan Löker's *Film and Suspense* (1976), which sees cinematic suspense as deriving mainly from the creation of a sense of guilt in the spectator. These psychological concepts are only lightly and intermittently applied in the bulk of Derry's book, which consists of often perceptive analyses of numerous thrillers and the categories into which they are grouped. The analytic sections of *The Suspense Thriller* rely primarily on the identification of recurring narrative patterns in the various thriller subgenres. Derry's approach here recalls that of the folklorist Vladimir Propp, whose methodology, famously used to analyze Russian fairy tales, has become a cornerstone of genre theory. Derry makes an especially convincing case in these terms for the "innocent-on-the-run" film as a coherent genre – quintessentially represented by the Hitchcock classics *The 39 Steps* (1935) and *North by Northwest* (1959) and also encompassing such films as the bleak conspiracy thriller *The Parallax View* (1974), the train-based comedy-thriller *Silver Streak* (1976), and the nightmarish farce *After Hours* (1985).

The thriller has been dealt with specifically as a literary form in Ralph Harper's *The World of the Thriller* (1969) and Jerry Palmer's *Thrillers* (1979). Harper, a humanities professor specializing in existential philosophy, interprets the thriller in terms of his specialty. He compares the central concerns of classic thriller authors, such as John Buchan and Graham Greene, to those of existential philosophers, such as Sören Kierkegaard and Karl Jaspers, and of major novelists frequently associated with existentialism, such as Fyodor Dostoyevsky and Franz Kafka.

According to Harper, thrillers (especially spy thrillers) simulate existentialism by envisioning a modern world filled with chaos and absurdity. Like the solitary individual examined and exalted by existentialism, the thriller hero is cut off from his previously secure bearings of community, habit, tradition, and religious assurance. He is thrust out in the cold (as spy novelist John le Carré might put it) or "thrown into the world" (in the words of existential philosopher Jean-Paul Sartre) and placed in crisis situations where he must nakedly confront absolute questions of identity, morality, faith, and death.[3] However, Harper notes, the thriller is a hybrid form, softening the stark extremes of existentialism with more reassuring notions of heroism and poetic justice, whereby individual effort is ultimately effective and a sense of moral order is at least temporarily restored.[4]

Although brief, Harper's book is quite diffuse, its ideas presented in the form of random observations rather than a structured argument. *The World of the Thriller* is peppered with intriguing insights that are left frustratingly underdeveloped. The book fails to establish that the existential dimension of thrillers amounts to much more than a miscellany of superficial resemblances, or that it accounts for more than a small fraction of the thriller's central concerns, or that it sufficiently distinguishes the thriller from other forms of action-oriented "crisis fiction," notably the war novel and the adventure tale.

Thrillers, by the British communications professor Jerry Palmer, is a wider-ranging effort, attempting to define the thriller in terms of its basic structure, literary roots, ideology, and sociological background. Palmer's central premise is distinguished by its elegant simplicity. In his view, the thriller can be reduced to just two essential components: a hero and a conspiracy. The basic thriller plot consists simply of the hero defeating the conspiracy.[5]

Palmer requires of the thriller hero a certain stature and ability: He (as in Harper's book, the possibility of a thriller heroine is neither excluded nor mentioned) must be "professional" and "competitive." In Palmer's terms, this means that the hero is uniquely competent. He is not an amateur or "average citizen"; he remains self-reliant and isolated (thereby diminishing the possibility of love); and he is successful – he always defeats the conspiracy. By these criteria, Palmer nominates as quintessential thriller heroes the superspy James Bond and the supertough private eye Mike Hammer.[6]

Moreover, Palmer insists that the thriller hero monopolize the reader's sympathy and allegiance. We must approve of the hero's actions and adopt his moral perspective to the virtual exclusion of all others; this unequivocal desire to see the hero succeed is what, in Palmer's view, creates thriller suspense. It is therefore possible to have suspense even if the outcome is predictable or the solution already known; what is important is that the reader identify wholeheartedly with a hero who is perplexed.[7]

The conspiracy is the evil design that the hero opposes. The common definition of conspiracy as a plural activity, involving a group of conspirators, is not specified by Palmer; he does not seem to exclude the possibility of a conspiracy involving a single evildoer. However, he does require that the conspiracy be serious enough to pose a broad threat against the normal social order and to require extraordinary measures for defeating it; purely personal injuries and vendettas do not qualify. Also essential is that the conspiracy be mysterious. The evil design must be largely hidden from the hero; otherwise, it is merely an obstacle, not a conspiracy.[8]

Palmer allows for the possibility of the *negative thriller,* practiced by such writers as Dashiell Hammett, Raymond Chandler, and John le Carré. The negative thriller offers some secondary variations but essentially conforms to the basic pattern. Our attitude toward the hero may be ambivalent, but it is still unchallenged – we do not approve of any character more than him. The hero's final triumph may be qualified by a sense of regret or impermanence, but he is still triumphant – outright defeat is not an option.[9]

Palmer's model for the thriller, though admirably concise, upon application seems both too loose and too restrictive. On the one hand, the generality of Palmer's definition allows him to include as thrillers many works commonly excluded or placed on the margins by other critics. For example, Palmer unequivocally includes the classical (or whodunit) detective story, because it fulfills the basic requirements of a hero and a conspiracy. (See Chapter 6 for a contrasting view of the whodunit.) This inclusion of the whodunit is a legitimately debatable position; however, Palmer's definition seems insufficiently precise to differentiate the thriller from many melodramas and courtroom dramas, particularly those in which a conspiracy operates to besmirch the reputation or otherwise inhibit the happiness of an undeserving victim. Examples include D. W. Griffith's wronged-woman melodrama *Way Down East* (1920), Frank Capra's greed-versus-decency fables *Meet John Doe* (1941) and *It's a Wonderful Life* (1946), Joseph L. Mankiewicz's scheming-actress tale *All about Eve* (1950), Jonathan Demme's anti-homophobia tract *Philadelphia* (1993), Jane Campion's Henry James adaptation *The Portrait of a Lady* (1996), and countless TV soap-opera plot lines. Perhaps some of these might be disqualified on the grounds of the hero/ine's insufficient professionalism or the narrowly personal focus of the conspiracy. However, such disqualifications would be less applicable to the thriller's sister genre, the adventure tale (discussed in the following section on G. K. Chesterton) – for example, *Tarzan and His Mate* (1934), in which the eminently heroic King of the Jungle prevails against an ivory-poaching conspiracy, and *Raiders of the Lost Ark* (1981), in which the indisputably professional and competitive Indiana Jones foils a Nazi scheme to obtain a potent religious relic.

On the other hand, the often categorical quality of Palmer's secondary requirements excludes many films and books and film versions of those books that are widely considered classic thrillers. Just a few examples include Graham Greene's 1939 espionage novel *The Confidential Agent* (agonizingly nonprofessional hero), Patricia Highsmith's 1955 novel *The Talented Mr. Ripley* and its 1960 film version *Purple Noon* (*Plein Soleil*) (told from the evil conspirator's perspective, thereby eliminating the mystery factor), Richard Condon's 1959 novel *The Manchurian Candidate* and its 1962 film version (perspective split between hero and antihero), Alfred Hitchcock's 1960 film *Psycho* (no dominant hero or moral perspective), Alan J. Pakula's 1974 film *The Parallax View* (hero defeated, conspiracy triumphant), and many other possible candidates whose exclusion would unnecessarily impoverish the history of the thriller.

In the absence of sufficiently comprehensive texts on the subject, I have attempted to construct piecemeal a general concept of the movie thriller by drawing from writings on (1) specific thriller-related literary genres, both popular (such as detective and spy fiction) and classical (such as comedy and heroic romance), and (2) certain relevant general topics, such as the labyrinth and suspense. The very breadth and vagueness of the thriller category understandably discourage efforts to define it precisely. Hopefully, the following discussion provides some useful parameters for mapping out this sprawling subject without defining it so narrowly as to exclude many works that, by common sense and common usage, belong within the wide domain of the thriller.

G. K. Chesterton: The Transformed City

As a starting point, I have selected G. K. Chesterton's "A Defence of Detective Stories," a pioneer statement of key thriller concepts. This brief essay is included in Chesterton's 1901 collection *The Defendant,* wherein the author declares his fondness for certain overlooked treasures of the familiar world. Chesterton, a prolific British author of the early twentieth century, particularly excelled as a journalist, essayist, and literary critic. However, he is best remembered today for the series of detective tales he wrote (beginning in 1910) featuring the amateur sleuth Father Brown, a clergyman whose humble, deceptively pedestrian manner offers a striking contrast to the eccentric flair of the most famous fictional detective of the day, Sherlock Holmes.

In the selected essay, Chesterton sets out to rescue detective stories from the low regard in which they are held for being specimens of popular literature. In terms similar to those that film critic Robin Wood would use over sixty years later to redeem the Hollywood output of Alfred Hitchcock, Chesterton establishes the detective genre's credentials as "a perfectly legitimate form of art" by comparing it to accepted classics such as Shakespeare's plays and Homer's *Iliad*.[10] Although specifically about the detective story, the essay advances concepts that are central to nearly all types of thriller. Particularly crucial is Chesterton's evocative description of how the detective story transforms the everyday world into a marvelous realm filled with menace and adventure. The essay's elaboration of this basic concept raises several other related issues that are applicable to thrillers in general.

The world of the thriller is an essentially *modern* world. Chesterton asserts that the detective story is "the earliest and only form of popular literature in which is expressed some sense of the poetry of modern life."[11] The world described by Chesterton is an *urban* world. He calls the detective story "a rude, popular literature of the romantic possibilities of the modern city" – much as the modern city is the primary (though not exclusive) locale of most types of thriller.[12] Chesterton sees a new and largely untapped source for romantic grandeur in such mundane details of urban life as chimney pots and lampposts:

Men lived among mighty mountains and eternal forests for ages before they realised that they were poetical; it may reasonably be inferred that some of our descendants may see the chimney-pots as rich a purple as the mountain-peaks, and find the lamp-posts as old and natural as the trees.[13]

The thriller invests this modern urban environment with an archaic and even *primitive* sense of the marvelous, the wild, and the adventurous. Chesterton's prose evokes mountain peaks, forests, princes, elves, goblins, and fairy ships, all shimmering through the mundane and "casual" surface of the now-transformed city:

No one can have failed to notice that in these stories the hero or the investigator crosses London with something of the loneliness and liberty of a prince in a tale of elfland, that in the course of that incalculable journey the casual omnibus assumes the primal colours of a fairy ship. The lights of the city begin to glow like innumerable goblin eyes, since they are the guardians of some secret, however crude, which the writer knows and the reader does not. Every twist of the road is like a finger pointing to it; every fantastic skyline of chimney-pots seems wildly and derisively signalling the meaning of the mystery.[14]

As intimated by Chesterton's pioneer appreciation of detective stories, the thriller characteristically takes place in modern times, not in the bygone, inherently adventurous days of knights, pirates, and cowboys. It is situated in the mundane, realistic world, not in a marvelous realm of dragons and genies. It is most often set in the cramped, crowded city, not in the traditionally heroic domain of vast forests and mighty mountains. Nonetheless, in the thriller, it is as if this modern, mundane, metropolitan context has become filled with the spirit of older, larger, wilder, more marvelous, and more adventurous realms.

These considerations – the thriller going against the grain of mundane modern life while at the same time remaining immersed in it – suggest that the thriller, in all its diverse and loosely defined variations, is an essentially modern form, whose rise coincides with the advent of urban industrialism, mass society, middle-class life-style, and the twentieth century. In other words, the thriller is a response to a modern world that is perceived under normal circumstances to be fundamentally not thrilling. As Alfred Hitchcock wrote in a 1936 magazine article, "Our civilization has so screened and sheltered us that it isn't practicable to experience sufficient thrills at firsthand."[15] The thriller seeks to redeem the nonadventurous modern world with a spirit of old-fashioned adventure. That this adventurous and heroic past may be more imaginary than real is not as important as the fact that it continues to function as a mythical standard against which the present is measured.

These concepts explain why one normally does not think of westerns as thrillers, even though they often contain a great deal of action, adventure, chases, and suspense. The crucial distinction is that the West – the frontier, the wilderness – is in itself *already* a highly adventurous environment. It does not need to be made adventurous or have adventure imported into it. In fact, in westerns the movement is in the opposite direction: The frontier is being tamed by the coming of civilization, which eventually transforms it into the type of nonadventurous environment from which the thriller may then emerge as a response. Only after the West is settled and civilized and urbanized does it become the appropriate setting for a thriller – as in the acclaimed detective thriller *Chinatown* (1974), which is set in the citified West, not the Wild West.

Similar considerations distinguish the thriller from a very closely related and often overlapping form: the adventure story. Represented by such novelists as Robert Louis Stevenson (*Treasure Island,* 1883), H. Rider Haggard (*King Solomon's Mines,* 1885), Rudyard Kipling (*Kim,* 1901), Joseph Conrad (*Heart of Darkness,* 1902), and many others, the adventure story precedes the thriller chronologically. It is historically connected to the heyday of imperialism, when the colonial empires of the major Western European powers (especially Great Britain) were at their peaks.[16]

Though less dominant after World War I, the adventure genre has survived in reasonably good health, as evidenced by the work of such popular authors as C. S. Forester (*The African Queen,* 1935), Desmond Bagley (*The Spoilers,* 1968), Wilbur Smith (*The Eye of the Tiger,* 1975), and Michael Crichton (*Jurassic Park,* 1990), and by such recent films as the Indiana Jones series (1981, 1984, 1989), *Romancing the Stone* (1984), *Cliffhanger* (1993), *Congo* (1995), *The Ghost and the Darkness* (1996), *Anaconda* (1997), and *The Mask of Zorro* (1998).

Like the western, the adventure shares several central elements with the thriller. The crucial distinction between thriller and adventure lies in the fact that the latter is predominantly set in an environment that is already exotic, often primitive, and clearly removed from the realm of mundane, modern-day urban existence [Fig. 2]: the Amazon jungle, the Arabian desert, the South Seas. The elements of enchantment discerned by Chesterton to be peering out so thrillingly from beneath the contemporary urban surface of the detective story are up front and ubiquitous in the exotic world of the adventure story. The primary operation in adventure tales is a movement away from the ordinary world into an adventurous environment, rather than the bringing of those adventurous elements into the ordinary world.

The dividing line between the thriller and the adventure is a hazy one, involving a great deal of overlap and hybridization. Spy stories – especially those set largely in exotic locales (such as several Alistair MacLean novels and James Bond films) – often straddle the boundary between thriller and adventure. Among the films mentioned later in

Figure 2. *Raiders of the Lost Ark:* The already exotic environment of the adventure film . . .

this book, examples of thriller–adventure hybrids include *The Perils of Pauline* (1914), *The Spiders* (*Die Spinnen*) (1919–20), *King Kong* (1933), *The Wages of Fear* (*Le Salaire de la peur*) (1953), *Topkapi* (1964), *The Poseidon Adventure* (1972), and *Jaws* (1975). For instance, *Jaws* starts out more on the thriller side of the spectrum, with an uncommon element (the shark) heightening a commonplace context of suntan lotion, Frisbees, and flabby bodies on a crowded public beach. However, the film moves toward the adventure side in its last section, when the heroes leave behind the sphere of everyday existence and venture out into the high-seas territory of *Moby-Dick* and *Captains Courageous* to do primal battle with the great white shark.

A crucial condition for the thriller is a strong sense of *contrast* between two different dimensions. On the one hand, there is the ordinariness of the initial context, encompassing such factors as the setting, the hero's life-style, and the sociohistorical background (e.g., modern urban life, modern mass warfare). On the other hand, there are those ingredients (a murder, a monster, a vital secret, supernatural forces) that invade the ordinary context, transforming it into something adventurous and charged with a sense of the marvelous [Fig. 3] . . . but not completely, not permanently. There still remains a sense of tension that is not completely erased by the presence of the transforming elements. The thriller gives us a double world, which is both extraordinary and ordinary, adventurous and nonadventurous, and it remains to a significant extent suspended between those two contrasting sides.

Northrop Frye: Heroic Romance and the Low-Mimetic Mode

Another method of approaching this transformative aspect of thrillers is suggested by Northrop Frye's *Anatomy of Criticism* (1957). The Canadian Frye was a leading literary scholar of the postwar period whose work stresses the continued relevance of long-standing patterns and archetypes to the current study and practice of literature. *Anatomy of Criticism,* Frye's most influential book, envisions the history of literature as a system of cyclical phases, subdivided into such interrelated components as mode, myth, symbol, and genre. As part of this system, Frye identifies four broad narrative categories, which he associates with the cycle of the four seasons: comedy (spring), romance (summer), tragedy (autumn), and irony/satire (winter).[17]

For the purpose of defining the thriller, the category of greatest interest is the romance. In terms of its mode (a quality determined by the elevation of the characters), Frye categorizes romance as being one step below myth. Myth concerns a realm of divine and superhuman beings who accomplish feats that are inconceivable in our recognizable, familiar world. Romance, on the other hand, concerns a realm that is midway between myth and realism. The hero of romance is superior in degree but not in kind to other men and his (or her) environment. His actions may partake of the marvelous, but he is still characterized as a human being, not as a god or supernatural being. Frye specifies, "The hero of romance moves in a world in which the ordinary laws of nature are slightly suspended."[18]

An exemplary romantic world is the enchanted forest, a somewhat marvelous, dreamlike realm where the hero might encounter dragons, ogres, sorcerers, witches, and other extraordinary beings. A familiar form of romance is the chivalric or Arthurian romance, concerning knights and their heroic quests. According to Frye, the essential element of a romance plot is adventure. The romance has a centrifugal, wandering structure, often in the form of a journey or quest, moving episodically from one adventure to the next. It typically involves or-

Figure 3. . . . versus the thrilleresque transformation of an ordinary environment: Harold Lloyd in *Safety Last.*

deals that the hero must undergo, including a descent into a labyrinth or underworld.[19]

Frye draws a descending scale in which we move down through:

1. the *mythic* mode of gods
2. the *romantic* mode of marvelous heroes
3. the *high-mimetic* mode (the term *mimetic* here indicates a tendency toward verisimilitude) of epic and tragedy, whose heroes are superior to other men but not to their environment
4. the *low-mimetic* mode of most comedy and realistic fiction, in which the hero is superior neither to other men nor to the environment – he is "one of us," as Frye says[20]
5. the *ironic* mode, originating in a realistic world akin to that of the low-mimetic mode, but with mythic undertones that move us full circle back toward the beginning of the cycle, and with the hero inferior to us in intelligence and power.[21]

The hypothesis I wish to extrapolate from Frye's model is that the thriller is a descendant of romance, but lifted out of the romantic realm and placed in the low-mimetic realm. On the one hand, the thriller, grounded in a strong sense of mundane reality, with a hero who is generally "one of us," seems to operate in a domain that aligns it with the low-mimetic mode (although certain forms of thriller, such as film noir, may edge into the ironic mode). Frye, classifying the Sherlock Holmes–type detective story as a form of comedy, characterizes it in terms that are remarkably similar to (and perhaps derived from) Chesterton's: "an intensification of low mimetic, in the sharpening of attention to details that makes the dullest and most neglected trivia of daily living leap into mysterious and fateful significance."[22] On the other hand, some of the thriller's plot elements (such as monsters, journeys, quests, combats) and some of the attributes of its heroes (such as the superspies and supercops discussed in Chapter 5) evoke the more marvelous domain of the romance narrative.

This concept corresponds with the one derived from Chesterton's essay in the previous section: The thriller infuses traditionally adventurous and marvelous elements into the nonadventurous, nonmarvelous modern-day world. In this configuration, one might see the enchanted forest of romance as being supplanted by the prime thriller locale of the city. In the low-mimetic mode, according to Frye, the city takes "the shape of the labyrinthine modern metropolis, where the main emotional stress is on loneliness and lack of communication."[23]

Of central importance here is the close interrelationship among three narrative modes: romance, comedy, and thriller. Frye, as we've just seen, identifies the low-mimetic mode as the site of both realism and most comedy. By moving its component of romantic adventure into the low-mimetic world, the thriller is moving into the domain where comedy usually operates. Also, as noted, Frye places comedy (spring) and romance (summer) next to each other in the literary cycle, which is conceptualized as a continuous spectrum rather than a series of separate compartments. At their mutual border, comedy and romance shade into each other.[24] Frye breaks down comedy and romance into six subcategories each, and, in the subcategory of comedy that is closest to the borderline of romance, he places "ghost stories, thrillers, and Gothic romances." He describes these forms as being characterized by "secret and sheltered places . . . the love of the occult and the marvelous, the sense of individual detachment from routine existence."[25]

In this brief mention of the thriller, Frye seems to see it as a form of comedy that is aspiring toward a more heroic, adventurous realm. One could just as easily conceive of the thriller in these terms as a form of heroic romance that is descending into a more ordinary, unheroic, and in some ways comic world. This is, in fact, the basic approach that is taken in the present book. In any event, these two concepts complement more than contradict each other, because they share the basic assumption that the thriller is a form that falls somewhere between romance and comedy, the marvelous and the low mimetic, bridging their distinct but adjacent realms. The close affinity between thriller and comedy is examined again, from a different perspective, in the discussion of Harold Lloyd's "comedy of thrills" in Chapter 3.

John G. Cawelti: The Exotic

John G. Cawelti is a leading scholar of popular literature and film who is strongly influenced by Frye and shares his preoccupation with genre and archetypal patterns. Cawelti's work centers on the basic formulas underlying such genres as the western (in his 1970 study *The Six-Gun Mystique*) and the detective story (in his 1976 book *Adventure, Mystery, and Romance*).

In the latter book, Cawelti conceptualizes the detective story in terms similar to Chesterton's, describing how the genre transforms the city "from a modern center of commerce, industry, and science into a place of enchantment and mystery."[26] He notes the prominent use of Asian and Middle Eastern elements in such formative detective and crime stories (all wholly or substantially set in London) as Wilkie Collins's dazzling mystery *The Moonstone* (1868), Robert Louis Stevenson's story collection *The New Arabian Nights* (1882), Arthur Conan Doyle's Sherlock Holmes novella *The Sign of the Four* (1890), and Sax Rohmer's Fu Manchu series (1913–59). Adding another dimension to Chesterton's concept, Cawelti calls detective stories a new form of *The Arabian Nights* and describes their transformed city as a place "where figures from the heroic past and Exotic East walk abroad."[27]

This concept of the *exotic* functions as the geographical and cultural equivalent of the archaic and marvelous factors pointed out by Chesterton. The thriller's practice of removing the everyday world from its familiar context is often underscored by the introduction of elements that are literally foreign and unfamiliar – that is, exotic. In the period of the thriller's development, the primary conventional site of the exotic was Asia, in the stereotypical form of the Mysterious East. As films cited in the following chapters demonstrate, a number of thrillers prominently feature exotic (typically Far Eastern) motifs, decors, costumes, objects, characters, and locales: the hara-kiri ceremony of the Japanese envoy in *Spies* (*Spione,* 1928), the Middle Eastern origins of the title object in *The Maltese Falcon* (1941), the precious jade (revered by "the great rulers of the East") and Polynesian hangout (complete with exotic dancer in full Oriental regalia) in *Murder, My Sweet* (1944), the Oriental decor of Geiger's cottage and bookstore in *The Big Sleep* (1946) [Fig. 4], the Chinatown connections of the femme fatale in the exotically titled *The Lady from Shanghai* (1948), and the title, final locale, and Asian servants in *Chinatown* (1974). The presence of such exotic and foreign elements serves to signal the mysterious, alluring, and exciting world of the thriller, and to differentiate it from the more solid, domestic world that the thriller transforms.

Cawelti sees the exoticized, glamorized cities of classical detective stories as having been largely supplanted by the grittier, disenchanted urban visions of the later, hard-boiled style represented by such authors as Raymond Chandler and Mickey Spillane.[28] However, it might also be argued that such developments have often sharpened the thriller's central sense of a double world, at once poetic and prosaic, mysterious and mundane. The use of exotic motifs in the thriller has become less prominent in the past twenty-five years, because of changing econopolitical alignments and increased consciousness of the racist assumptions of "Orientalism" (famously analyzed by engagé literary scholar Edward W. Said).[29] The device has persisted, however, in such prominent thrillers as *Blade Runner* (1982), in which future Los Angeles seems to have become a suburb of Tokyo; *Gremlins* (1984), in which the troublesome critters originate from a Chinatown curio shop; and *Fatal Attraction* (1987), in the more muted form of the Japanese restaurant where the hero first meets his nemesis and the frequent references to the Japan-set opera *Madama Butterfly.* Other of Cawelti's concepts, more specific to the detective genre, are discussed in Chapter 6.

W. H. Matthews: Mazes and Labyrinths

A key descriptive figure for the heightened world of the thriller is the *labyrinth.* The origins of the labyrinth date back to the ancient Egyptians, who built such structures in connection with religious rituals and tombs. The most famous early labyrinth is found in the Greek myth of Theseus and the Minotaur. The following summary of this ancient tale is based primarily on the graceful rendition in H. A. Guerber's often-reprinted 1907 anthology *The Myths of Greece and Rome:*

Figure 4. *The Big Sleep:* Los Angeles sleuths (Humphrey Bogart, Lauren Bacall) amid exotic decor.

The island of Crete was ruled by King Minos. Minos' wife, Pasiphae, engaged in a passionate relationship with a bull. From this bestial union there resulted a monstrous offspring, half-bull and half-man, known as the Minotaur. King Minos engaged the services of Daedalus, a renowned builder and inventor, to fashion a structure to house the Minotaur. This was called the labyrinth, and it was a maze so devious that no one who went into it could find the way out.

The purpose of the Cretan labyrinth was twofold. One was to imprison the Minotaur – to conceal this shameful, man-eating monster and prevent him from preying upon the citizens of Crete. The other was to trap the Minotaur's victims. Every year, as a tribute, seven youths and seven maidens were sacrificed to the Minotaur. They were thrust, one by one, into the labyrinth, where they wandered around, hopelessly lost, until they fell into the clutches of the beast.

The Minotaur's victims were obtained forcibly by Minos from the city-state of Athens. The ruler of Athens was King Aegeus, and his son was Theseus, a great traveler and adventurer. Upon returning to Athens from one of his journeys, Theseus found the city plunged into gloom because the time was nigh to offer up fourteen young people for the Minotaur's consumption. Theseus resolved to put a stop to this cruel ritual, so he included himself among the tribute of fourteen and set off with them to Crete.

Arriving in Crete, Theseus caught the eye of Minos' daughter, the fair Ariadne, who immediately fell in love with him. Going behind her father's back, she secretly supplied Theseus with a sword and a ball of thread. As Theseus made his way into the labyrinth, he unwound the ball of thread to mark his path. He slew the Minotaur with the sword and then, retracing his steps, "made his way out of the mysterious maze and into the light of day."[30]

The story of Theseus' escape from the Minotaur contains, in implicit form, many of the ingredients of an archetypal thriller: a hero descending into a complicated, mazelike world in order to defeat the villain in a climactic duel and finally (to borrow Guerber's felicitous phrase) making his way out of the mysterious maze and into the light of day. That final phrase fits the conclusions of a remarkable number of movie thrillers, including several of those discussed elsewhere in this book, such as *Man Hunt* (1941), *The Lady from Shanghai, The Poseidon Adventure, The Texas Chain Saw Massacre* (1974), *The Funhouse* (1981), and *A Nightmare on Elm Street* (1984). One could even read the story as an embryonic spy thriller. Theseus is like an undercover agent, dispatched on a secret mission into enemy territory and posing as one of the tribute victims in order to infiltrate the labyrinth. Somewhat like James Bond, he uses his irresistibility to women to help him attain his goal. Finally, Theseus accomplishes his mission by cracking the secret, the code, the way out of the maze.

More broadly, the concept of the labyrinth is relevant to certain general properties of storytelling that are especially intensified in the thriller. This relationship is illuminated by W. H. Matthews's *Mazes and Labyrinths* (1922), a guide for designing mazes that was for many years a standard text on the subject. There are some striking parallels between the strategies Matthews describes for constructing a maze and the strategies frequently employed to construct stories in general and mystery and thriller stories in particular.

For instance, Matthews asserts that the design of the maze should attain a certain degree of complexity. If the maze is too easy to get out of, the pleasure of following it will be lost.[31] This guideline is similar to the mystery-story maxim that the solution should not be too simple or the culprit too obvious. It should be possible to reach the exit by deduction, by figuring out the design, rather than just by aimless trial and error, much as the solution to a good mystery should not be arbitrary or based on information withheld from the reader.[32] According to Matthews, the design of a labyrinth may be "compact" (wherein every bit of space is taken up by either the paths or the walls between them) or "diffuse" (wherein there are incidental areas beyond the path itself).[33] One could draw an analogy between the compact maze and the tight, centripetal structure of the whodunit, in which everything contributes to the final solution. Similarly, one could compare the diffuse maze to the looser, centrifugal structure of the detective thriller, in which there is more room for digressions and deviations from the main path, as discussed in Chapter 6.

A frequent explorer of the relationship between stories and labyrinths is the illustrious Argentinean tale spinner Jorge Luis Borges. Perhaps the best-known Borges story on this theme is "The Garden of Forking Paths" (1941), which centers on a Chinese spy whose great-grandfather was famous for constructing a labyrinth and writing a novel, both of which are thought to be lost. This characteristically convoluted Borges tale eventually collapses the distinction between novel and maze: "Everyone assumed these were separate activities. No one realized that the book and the labyrinth were one and the same."[34]

Following a labyrinth can be seen as a metaphor for following a story. A story is like a trap into which we enter willingly, for the pleasure of being entrapped, with the understanding that the trap will eventually have an outlet. When we enter a story, we enter a maze, down whose forking paths we are led by the author, who unwinds the route little by little, conceals things from us, creates blind spots and false turnings and barriers around which we cannot see, in order to prolong the suspense and give us the pleasurable anxiety of being lost . . . for a little while.

Pascal Bonitzer: Partial Vision

The concept of the labyrinth is extended to the domain of the movie thriller in Pascal Bonitzer's dense but suggestive article, "Partial Vision: Film and the Labyrinth." Bonitzer is a French film critic who, like many of his colleagues, turned from the theory to the practice of film-making. In recent years, he has collaborated on the screenplays of several important films, including Jacques Rivette's parable of art making, *La Belle Noiseuse* (1991), and Raul Ruiz's Borgesian anthology on the power of fictions, *Three Lives and Only One Death* (*Trois vies et une seule mort,* 1996).

Bonitzer's essay, which was originally published in 1979 in the influential French film journal *Cahiers du cinéma,* draws an essential relationship among three different elements: (1) the labyrinth, (2) the nature of cinema, and (3) the use of suspense in film storytelling. The central, underlying quality shared by these three elements is (as the title of the article indicates) "partial vision." What Bonitzer means by this phrase is that we can see only so much, but *what we cannot see* is also an active part of the system and always on the verge of being revealed – it is just around the next bend of the labyrinth, or just outside the frame line of the film image, or just about to be divulged in the next passage of the plot.

Bonitzer's argument draws heavily on a concept developed by the important French film theorist André Bazin. In his often-cited essay "Theater and Cinema" (1951), Bazin states that a defining property of cinema is the special relationship it creates between onscreen and off-screen space.[35] A film image, like a painting or a proscenium stage, delimits its represented world by placing a border around the part that is shown. However, unlike (or, at least, more dynamically than) in painting or theater, the off-space in cinema is always accessible, always imminent, even when it is not shown, because the field of vision can expand, instantly and nearly infinitely, in order to include that off-space. For example, if a character is standing offscreen, the camera can pan over or pull back to include that character. The frame line is exceptionally fluid and permeable in movies.

Cinema is based on a play between onscreen and offscreen space, a dialectic between withholding and revealing visual information, between restricting our vision and expanding it. Cinema creates blind spots; it has a now-you-see-it-now-you-don't quality. These properties connect cinema to the basic principles of both suspense and the labyrinth, which are similarly based on withholding and revealing – showing us only so much, blocking our vision in order to intensify our awareness and anticipation of what we cannot see.

Bonitzer goes on to call the labyrinth a contradictory space because it connotes both confinement and infinitude. In other words, one is

Figure 5. *North by Northwest:* Accidental spy (Cary Grant) caught in "an unlimited prison."

trapped inside a labyrinth, with one's vision blocked and one's steps confined to following the path; yet that path is potentially endless, and there are an infinite number of different routes that can be taken. Citing the famous scene in Hitchcock's *North by Northwest* of Cary Grant being chased by an airplane across an open, sunlit cornfield [Fig. 5], Bonitzer defines the labyrinth as "an unlimited prison."[36]

The general connection that Bonitzer points out between film (especially narrative film) and the labyrinth becomes even stronger in the movie thriller because the thriller emphasizes and intensifies these labyrinthine elements in at least three central ways. First, thrillers tend to feature especially labyrinthine, convoluted plot structures. In contrast to the related but less thrilleresque form of the whodunit detective story, the structure of the thriller plot tends to be diffuse, digressive, meandering, full of twists and turns and tangles and opportunities to wander into side streets and blind alleys, where one has the feeling of being lost in a maze (see Chapter 6).

Figure 6. *The Lady from Shanghai:* Ill-fated lovers (Orson Welles, Rita Hayworth) in the labyrinth.

Second, besides creating labyrinthine plots, the movie thriller often crystallizes these associations by showing and vividly articulating actual physical labyrinths or labyrinthine spaces. Striking examples can found in many of the films cited in this book, including the foggy London waterfront in *Man Hunt,* the Hall of Mirrors in *The Lady from Shanghai* [Fig. 6], the Vienna sewers in *The Third Man* (1949), the network of tubular drainage tunnels through which James Bond escapes in *Dr. No* (1962), the hedge-maze adjoining the hotel in *The Shining* (1980), the endless corridors of the Pentagon in *No Way Out* (1987), the twisting innards of the besieged freighter in *The Usual Suspects* (1995), and the Los Angeles storm drains that climax *He Walked by Night* (1949), *Them!* (1954), and *It's Alive* (1974).

There can be more than one variety and more than one level of labyrinth in a particular film. For instance, on a macrocosmic level, the city is a prime thriller labyrinth; the thriller tends to transform the shape

Figure 7. *The Big Sleep:* Labyrinths within labyrinths.

of the modern city from a grid into a maze. In *The Big Sleep* (see Chapter 6), Los Angeles is a labyrinth, and, within that, General Sternwood's hothouse (with its tangle of intertwined tropical flora), Eddie Mars's casino (with its spokelike layout of different chambers and passages branching off a central entrance area), the casino parking lot (where the detective hero Philip Marlowe lies in wait for a would-be thief), and the Fulwider office building (where Marlowe witnesses a murder through a zigzag of cracked doorways and frosted-glass windows) [Fig. 7] are presented as labyrinths. In *The French Connection* (1971; see Chapter 9), New York City is a labyrinth; the subway station where the police hero Doyle loses his man, the city avenue down which he pursues a would-be assassin, and the run-down building at the film's climax are labyrinths within that labyrinth.

The third especially labyrinthine dimension of the thriller concerns the very central and heightened importance of *suspense*. Bonitzer's essay points out the close interconnection between suspense and the labyrinth. He asserts that it is not so much the labyrinth that creates suspense, but suspense that creates the labyrinth.[37] In other words, once a suspenseful element – such as a deadline to meet or a killer to catch – is introduced into a plot situation, then any space can become labyrinthine, filled with potential obstructions, delays, wrong turns, and unseen pitfalls. To illustrate this point, Bonitzer quotes a passage from François Truffaut's introduction to his well-known interview with Alfred Hitchcock:

A man leaves his home, hails a cab and drives to the station to catch a train. This is a normal scene in an average picture. Now, should that man happen to look at his watch just as he is getting into the cab and exclaim, "Good God, I shall never make that train!" that entire ride automatically becomes a sequence of pure suspense. Every red light, traffic signal, shift of the gears or touch on the brake, and every cop on the way to the station will intensify its emotional impact.[38]

The celebrated car chase in *The French Connection* is an example of how suspense can transform a straight city avenue into a labyrinth filled with traps and missteps (see Chapter 9).

Lars Ole Sauerberg: Concealment and Protraction

Suspense is one ingredient that everybody seems to agree is central to the otherwise cloudy, ill-defined concept of the thriller. (However, as noted in the discussion of *The Big Sleep* in Chapter 6, it is possible for a film to qualify as a thriller even when suspense is not a significant factor.) Much like the thriller itself (see Chapter 1), suspense involves a quantitative relationship – that is, it is an issue of "How much?" rather than either/or. The basic elements of suspense are inherent in virtually all storytelling; but in the case of full-fledged, thriller-level suspense, these elements become so acute that other aspects of the narrative are overridden by our curiosity and anxiety over what is going to happen next.

In this respect, suspense relates to the sensational, sadomasochistic aspect of the thriller discussed in Chapter 1. The expression "keeps you on the edge of your seat" is commonly used to describe the effect of suspense. This telling phrase demonstrates that suspense involves a significant amount of discomfort for the spectator: Sitting on the edge of one's seat is a very different matter from lounging back and relaxing. In a thriller, we find pleasure in intense sensations – discomfort, anxiety, fear, tension – that might ordinarily be considered unpleasurable, as well as in the ultimate release from such pleasurably unpleasurable sensations.

Suspense centrally involves two basic dynamics, two pulls on the spectator. Lars Ole Sauerberg treats this issue in *Secret Agents in Fiction* (1984), a book with a strong attention to theoretical issues whose implications extend beyond the specific topic of spy fiction. Sauerberg calls these two basic suspense factors *concealment* and *protraction*. In the first case, suspense is created by hiding something from us; in the second, by delaying an expected outcome. Sauerberg writes, "Whereas concealment is the author's deliberate withholding of information, protraction is a matter of stretching an issue and a result as much as may be tolerated."[39] Although the two factors usually interact, Sauerberg separates them, allowing for cases in which one or the other may be dominant.

As an example of a story that highlights protraction with little sense of concealment, he cites the espionage/adventure tales of Alistair MacLean, which often center on a countdown toward an expected event, such as a bomb going off – as in *The Guns of Navarone* (1956; film version, 1961), about a commando team sent to blow up a Nazi gun emplacement on a Mediterranean island.[40] Other examples might be drawn from the "psychological crime thriller" (see Chapter 7), in which the identity and intentions of the villain (such as Bruno Anthony in *Strangers on a Train*, 1951) are revealed early in the story.

As an example of "pure concealment," Sauerberg cites "much horror fiction, as the reader is impatient to learn about the nature of whatever dreadful thing threatens the hero."[41] His reasoning here is not entirely clear, because the horror genre often involves a great deal of protraction (as noted in my discussion of Gothic fiction in the section "Precinematic Forerunners" in Chapter 3). Perhaps Sauerberg is referring to protraction strictly in relation to a clearly announced and expected result, whereas in some examples of the horror genre (such as the films *Psycho* and *The Texas Chain Saw Massacre*) the overall direction of the story may be unclear and/or unexpected, with the viewer or reader kept continually off balance.

In any event, Sauerberg's identification of the stronger case in which protraction is dominant raises the possibility (sometimes underemphasized by writers on the subject) that suspense can function even when little or no mystery attends the end result. This accounts for the presence of suspense in stories that involve well-known historical events and figures, such as Frederick Forsyth's novel *The Day of the Jackal* (1971; film version, 1973), about an attempted assassination of French President Charles de Gaulle, and Ron Howard's film *Apollo 13* (1995), about a nearly disastrous space mission. As these examples illustrate, the sheer experience of waiting for a strongly anticipated and relentlessly approaching event may be sufficient to generate considerable suspense.

Delay is like a labyrinth, a web – a state of being caught or suspended. As Bonitzer suggests, the labyrinth is in some ways the spatial equivalent of the emotion of suspense, and, by the same token, suspense is the emotional equivalent of the labyrinth: We do not proceed straight to the exit, we advance without getting anywhere; we move toward the goal, the resolution, the exit, and at the same time we move away from it.

Noël Carroll: The Question–Answer Model

Another, more thorough definition of suspense is offered in the essay "Toward a Theory of Film Suspense" (1984) by Noël Carroll, an uncommonly lucid film theorist who has also written extensively on the horror film. Adapting a concept taken from the Russian film director and theorist V. I. Pudovkin, Carroll bases his theory of suspense on an "interrogatory" or *question–answer* model: The narrative poses questions. The posing of these questions arouses in the audience an intense desire to know the answers. This creates suspense.[42]

Of course, many narratives pose questions without being especially suspenseful. Carroll specifies two further qualifications that distinguish full-scale suspense from milder varieties of narrative propulsion. The first is the element of expectation: We must be informed, we have to be made strongly aware that a question has been posed, so that we can then suspensefully anticipate a result. The second qualification is that the question must present a clearly defined choice between a limited number of possibilities, usually only two – for example, will the hero live or die? Carroll uses this qualification to distinguish between questions posed by suspense and those posed by a whodunit mystery, in which the potential answer to the central question "Who committed the murder?" is usually dispersed among a large gallery of suspects.[43]

Carroll also emphasizes the importance of what he calls "moral" and "probability" factors in determining suspense. The *probability factor* involves the notion that the less likely a desired result appears to be, the more suspense will be generated. A "sure thing" will not generate much suspense, as opposed to an against-all-odds situation. The *moral factor* might be rephrased more crudely (though less troublesomely) as "rooting interest," or more mildly (as Carroll surmises in an appendix to his essay) as "desirability." According to Carroll, the presentation of a "morally right" outcome as one of the possible answers to a suspense question (e.g., will the maiden save her virtue or surrender it to the villain?) intensifies our involvement in the action and so sharpens the suspense. This moral factor need not depend on conventional notions of good and evil but may simply center on the attractiveness of the protagonist's character – as in heist films, in which a strong rooting interest is created for characters who attempt daring robberies (see Chapter 5). Combining these two factors, Carroll concludes that maximum suspense will be achieved when the morally most desirable outcome appears to be the least probable.[44]

Although the presence of a clearly desirable alternative is undoubtedly a powerful factor in creating suspense, Carroll perhaps underrates the possibility of more ambivalent cases in which suspense can still be strongly (even just as strongly) operative. In an appendix, Carroll does take note of one such possibility, acknowledging that Alfred Hitchcock's films contain suspenseful situations in which the moral factor is weakened and even contradicted. These include such tour-de-force sequences as the one in *Strangers on a Train* wherein the villain Bruno Anthony (Robert Walker) reaches down a storm drain to retrieve the lighter that he intends to use to incriminate the hero [Fig. 8], and the one in *Frenzy* (1972) wherein the sex-murderer Rusk (Barry Forster) struggles to extract his monogrammed tiepin from the rigor-mortis grasp of his latest victim. In both cases, Hitchcock prided himself on having created situations in which the audience is encouraged to root for the bad guy, or, in Carroll's terms, to desire an immoral result. Carroll finally accounts for these deviations by classifying Hitchcock as an original and even subversive artist who defines himself against the established norm.[45] However, it could be argued that Hitchcock, as the acknowledged Master of Suspense, with a massive continuing influence on other filmmakers (see "Hitchcock's Golden Period" in Chapter 4), might himself be considered part of the norm. Accordingly, such morally clouded suspense situations, although certainly less common than the lopsided variety, might not be as unusual or even as problematic as Carroll implies.

In addition to individual sequences in which a significant part of our allegiance is at least temporarily diverted to the villain, there are suspenseful films in which our allegiance is strongly and/or consistently divided along the moral lines proposed by Carroll. In Michael Mann's *Heat* (1995), a hybrid of heist film and police thriller, the audience's sympathy is elicited with virtually equal intensity for the dedicated thief (Robert De Niro) who is attempting to pull off a major bank robbery and the dedicated cop (Al Pacino) who is attempting to catch him. However, this divided allegiance does not seem to diminish the tension and suspense of such passages as the harrowing bank-robbery shootout, the powerful scene in which a thief's wife (Ashley Judd) must decide whether to betray her husband (Val Kilmer), and the melancholy showdown in which Pacino chases De Niro across an airfield.

Such consistently sustained ambivalence is an uncommon but still potentially effective strategy in thriller movies; other notable examples include the objective police–assassin procedural *The Day of the Jackal* and the fervent black dealer–white cop crime drama *Clockers* (1995). More common are individual suspense sequences in which two morally opposed alternatives are clamoring for our allegiance at the same time – for instance, scenes in which protagonists are torn between emotionally satisfying vengeance and pragmatic restraint (as in *The Big Heat*, 1953; *Cutter's Way*, 1981; *Seven*, 1995), scenes in which murderous protagonists are hazardously attempting to dispatch somewhat sympathetic victims (as in *The Postman Always Rings Twice*, 1946; *Taxi Driver*, 1976; *Martin*, 1978), scenes in which our allegiance with protagonists on vengeful crusades begins to curdle (as in *Fury*, 1936; *Ms. 45*, 1981; *To Live and Die in L.A.*, 1985), and horror-film scenes in which we are torn between desiring the destruction and survival of ambivalently sympathetic monsters (as in *King Kong*, 1933; *I Was a Teen-age Werewolf*, 1957; *Species*, 1995).

As discussed in Chapter 1, the ambivalence and instability resulting from such divided responses can even contribute mightily to the thrilleresque impact of a film. Carroll describes how he found the fingerbreaking scene in *Frenzy* hilarious in a black-humorous way and maintains that such laughter detracted from the suspense.[46] His response illustrates how the strong subjective dimension of suspense (i.e., what one person finds agonizingly suspenseful, another may find boring or merely amusing) necessarily qualifies any attempts to evaluate its effects in a movie (see Chapter 10). Still, as demonstrated throughout this book, the thriller thrives on emotionally conflicting responses,

Figure 8. *Strangers on a Train:* Plight of the villain (Robert Walker) causes us to desire an immoral result.

and laughter and suspense can easily coexist and even intensify each other.

Suspense centrally involves the idea of suspension. We are suspended between question and answer, between anticipation and resolution, between alternative answers to the question posed, and sometimes between ambivalent emotions and sympathies that are aroused by a suspenseful situation. There is a close relationship between the concept of suspense and the term *entertainment,* which literally means "to hold between." This aspect of suspense also relates to the sense of being captured or enthralled that is so central to the thriller and the way it entertains us (see Chapter 1). More specific issues of suspense (concerning such factors as time, knowledge, and identification) are discussed in Chapter 7.

All of these critical and theoretical concepts – transformation of the ordinary, the exotic, the labyrinth, suspense – contribute to the specially charged world of the thriller. They work together to create a realm that, at its most effective, transports us to a heightened state of suspension – between the mundane and the marvelous, the modern world and the heroic past, the seen and the unseen, pain and pleasure, concealment and revelation. Thrillers have coalesced into specific historical movements and generic categories that articulate these concepts in distinct but related ways. Some of the most important of those categories, and individual thrillers that represent them, are the subject of the chapters that follow.

PART TWO

Historical Overview

3

Formative Period

Because of the wide, imprecise scope of the thriller, it would be unwieldy and impractical to attempt a comprehensive history of each individual genre – detective, film noir, horror, police, spy, and so on – that this metagenre comprehends. Instead, the overview presented in Part II of this book concentrates on selected "hot" cycles that were especially active and especially relevant to the development of the movie thriller (e.g., not the entire detective-movie genre, but the hard-boiled cycle of the early 1940s; not the entire science-fiction genre, but the alien-invasion cycle of the 1950s). These different cycles are dealt with not in isolation but in terms of their relationship to other thriller cycles (e.g., the hard-boiled detective movie feeds into film noir, which in turn feeds into the 1950s police film). Accordingly, Chapters 3–5 have a double focus: (1) a series of movements arising within different individual genres, (2) each strand contributing to an overall tapestry of the general development of the movie thriller.

Although the survey of the movie thriller in Part II is lengthy, it is by no means comprehensive. Many important examples are left out or barely mentioned: Val Lewton–produced horror classics such as *Cat People* (1942) and *The Seventh Victim* (1943); major middle-period Hitchcock films such as *Shadow of a Doubt* (1943) and *Notorious* (1946); low-budget sleepers such as *The Window* (1949) and *The Narrow Margin* (1952); Japanese master Akira Kurosawa's great police thrillers *Stray Dog* (1949) and *High and Low* (1962); couple-on-the-run chase films such as *Gun Crazy* (1949) and *Thelma & Louise* (1991); several important French crime films by Claude Chabrol and Jean-Pierre Melville; psychopath sagas such as *Hangover Square* (1945) and *Henry: Portrait of a Serial Killer* (1990); the flamboyant *giallo* ("yellow") shockers of Italian stylists Mario Bava and Dario Argento; Kathryn Bigelow's offbeat contributions to the horror film (*Near Dark*, 1987) and police thriller (*Blue Steel*, 1990); and Hong Kong action epics such as *The Killer* (1989) and *Full Contact* (1992) – to name just a few. The exclusion of these and similarly worthy films should not be taken as a reflection on their quality, significance, or eligibility as thrillers. The vast scope of the subject and the limited length of the present volume have made it necessary to stick as closely as possible to a coherent, highly selective sequence of major categories and historical periods. This sequence, however, represents only one of numerous possible paths that could be taken through the many-chambered maze of the movie thriller.

Precinematic Forerunners: Fiction, Melodrama, Amusement Parks

As noted in Chapter 2, this book takes the position that the thriller is an essentially modern form, one that did not fully emerge, in literature as well as film, until the early part of the twentieth century. However, this emergence was the result of a broad-based evolutionary development reaching back to the eighteenth century, especially in the field of fiction. Of the various literary antecedents of the twentieth-century thriller, three are particularly important.

The first is the Gothic novel, a series of horrific tales whose heyday ran from Horace Walpole's *The Castle of Otranto* (1765) to Mary Shelley's *Frankenstein* (1818) and Charles Maturin's *Melmoth the Wanderer* (1820), with a peak achieved in the 1790s by such works as Matthew Lewis's *The Monk* (1796) and Ann Radcliffe's *The Mysteries of Udolpho* (1794) and *The Italian* (1797). Although the Gothic novel proper declined after 1820, the Gothic strain continued to run strong in the fiction of Edgar Allan Poe, Nathaniel Hawthorne, Charlotte Brontë, Emily Brontë, Robert Louis Stevenson, Sheridan LeFanu, Henry James, Bram Stoker, and many others.

A central element of the Gothic novel is its strong sense of atmosphere. The traditional Gothic setting is a haunted, medieval landscape of forbidding castles, crumbling ruins, abbeys, dungeons, shadows, moonlight, ghosts, and graveyards. There is a tendency to linger on atmosphere to the point of greatly slowing down and stretching out the action. The "protraction" or "delay" factor of suspense (see Chapter 2) is often extended to an unusual degree in Gothic fiction, which gravitates toward in-between states and limbos of ambiguous suspension.

Other key ingredients of the Gothic novel are sex and violence. As William Patrick Day observes in his stimulating study *In the Circles of Fear and Desire* (1985), the traditional Gothic tale involves two basic characters: a male persecutor and a female victim. The purest form of this Gothic pattern (on which twisted variations, such as a feminized male protagonist, are possible) involves the pursuit, abduction, and persecution of a maiden by a diabolical villain or antihero. The action typically depicts the female being held captive or enthralled in some way, while the villain tries to terrorize her, bend her to his will, force her to surrender her virtue, or simply exercise the sheer joy of domination. The sadomasochistic element, mentioned earlier as being widely implicit in the thriller, is strongly foregrounded in many Gothic novels.[1]

The acute and extended vulnerability of the enthralled protagonist/victim is another of several Gothic elements that strongly anticipate the thriller. Literary scholar Robert D. Hume, in a 1969 essay, asserts that the Gothic novel involved the reader in a new way, with an increased emphasis on suspense, sensation, and emotion, as opposed to the more moral and intellectual focus found in previous forms of fiction.[2] Frederick S. Frank, in a 1981 catalog of Gothic fiction, similarly describes the form in terms that place it as a predecessor of the thriller, specifying works "whose principal literary goal is to terrify, horrify, startle, or thrill the audience. . . . To be classified by the bibliographer as 'pure' Gothic or 'high' Gothic, a work must aim to electrify and not to edify its readership."[3]

However, in terms of the parameters proposed in Chapter 2, the Gothic tale's status as a thriller is problematic. Gothic fiction, in its traditional form, is set in an antiquated, decaying world that is fundamentally not modern, even in terms of the period when the books were written. Also, the Gothic tale is not grounded in a commonplace context that becomes transformed by the introduction of thrilling elements. Instead, it takes place in a world that is already quite heightened, exotic, extraordinary. The Gothic novel (and horror films conceived in the Gothic tradition) can be seen as transitional, borderline forms of thriller. These forms move closer toward the mainstream of the thriller as they move out of the traditional setting of isolated castles and into the domain of the commonplace and contemporary, where the Gothic features can then operate as exotic, adventurous elements that heighten and transform the mundane modern world. Several examples are cited in the discussions of horror films at the end of this chapter ("Monsters of the Early 1930s") and in Chapter 5 ("Splatter").

A second literary antecedent, the Victorian sensation novel, adapted the sensational and atmospheric effects of Gothic fiction to the contemporary and familiar world. The first full-fledged example of the form was Wilkie Collins's popular success *The Woman in White* (1859–60), centering on a cruel and ingenious scheme to separate a young heiress from her fortune. From the start, the sensation novel was perceived by critics as a new form of the Gothic, stripped of its mysticism, brought up to date, and placed closer to everyday life.

This enhancement of "proximity" (as an 1863 reviewer termed it) made the sensations of the sensation novel all the more intense.[4] In an important 1862 magazine review entitled "Sensation Novels," the novelist and essayist Mrs. [Margaret] Oliphant cites the famous episode that sets the plot of *The Woman in White* in motion: The hero, Walter Hartright, is strolling alone one moonlit night when he is frozen by the touch of a hand upon his shoulder; he turns and finds himself facing "a solitary Woman, dressed from head to foot in white garments . . ."[5] As Mrs. Oliphant describes the moment, "Few readers will be able to resist the mysterious thrill of this sudden touch. The sensation is distinct and indisputable. The silent woman lays her hand upon our shoulder as well as upon that of Mr. Walter Hartright. . . ."[6]

One could say, then, that the sensation-novel movement begins with the description of a literal, physical sensation: a touch that chills the blood. This visceral dimension, along with the intrusion of the extraordinary into an ordinary context (the setting is described as a "well-known, uneventful road, where holiday people strolled on Sundays"), point toward the future development of the thriller.[7]

Victorian sensation novels were often originally published in serial form, producing what many reviewers considered an unhealthy excess of lurid climaxes. These serialized novels sometimes concluded their installments with a cliff-hanger – although the term used at the time was "climax and curtain."[8] The theatrical origin of this phrase indicates another form that both influenced and was influenced by the sensation novel: the stage melodrama (discussed later in this section). With its emphases upon victimized innocence, evil conspiracy, dark mysteries, and spectacular incident, Victorian sensation fiction was in many ways a novelistic equivalent of the contemporary melodramatic theater. Indeed, several adaptations of these novels (notably Mrs. Henry Wood's 1861 *East Lynne* and Mary Braddon's 1861–2 *Lady Audley's Secret*) became staples of the melodramatic stage.

The third of these prototypical forms is the early detective/mystery story, pioneered by such authors as Edgar Allan Poe, whose "The Murders in the Rue Morgue" (1841) is widely considered the first detective story; Émile Gaboriau, whose Monsieur Lecoq, featured in several

French novels of the 1860s, was the first important fictional police detective; and Arthur Conan Doyle, creator of Sherlock Holmes, who first appeared in print in 1887. The developing detective story drew upon both of the previously mentioned forms. The Victorian sensation novel often employed detective figures (usually amateur) and evidence-gathering procedures to clear up the mysteries that haunted its post-Gothic world. The detective story has also been interpreted by several critics, including John G. Cawelti and William Patrick Day, as both an outgrowth and a domestication of the Gothic tradition. The classical detective's eccentricity and isolation mark him as a descendant of the Gothic villain/antihero, turned to more constructive purposes as he exercises a combination of reason and imagination to tame the chaotic ambiguity that had ruled the Gothic world.[9] This Gothic heritage is most vividly displayed in the classic Sherlock Holmes novel *The Hound of the Baskervilles* (1901–2), set on a desolate moor with a lonely manor house, creeping fog, mysterious prowlers, and unearthly howls. The history of the detective story is further discussed in Chapter 6.

The roots of the thriller can be more generally related to the rise of urban-industrial society in the nineteenth century, which created a new and expanded mass audience, along with new popular entertainment forms to serve that audience. One of the most important of these nineteenth-century entertainment forms was the melodramatic theater. Whereas the theater of previous eras had been based upon the spoken word, delivered by actors in a predominantly abstract setting, the melodrama placed a premium on action and visual spectacle.

A perennial high point of the frequently performed stage versions of *Uncle Tom's Cabin* (first adapted in 1852) was the escaped slave Eliza's flight across an ice-choked river, with bloodhounds in hot pursuit. The rural melodrama *Blue Jeans* (1890) featured a scene in which the heroine unties the hero just as he is about to be bifurcated by an advancing buzz saw. In the sensational climax of *Under the Gaslight* (1867), the heroine, locked in a shack, sees the villain tie a one-armed man to a nearby railroad track. She furiously hacks her way free with an ax and rescues the victim mere seconds before a locomotive thunders past (moving the grateful man to exclaim, "And these are the women who ain't to have a vote!").[10] The concept was recycled in the cheap-theater favorite *Saved from the Storm* (ca. 1878), but this time the bound victim was (trendsettingly) the heroine, and her rescuers were two resourceful dogs! Melodramas sometimes used rapid scene changes and lighting shifts to switch back and forth between two suspensefully converging lines of action. For instance, the popular potboiler *The Octoroon* (1859) showed the suicidal heroine preparing to take poison while the hero races through swamps in an attempt to bring life-saving news. There is a clear lineage from these stage antecedents to the types of scenes that would be found in many thriller movies of the next century. For example, the buzz saw from *Blue Jeans* becomes a laser beam that threatens to geld James Bond in *Goldfinger* (1964), and a variation on the bound-heroine/speeding-train scenario occurs at the end of *Speed* (1994).

Another relevant area of nineteenth-century popular entertainment encompasses fairgrounds, amusement parks, and the thrill-oriented rides and attractions that were featured in those venues. The first roller coasters appeared in America in the 1880s; the original Ferris wheel was a top attraction at the 1893 World's Columbian Exposition in Chicago. During this period, other rides were developed whose appeal was based on speed, disorientation, and the providing of sharp sensations: the Shoot-the-Chutes (a water slide), the Tickler (whirling tubs), the Steeplechase (wooden horses on an undulating track). The connection between amusement-park rides and the visceral side of the thriller has already been pointed out in Chapter 1.

In addition, amusement parks and thrillers both offer a departure from humdrum reality that is merely a heightened version of that same humdrum reality. In an insightful monograph on Coney Island, cultural historian John F. Kasson points out that people who endured crowded, noisy, jerking subway or elevated-train rides every working day would find pleasurable, heightened equivalents of those same sensations on roller coasters and other amusement-park attractions.[11] Similarly, latter-day movie patrons might find in a frenetic car chase a pleasurable, heightened version of the freeway traffic they tediously battle every rush hour.

Attraction Films and Chase Films

Arising around the same time as these amusement-park attractions and pitched at the same mass audience was the nascent art form of the motion picture. Amusement parks and fairgrounds were in fact one of the main venues for early motion-picture exhibition, first presented in peep-show arcades, then projected on screens, and later incorporated into simulated train trips, car rides, and balloon ascensions. The link between early cinema and amusement-park attractions was further underlined by what film historian Tom Gunning has labeled the "cinema of attractions."[12] This term refers to early, novelty-oriented short films that were designed more to provide individual sensations (such as surprise, amazement, laughter, sexual stimulation) than to develop continuous story lines. A large group of these attraction films highlighted the cinema's ability to convey the sensation of motion by placing the camera on moving vehicles such as trolleys, trains, boats, and elevators.

As the motion-picture industry moved toward its eventual domination by the story-based film, the sensation of motion featured in many attraction films was incorporated into a rudimentary narrative framework known as the "chase film," an important stepping-stone to the full-fledged narrative cinema. Coming to prominence around 1903, these chase films – some of them based on true events, some comic in nature, some of the most influential of them produced in Britain and France – usually employed a minimal narrative setup as the springboard for an extended chase scene that constituted the bulk of the film. Typical of these early chase scenes was their inclusion of pursuer and pursued within the same shot, rather than cutting back and forth between them.

The chase film was one of several forms that contributed to the most celebrated and commercially successful American film of this period, *The Great Train Robbery* (1903), produced by the Edison Company and supervised by the important early filmmaker Edwin S. Porter. Derived in part from a popular stage melodrama of the same name, *The Great Train Robbery* demonstrates the melodramatic theater's flair for spectacle and sensationalism. Depicting the holdup of a passenger train and a posse's subsequent capture of the robbers, *The Great Train Robbery* also treats themes that would later cause it to be considered a pioneer film in the western genre. However, it spends less time in developing these themes than it does in detailing the process of the robbery itself. We see the bandits subduing a telegraph operator, sneaking onto the train, shooting a guard, blowing open a safe in the mail car, overpowering the engineer, uncoupling the engine, robbing the passengers, and then using the detached engine to reach a rendezvous point where their horses are waiting to carry them away. In this respect, the film anticipates a category of thriller known as the "heist film," centering on the detailed depiction of an ingeniously planned robbery, which is discussed in Chapter 5 (see "European Influences, American Censorship, and Heist Films").[13]

The Great Train Robbery also points toward the thriller's central emphasis on accelerated motion – especially in the action scenes set upon the speeding train and in the final horseback pursuit by the posse. Unlike almost all other chase films of the period, *The Great Train Robbery* attempts some crosscutting (a.k.a. "parallel editing" and "switchback editing") to go back and forth between actions occurring in different places. The film cuts away from the fleeing robbers to scenes of the robbery being discovered and a posse being raised; however, the temporal relationship between these converging plot lines is unclear. After that interlude, the film conforms to the more typical chase-film format, with deep long shots that include both bandits and lawmen as the latter sweep toward the foreground to overwhelm the fugitives. Porter added one final touch to his action-packed spectacle: a close shot of one of the robbers firing his pistol directly toward the camera. This sensational effect, whose impact is somewhat independent of the story line (the exhibitor had the option of placing it at either the film's beginning or end), links *The Great Train Robbery* to the aforementioned "cinema of attractions." It also anticipates the movie thriller's characteristic emphasis on high points and thrills whose individual impact sometimes undermines the overall coherence of the narrative.

A purer example of the early chase film is *Capture of "Yegg" Bank Burglars,* an Edison–Porter production of 1904. The opening scenes show a gang of thieves (known as "yeggs" in the slang of the day) planning and executing a bank robbery, which is depicted more perfunctorily here than in *The Great Train Robbery.* The film then turns into an extended chase, with bandits and pursuers passing diagonally through the same shots. The chase rapidly moves through a series of different locales and modes of locomotion: by foot, horse, rowboat, and finally railroad. *Capture of "Yegg" Bank Burglars* concludes with a truly spectacular effect: The locomotive that the bandits are riding suddenly collides head-on with another speeding locomotive, ending the film in a tangle of twisted metal and splintered wood. Although this final effect is more fully integrated into the story line than is the in-your-face gunshot that concludes (or begins) *The Great Train Robbery,* it still has an excessive, autonomous quality – and, in fact, the final crash footage was lifted from an entirely different film.

Although the chase film was too limited in scope to enjoy more than a brief prominence in cinema history, its legacy can be found throughout the history of the movie thriller, especially in films dominated by abnormally extended chase sequences that pile one climax on top of another with barely a moment for spectators or characters to catch their breaths. Examples include *On Her Majesty's Secret Service* (1969), the most kinetic of the early James Bond films, whose second half contains an astonishing series of chase scenes; *Vanishing Point* (1971), whose rebel hero guns his supercharged white Challenger across the western United States, evading one roadblock after another in an enigmatic duel with Authority; and *Speed* (1994), which consists mostly of a nonstop dash that, similarly to *Capture of "Yegg" Bank Burglars,* moves from one mode of transportation to another (jeep, foot, sports car, bus, dolly, subway).

D. W. Griffith and the Rise of Narrative Film

The period 1907–13 saw the solidification of the movie industry's domination by narrative filmmaking, accompanied by the development of more sophisticated techniques of film storytelling. The person most closely identified with this development is D. W. Griffith, who between 1908 and 1913 directed for the Biograph Company more than four hundred short films (ca. 12–25 minutes long) in which many basic elements of narrative film style were, though perhaps not invented, employed in a more expressive and artistically coherent manner than ever before. The techniques that Griffith refined for enhancing suspense, psychological depth, and spatial orientation were crucial to all narrative cinema, but some were also especially relevant to the still embryonic form of the movie thriller.

The importance of the stage melodrama as an antecedent of the movie thriller has been noted above. Griffith, whose prefilm background was as an actor and aspiring playwright in the melodramatic theater, maintained this link and extended it into more specifically cinematic directions. Perhaps the most celebrated technique developed by Griffith was the use of crosscutting, which he applied to last-minute rescue situations derived from the stage melodrama. As previously mentioned, early chase films had included the chasers and the chased within the same shot; crosscutting was used either not at all or only in a limited manner (as in *The Great Train Robbery*). Crosscutting was first fully employed in early 1908, a few months before Griffith's debut as a film director, but he proceeded to utilize this prime suspense device more extensively than did any of his contemporaries.[14]

An example of Griffith's development of crosscutting to enhance suspense and action is his 1912 Biograph short *The Girl and Her Trust.*

A semiremake of Griffith's important earlier film *The Lonedale Operator* (1911), *The Girl and Her Trust* centers on Grace (Dorothy Bernard), a telegrapher at a remote railroad station. Left alone with a strongbox of money, she finds herself besieged by two larcenous tramps. Grace telegraphs for help and then ingeniously contrives to delay her attackers. The climax is a high-speed chase between a locomotive and a railway handcar on which the thieves are attempting to flee, with the abducted heroine aboard.

The Lonedale Operator, Griffith's earlier version, climaxes with the train rushing to the rescue while the heroine is trapped in her office. *The Girl and Her Trust* peaks more dynamically with a chase involving two rapidly moving points: the train and the handcar. In addition, Griffith orchestrates the relationship of the camera to the action in a dynamic variety of ways, juggling

1. shots in which the camera is static while the train or handcar whiz by,
2. shots in which the camera is mounted upon those moving vehicles [Fig. 9], and, most strikingly,
3. shots in which the camera, apparently mounted on an unseen automobile, speeds alongside the racing vehicles.

The third category includes a spectacular shot in which the camera hurtles at top speed beside the rushing locomotive from a medium distance. Griffith holds the shot for a relatively long time, until it becomes an almost abstract contemplation of the visual effects of accelerated motion, with trees and buildings flying by in distorted, blurred shapes. This shot's intoxication with the sheer sensation of speed relates it to the attraction films of earlier cinema history (especially those whose primary function was to display motion from a moving platform) and also to later thriller movies, which often pursue visceral sensations in an overloaded manner that outstrips the needs and coherence of the narrative.

In addition to presenting its action in an exciting and varied manner, *The Girl and Her Trust* provides a psychological context for that action. This psychological dimension involves an underlying discontent within the heroine, which surfaces in her conflicted attitude toward the opposite sex. The film opens with some humorous business of two different suitors approaching Grace and being rudely rebuffed. When the second one impetuously steals a kiss, she reacts not merely with conventional coyness and maidenly modesty (as the heroine does

Figure 9. *The Girl and Her Trust:* Thieves give dissatisfied heroine (Dorothy Bernard) the ride of her life. (The Museum of Modern Art Film Stills Archive)

in a parallel situation in *The Lonedale Operator*), but with genuine and drawn-out repugnance, as if she had been slobbered upon by a barn-yard animal. A few moments later, when Grace is alone, we can see that she is having second thoughts about her hostile behavior, but she keeps these regrets to herself.

The heroine's frustration in romantic matters, her inability to find an outlet for her deepest feelings, is linked to a general dissatisfaction with her everyday life. When the second suitor, before departing, warns Grace to be cautious, she scoffs (in an intertitle), "Danger? Nothing ever happens here." Such frustrations over the inadequacy of hum-drum reality have been the bane of many a thriller hero and heroine. John Buchan's trendsetting spy novel *The Thirty-Nine Steps* (1915) opens with the hero, Richard Hannay, going stir-crazy in London; he declares himself to be "the best-bored man in the United Kingdom."[15]

In Fritz Lang's film noir *The Woman in the Window* (1945), middle-aged professor Richard Wanley (Edward G. Robinson) sinks back in a plush armchair and bemoans the solidity and stodginess of his sedentary existence: "To me, it's the end of the brightness of life, the end of spirit and adventure." In Alfred Hitchcock's suspense classic *Rear Window* (1954), globe-trotting photojournalist L. B. Jeffries (James Stewart), immobilized with a broken leg, sits restlessly by his apartment window, scanning the domiciles of his seemingly all too ordinary neighbors. In Steven Spielberg's influential hit *Jaws* (1975), a former New York City cop (Roy Scheider) becomes police chief of a tranquil beach resort; as he sets off for work, his wife urges, "Be careful!" and he scornfully replies, "In this town?" In such cases, it often seems as if the hero summons up, from the depths of his dissatisfaction, the disruptive element that will break the spell of deadening routine: the fugitive whom Hannay finds knifed to death in his apartment; the beautiful woman whose ghostly apparition leads Wanley into a nightmare of murder and guilt; the mysterious scream in the middle of the night that arouses Jeffries's eager suspicions; the half-eaten body that washes up on the beach of the peaceful resort.

 The Girl and Her Trust contains a similar pattern. The heroine seems to sense subconsciously the presence of the prowling tramps before they actually appear to her. In *The Lonedale Operator,* the heroine first spots the tramps when they are offscreen, in a separate shot, and they remain separated from her until they finally break through the door in the film's last moments. In *The Girl and Her Trust,* however, Grace first confronts her nemeses within the same shot, turning slowly as they rise up in a window behind her. To a certain extent, these tramps seem like an apparition conjured up by the heroine's own submerged conflicts rather than a purely external force invading a previously stable existence, as is the case in *The Lonedale Operator* and several other Griffith besieged-room thrillers of the Biograph period.

Evolution of the American Serial

An eccentric but influential contributor to the evolution of the movie thriller was the serial – that is, a continuing story broken up into a number of regularly scheduled episodes. A transitional form between the previously dominant short film and the rising (but riskier) feature film, the early movie serial provided a format for sustaining and extending the action/suspense devices pioneered by the chase films, the Biograph films, and other early narrative shorts. Within the loose and episodic structure of the serial, action and suspense sequences could dominate the film with a nearly constant succession of thrills, as opposed to early feature films in which chase sequences (such as the Klansmen's ride to rescue in Griffith's 1915 historical epic *The Birth of a Nation*) or cliff-hanging situations (such as the mountaintop struggle in Erich von Stroheim's 1919 Alpine melodrama *Blind Husbands*) appear only as interludes or final climaxes in otherwise nonthriller films.

There is a hazy line of distinction between serials and what are more properly termed *series films* – that is, series of otherwise self-contained individual films in which leading characters and, often, a limited number of plot elements are repeated from one film to the next. The James Bond movies are a recent instance, although series films were established early in American film history – for example, the "Broncho Billy" Anderson series of westerns (ca. 1910–15) and the John Bunny–Flora Finch series of domestic comedies (ca. 1912–14). The earliest films commonly included in histories of the motion-picture serial combine aspects of both the series film and the serial.

The first movie serials had their origins in the intensely competitive American newspaper business of the early twentieth century. Since the mid-nineteenth century, it had been a common practice for newspapers and magazines to run fictional stories in installments; as noted above, many Victorian sensation novels were originally published as magazine serials. In late 1913, the *Chicago Tribune,* embroiled in a fierce circulation war with six other Chicago dailies, hit upon the idea (previously employed, to a more limited degree, by a magazine called *The Ladies' World*) of increasing its readership by running a serialized story simultaneously in both a newspaper version and a movie version. The paper joined forces with Chicago-based film magnate William Selig to produce *The Adventures of Kathlyn,* a serial in thirteen parts, released over a five-month period, concerning the travails of a young heiress who journeys to India, where she defends her honor and her fortune from an exotic villain named Umballah. The *Tribune's* strategy was a tremendous success, resulting in a reported 10-percent circulation boost, with especially heavy gains among a lower-class and immigrant clientele previously underrecruited by the upscale paper.[16]

The success of the *Tribune's* experiment led to a number of similar newspaper–movie tie-ins. In 1914, the *Tribune* itself followed up *The Adventures of Kathlyn* with *The Million Dollar Mystery,* which was even more successful at the movie box office, and the rival *Chicago Herald* combined with Universal Film Manufacturing Company to produce *Lucille Love, Girl of Mystery,* a globe-trotting spy-themed serial. Also in 1914, the Hearst newspaper empire collaborated with the powerful Pathé Film Company on the most famous silent-movie serial, *The Perils of Pauline,* starring Pearl White as a resilient damsel whose fat inheritance is coveted by her false friend Owen and whose life is threatened by Gypsies, American Indians, and other, less exotic adversaries. Pathé, a French entertainment giant with an active branch in the United States, went on to become the leading producer of American silent serials (known, in fact, as the "House of Serials"), while at the same time providing a direct link to the flourishing French serial scene of the same era (see the following section).

Having established its commercial viability beyond the realm of newspaper publicity stunts, the American movie serial continued to thrive, averaging around twenty productions per year for the rest of the decade. As the United States approached its entry into World War I, stories centering on the favorite serial theme of the heroine's threatened birthright were increasingly supplemented or supplanted by plot lines featuring far-reaching conspiracies hatched by secret societies and foreign governments (most often not the Germans but the Japanese, Russians, and even Mexicans). After peaking in 1920 with over thirty productions, the American serial tailed off in both prestige and profitability, becoming ensconced in a more secondary position within the film-exhibition hierarchy, now aimed primarily at second-run houses and juvenile audiences.[17]

The most significant element developed by the serials of this era was the cliff-hanger (a.k.a. "hold-over suspense"), wherein each episode (except the last) ends with the hero or heroine in a seemingly hopeless predicament that is not resolved until the beginning of the following week's episode. Employed irregularly or not at all in early serials like *The Adventures of Kathlyn* and *The Perils of Pauline,* the cliff-hanger chapter ending soon became an entrenched convention of the American movie serial. The cliff-hanger represents an extreme case of the central suspense principle of protraction (see Chapter 2): The audience sees the heroine, say, about to be butterflied by a buzz saw and has to wait until next Saturday to find out how she escapes.

Although serials declined in prominence and were subsequently eclipsed by feature-length thrillers, they left their mark upon the movie thriller, especially in terms of structure. Even in later, more sophisticated varieties, thriller films have often gravitated toward loose, episodic structures whose form is more serial than cumulative (a property that is by no means exclusive to thrillers). The thriller tends to break up into a series of self-enclosed set pieces, a string of semiautonomous climaxes. The serial makes unusually explicit the primacy of sheer suspense, of visceral impact, of immediate thrills, over the continuity and coherence of the narrative – priorities that, in less eccentric form, remain forceful throughout the history of the movie thriller.

Notable examples of this episodic tendency include many of the films in the James Bond series – for example, *GoldenEye* (1995), which, after reaching a series of spectacular, seemingly definitive action climaxes in Russia, jarringly shifts its scene to the Caribbean in order to serve up another crescendo of thrills. The detective thriller *The Big Sleep* (1946), analyzed in Chapter 6, is a famed (even notorious) example of a film that privileges episodic punch over narrative coherence. Alfred Hitchcock's *Strangers on a Train* (1951), the focus of Chapter 7, is much more tightly constructed, but even that film's structure tends toward a series of set pieces: the murder of Miriam, the party scene, Guy's trip to Bruno's house, the tennis match, the cigarette-lighter scene, the merry-go-round scene. Other Hitchcock thrillers, such as *The 39 Steps* (1935) and *North by Northwest* (1959), are even more overtly episodic. Hitchcock himself said of the former, "What I liked about it were the sudden switches and the jumping from one situation to the other with such rapidity."[18]

Another distinctive trait of early movie serials is their predominant use of female protagonists, as indicated by such typical titles from the period 1914–17 as *The Adventures of Kathlyn, The Perils of Pauline, The Exploits of Elaine, The Ventures of Marguerite, Lass of the Lumberlands, The Mysteries of Myra,* and *Perils of Our Girl Reporters.* It should be noted, however, that there is a tendency (becoming more pronounced as time goes on) for these eponymous heroines to be curiously passive figures who are constantly being tied up or otherwise placed in situations of helpless entrapment [Fig. 10], often while an active male co-star scurries around trying to save them.

In this respect, the early serial points both backward toward the stage melodrama and forward toward a thriller subcategory that could be called the "damsel-in-distress" thriller. Examples include *The Spiral Staircase* (1946), which blends Gothic and expressionist elements to depict a mute servant girl (Dorothy McGuire) menaced by a maniac in a Victorian mansion; *Lady in a Cage* (1964), which epitomizes modern-day social decay through the predicament of a cut-off shut-in (Olivia de Havilland) terrorized by lowlifes and juvenile delinquents; the influential horror movie *Rosemary's Baby* (1968), in which a pregnant young woman (Mia Farrow) is entrapped by a satanic cult in her Manhattan apartment building; the pioneer stalker film *Halloween* (1978), pitting a virginal baby-sitter (Jamie Lee Curtis) against an escaped psychopath; and the feminist-themed *Lady Beware* (1987), in which a young professional woman (Diane Lane) is viciously harassed by an insinuating sexual deviate. The form of such films (especially when they center on a woman trapped alone in a house) is somewhat different from that of thrillers centered on male action-heroes – less wide-ranging, more confined. These characteristics link the damsel-in-distress thriller to the Gothic horror story, from which it partly derives and with which it sometimes overlaps.

The heroine-centered serial began to lose its ascendancy with the increase of war-themed serials in 1916–18. The trend became more pronounced after 1920, when, in part because of censorship pressures and the serial's changing audience, there was a predominant shift to male heroes. This shift was accompanied by the use of more masculinized, adventure-oriented settings, such as the jungle, the pirate-infested high seas, the Far North, and, especially, the Wild West, which became the most common venue for serial stories.[19] At this point, the serial edged further away from the realm of the thriller and toward that of its sister genre, the adventure film.

Louis Feuillade and the French Serial

The development of the movie serial in the United States was paralleled and in some ways surpassed in Europe, where the form achieved an artistic significance well beyond that of its American counterparts. The leading country in the development of the European serial was France, and the most important figure involved was Louis Feuillade. A very prolific filmmaker, active since 1906, Feuillade had served his apprenticeship writing and eventually directing chase films, primarily of the comic variety.

As in the United States, there was a hazy line of evolution in France from the series film to the more tightly connected serial. Beginning with the Nick Carter detective adventures of 1908, there had been a number of popular French film series centered on crime themes. In 1913 Feuillade directed a film in this vein, *Fantômas*, based on a series of best-selling novels. The enormous success of the first *Fantômas* film

Figure 10. *Trail of the Octopus* (1919–20): Serial heroine (Neva Gerber) under constraint in exotic setting. (Academy of Motion Picture Arts and Sciences)

led to four sequels, each approximately one hour long, released in 1913 and 1914. They all feature the exploits of the ingenious master criminal Fantômas, who employs chicanery (such as making a glove from the skin of a dead man's hand in order to leave misleading fingerprints), bizarre devices (most famously, a murderous boa constrictor), and multiple disguises to outwit his two persistent antagonists, the police inspector Juve and the newspaperman Fandor.

The directions explored in *Fantômas* were further refined in Feuillade's next major crime series, *Les Vampires,* which is widely considered his masterpiece. Released in ten loosely connected parts (ranging from ca. 35 to 80 minutes long) in 1915 and 1916, *Les Vampires* is, like *Fantômas,* a hybrid of the series film and the evolving serial film. Unlike *Fantômas,* however, *Les Vampires* entirely lacks cliff-hanger endings. It also features an oddly proportioned and sometimes inconsistent story line, occasioned in part by the off-the-cuff manner in which the film was shot.

The convoluted plot centers on a flamboyant gang of criminals, the Vampires, and their dauntless opponent, the Parisian reporter Philippe Guérande. The Vampires, masters of disguise who often dress in black hoods and leotards while carrying out their crimes, are a shadowy, amorphous organization whose members don't always know each other and sometimes battle among themselves. In the course of the series, they are led by four successive Grand Vampires, each killed off in turn, each served, sexually as well as criminally, by the vampish Irma Vep (her name an anagram of Vampire), who constitutes the heart and soul not only of the Vampires but also of *Les Vampires* itself. Portrayed with fierce vitality by the music-hall actress Musidora, who became a movie star as a result, Irma Vep is the film's most attractive character, clearly surpassing the pallid hero Guérande and his obnoxious comic sidekick Mazamette. Irma's charisma undercuts the film's good-versus-evil schema and contributes to its somewhat amoral tone, reinforced by the fact that the good guys often use the same duplicitous methods as the bad guys and by the disturbingly ferocious slaughter of the Vampires at the end.

In a manner similar to that of the detective story (see Chapter 6) and the haunted-house story, *Les Vampires* creates a sturdy-looking world of bourgeois order and then undermines it. The thick floors and walls of châteaux and hotels become porous with trapdoors and secret panels. Massive fireplaces serve as thoroughfares for assassins and thieves, who scurry over the rooftops of Paris and shimmy up and down drainpipes like monkeys. Taxicabs bristle with stowaways on their roofs and disclose false floors to eject fugitives into convenient manholes. At one point, the hero unsuspectingly sticks his head out the window of his upper-story apartment, only to be looped around the neck by a wire snare wielded from below; he is yanked down to the street and bundled into the trunk of a departing taxicab in less time than it takes to say "Irma Vep!" In another scene, a wall with a fireplace opens up to disgorge a large cannon, which slides to the window and lobs shells into a nearby cabaret. In the film's most impressive set piece, gas is wafted into a high-society party. The panicked merrymakers try to flee, fists frantically pounding on the locked doors, and slowly collapse. Sprawled bodies cover the floor of the darkened salon; all is still . . . then two doors fly open in the deep background, and hooded, black-clad Vampires advance catlike into the room, picking over the wallets and jewelry of the unconscious guests.

Augmenting this atmosphere of capricious stability, the plot is built around a series of tour-de-force reversals, involving deceptive appearances on both sides of the law: "Dead" characters come to life, pillars of society (a priest, a judge, a policeman) turn out to be Vampires, and Vampires are revealed to be law enforcers operating in disguise. It is Feuillade's ability to create, on an extensive and imaginative scale, a double world – at once weighty and dreamlike, recognizably familiar and excitingly strange – that is of central importance to the development of the movie thriller and marks him as an important pioneer of the form.

Fritz Lang and the Thriller Metropolis

Next to France, the most significant venue for serials production in Europe was Germany – although these films were often hybrids of the serial and the series film, much like *Fantômas* and *Les Vampires.* From this context emerged Fritz Lang, who is equaled only by Hitchcock for his importance in the evolution of the movie thriller. In the late 1910s, Lang, an Austrian war veteran and art student, began working as a writer and assistant on German films, including Joe May's *The Mistress of the World* (*Die Herrin der Welt,* 1919), a series of eight feature-length episodes concerning a young woman's search through various exotic locales for a lost treasure with magical powers.

Lang soon got his own chance to direct a film of this type: *The Spiders* (*Die Spinnen*), a projected series of four feature-length episodes, of which only two were completed, released in 1919 and 1920. Similarly to *The Mistress of the World,* the plot concerns a globe-spanning search for exotic treasures. The Feuillade influence can be seen in the depiction of the Spiders, a Vampires-like secret organization of top-hatted criminals, operating under the command of the Asian villainess Lio Sha. Much of *The Spiders* is set in far-flung exotic locales, ranging from a ruined Inca city to a temple in India to a rocky island in the Falklands, inclining the film toward the sphere of the adventure story. Most relevant to the development of the thriller is an episode set in San Francisco. The city is revealed to contain a second, secret Chinatown beneath the visible one, its gates guarded by live tigers, its subterranean streets clogged with dissolute pedestrians. The key thriller concept of the modern city as a double world, at once ordinary and exotic, is here given a fanciful and unusually literal twist.

Lang took *The Spiders*'s sense of the exotic and the adventurous and inserted it into a more familiar modern-day context in *Dr. Mabuse, the*

Gambler (*Dr. Mabuse, der Spieler*), a four-hour crime drama released in two closely linked parts (the first ending with a cliff-hanger) in 1922. The subtitles of the film's two parts, *The Great Gambler: A Picture of the Time* and *Inferno: A Play about People of Our Time,* announce its intention to deal with close-to-home contemporary themes. The dissolute underworld so fancifully located beneath the streets of San Francisco in *The Spiders* is raised to the surface and explicitly related to the here and now of postwar society. *Dr. Mabuse, the Gambler,* especially in its first part, paints a broad canvas of the chaos and decadence of Weimar Germany, infected with financial uncertainty, widespread crime, drug use, promiscuity, gluttony, gambling, and other vices mechanically pursued by jaded pleasure seekers.

Dominating this lurid world from behind the scenes and manipulating it to his own ends is the title character, Dr. Mabuse, one of Lang's most famous creations (revived in two sequels by Lang and at least five additional films by other directors). Mabuse is a master criminal, descended from the archvillains of Feuillade and the American serials, but with a larger and more abstract dimension. At times Mabuse's elaborate schemes, whose aims range from the grandiose (manufacturing a stock-market panic) to the sordid (raping a world-weary countess), seem motivated less by profit or even survival than by an indiscriminate compulsion to spread disorder – to roll the dice and pull the strings. At one point, Mabuse fleeces a rich young American at cards but never collects the money; at another, he abducts his chief nemesis, a determined public prosecutor, but, rather than killing him, leaves him unconscious in a drifting rowboat from which he is soon rescued.

The German word *Spieler* (like its English equivalent "player") can mean both "gambler" and "actor," a reference to Mabuse's gaming activities and to his abilities as a performer. Like Feuillade's Fantômas, Mabuse is a supreme trickster and master of disguises. His many impersonations in the course of the film include a haughty financier, white-haired Dutch professor, black-bearded peddler, high-society psychoanalyst, and stage hypnotist. Mabuse is more imposing in his various masks than he is as his undisguised self, at which points he resembles a megalomaniacal gangster with an erratic temper. Mabuse finally seems less a flesh-and-blood character, or even a larger-than-life villain, than an abstract principle of chaos that pervades postwar Europe and produces a collective loss of will.

The social implications of *Dr. Mabuse, the Gambler,* as well as much of its excitement, diminish in the second part, *Inferno,* when Mabuse's far-reaching evil is reduced to the more familiar dimensions of a stock

Figure 11. *Dr. Mabuse, the Gambler:* Twisting back alleys of the thriller metropolis. (The Museum of Modern Art Film Stills Archive)

melodramatic villain, leering after the virtue of an abducted woman. The opening scenes of the first part (*The Great Gambler*), interweaving the various machinations that enable Mabuse to seize control of the stock market, display the intricate structuring techniques that would characterize later Lang masterpieces such as *Spies* and *M,* but this aspect is not as impressively sustained in the rest of *Dr. Mabuse, the Gambler.* The film's importance in the history of the thriller lies mainly in its elaboration of the thriller environment. *Dr. Mabuse, the Gambler* creates a duplicitous, labyrinthine network of decadent nightspots and secret dens that are linked together by murky thoroughfares, twisting back alleys, and subterranean passages [Fig. 11]. Concrete yet nightmarish, this world is infused with a mood of pervasive conspiracy – a mood made tangible through the film's visual design, keyed on a series of deep, compartmentalized spaces that entrap the characters and expose them to the menace of the master villain.

This environmental dimension is most elaborately developed in Lang's science-fiction classic *Metropolis* (1926). Although *Metropolis* itself is not primarily a thriller, its stunning vision of the modern city as a darkly dazzling dystopia – alienating, awesome, both primitive and overcivilized, riddled with labyrinths, and stratified into a shadowy underworld and a flashy overworld that disconcertingly mirror one another – has been enormously influential on a number of later thriller movies. These include Carol Reed's *The Third Man* (1949), which explores the confusion of postwar Vienna from the top of a Ferris wheel to the depths of the city sewers; the crime film *He Walked by Night* (1949) and the influential police movie *Dirty Harry* (1971), described in greater detail in Chapters 4 and 5, respectively; Ridley Scott's futuristic police film, *Blade Runner* (1982), set in an entropic high-tech, low-rent Los Angeles; and Lang's own later films, including the Mabusean thriller *Spies* (*Spione,* 1928), the crime classic *M* (1931), the impressive sequel *The Testament of Dr. Mabuse* (*Das Testament des Dr. Mabuse,* 1933), the spy film *Man Hunt* (1941; see Chapter 8), and *While the City Sleeps* (1956), a late variation on *M*'s theme of a psychopathic killer at large in a stratified metropolis.

In Lang's 1928 thriller *Spies,* which resembles *Dr. Mabuse, the Gambler* in many of its basic plot elements, the paranoid design of Lang's world goes beyond the physical settings and the composition of individual shots to encompass the overall design of the film, realized through structure and editing. Like Griffith, Lang makes extensive use of crosscutting, jumping back and forth between different locations and plot strands. However, in Lang's films, the device is used not only to enhance suspense and draw thematic parallels but also to develop a paranoid vision of a world where everything seems to fit together as part of an ever-widening web of conspiracy. In *Spies,* Lang frequently cuts between one locale and another, at times punctuating sequences with individual shots that show seemingly unrelated events or the looming presence of the master villain. These initially mysterious connections eventually stand revealed as interlocking pieces in a vast conspiratorial pattern, links in a chain that inexorably encircles the protagonists.

For instance, in one sequence of *Spies,* the following obscurely related pieces in the pattern are laid out before us: the master villain

Figure 12. *Spies:* Master criminal (Rudolf Klein-Rogge) spinning the web. (The Museum of Modern Art Film Stills Archive)

Haghi, seated behind the control-panel desk at his headquarters [Fig. 12]; a secret agent in clown makeup; the hero, Donald Tremaine, on board a train; his beloved, Sonia, on another train; and the number 33-133, glimpsed by Sonia on a slip of paper in Haghi's office and then on the side of Tremaine's departing train. The railroad car carrying Tremaine is clandestinely uncoupled in the middle of a tunnel. An oncoming train plows into it. At the station, Sonia hears news of a train wreck. Cut to a flashback image of the number 33-133 on the side of Tremaine's departing train. Cut to a flashback image of the same number on the slip of paper in Haghi's office. Dissolve to Haghi icily folding the slip of paper in his fingers. Cut to the number 33-133, "folded" on the crumpled, smoking wreckage of Tremaine's railroad car. Cut to Sonia, realizing in horror that Haghi has tricked them. Cut to a dramatic close-up of Haghi, staring into the camera, his face enveloped in a cloud of cigarette smoke that clears to reveal his sinister expression;

fade-out. And the secret agent in clown makeup? That piece, too, will fall into place, in the very last scene of the film.

Although rarely so intricately and rigorously realized, a similar sense of an underlying conspiratorial pattern is conveyed through the initially fragmented, ultimately interlocking structures of later thrillers. Such dark designs color the complex flashback structures of several films noirs, such as Robert Siodmak's *The Killers* (1946), which reconstructs a payroll robbery and its bloody aftermath through a series of temporally scrambled flashbacks, and Stanley Kubrick's *The Killing* (1956), which uses a baroque structure of flashbacks-within-flashbacks to similar effect in narrating a racetrack heist. Recent examples of Langian paranoia-shaped structures include Oliver Stone's *JFK* (1991), which takes a thrilleresque approach to the Kennedy assassination, and Bryan Singer's *The Usual Suspects* (1995), a heist story whose disparate pieces ultimately reveal a conspiratorial pattern and whose shadowy mastermind, Keyser Söze, has something in common with Lang's Haghi and Dr. Mabuse.

In Lang's *M* (1931), a harrowing account of a police manhunt, the film's network of interlocking events is no longer tied to a fantastic villain like Mabuse or Haghi. It becomes instead a generalized condition of entrapment that transcends any single individual or group, arising from both a concrete analysis of the social structure and an abstract sense of Fate. The police and organized crime converge on a doomed child-murderer, and questions of justice become inextricably entangled with institutional power, business interests, and maintenance of the status quo. Using sound for the first time, Lang employs *sound bridges* (i.e., a sound carries over from one scene or one locale into another) and *sound–image bridges* (i.e., something mentioned at one locale is immediately followed by an image of that thing at another locale) to strengthen the sense of linkage, of an all-enveloping pattern. After Lang's move to Hollywood in the mid-1930s, his epic style became more hero-centered, and his interlocking structures less intricate and overt, though still rigorous and expressive. One of his American films, *Man Hunt,* is analyzed in Chapter 8.

In contrast to the freewheeling narratives of Feuillade and the American serials, Lang's films delineate a rigorous geometric pattern within which everything falls into place, expressing a sense both of pervasive conspiracy and, beyond that, of larger forces that transcend any human conspirator. As critic Eric Rhode has suggested, there are implicit parallels between Lang's master villains, such as Mabuse and Haghi, and the director himself, each working to fashion the elements at his disposal into an airtight design.[20] The film itself becomes a labyrinth, not just in its mazelike physical settings and the convolutions of its plot line but in its very shot-to-shot structure, as intricate and painstakingly constructed as a spider's web. No filmmaker has conveyed more powerfully than Lang a sense of overwhelming entrapment, of a world whose every circumstance, every twist and turning, every corner and corridor, seem to conspire against the individual and draw her or him more deeply into the web.

This aspect of Lang's films can be related to a general sense of looming, nebulous anxiety that also informs the work of such early twentieth-century dread masters as the novelist Franz Kafka (*The Trial*, 1915; published 1925), the composer Alban Berg (*Wozzeck*, 1925), and the artist Giorgio de Chirico, whose famous painting *The Melancholy and Mystery of a Street* (1914) could easily serve as a poster for *M*. Lang adapted this high-culture concept to the entertainment formulas of commercial cinema, at the same time taking the lively pulp fancies of Louis Feuillade, Joe May, and *The Perils of Pauline* and investing them with greater artistic rigor and symbolic depth.

German Expressionism

These early thriller forms – the Feuilladean crime series, the American serial, the Langian paranoid thriller – can be interpreted against the background of World War I and, especially in Germany, its chaotic aftermath. Such events brutally demonstrated the powerlessness of the individual and the encroachment of mass warfare, mechanization, and nationalism into modern life – sinister trends for which the thriller is especially well equipped to provide both a reflection and an alternative (see Chapter 8). In his history of French silent cinema, Richard Abel observes that Feuillade's major serials, although they never deal with the war that is raging concurrently, reflect it indirectly through their unsettling juxtapositions of ordinary life with sudden, dreamlike eruptions of terror and violence.[21] The previously described use of gas attacks and heavy artillery by the criminal gang in *Les Vampires* makes such associations especially apparent.

Among moviegoers of the day, the antisocial activities of Fantômas and the Vampires uncomfortably recalled waves of criminal and political violence that had shaken France in recent years, including a highly publicized rampage by the anarchist Bonnot gang in 1912.[22] Similarly, the disorder and violence portrayed in Lang's *Dr. Mabuse, the Gambler* (especially the final battle between Mabuse's minions and the police) reminded many of the bloody Spartacist uprising, pitting leftist insurgents against government troops, that had convulsed Germany in 1918–19. Mabuse's schemes to destabilize the stock market and devalue paper currency have a clear relationship to the economic disarray and runaway inflation afflicting Germany at the time. In his well-known history of German cinema, *From Caligari to Hitler* (1947), Siegfried Kracauer, controversially and somewhat hindsightfully, sees in Mabuse's sinister power a foreshadowing of the fascist nightmare that was to rise from the chaos of postwar Germany.[23]

Although German society was in a state of breakdown in the 1920s, German cinema was enjoying the richest and most innovative period in its entire history. This period is usually referred to as "German expressionist cinema," in recognition of its relationship to the expressionist art movement, which was especially active in Germany from 1905 on. The expressionist movement affected all fields of art. Its influence upon the cinema is most apparent in the field of painting, in the work of such forerunners as Vincent van Gogh and Edvard Munch, and of such German artists as Otto Dix, Conrad Felixmüller, George Grosz, Ernst Kirchner, and Emil Nolde. Expressionism was an antinaturalistic (but, for the most part, nonabstractionist) movement, based on the principle of outer reality being transformed by a more essential inner reality that is subjective, emotional, spirit-centered, and visionary. Expressionist painting depicts a visible world that is vividly, even violently reshaped by extreme states of feeling and abstract underlying forces.

The flagrantly distorted sets and stylized gestures of the groundbreaking expressionist film *The Cabinet of Dr. Caligari* (*Das Kabinett des Dr. Caligari*, 1920) are explicit and somewhat overpronounced examples of this tendency in postwar German cinema. Expressionist techniques are used in a selective and modulated but still forceful manner in later works by leading German filmmakers – including F. W. Murnau's psychological portrait *The Last Laugh* (*Der letze Mann*, 1924) and fablelike romance *Sunrise* (an American production of 1927); G. W. Pabst's epic femme-fatale drama *Pandora's Box* (*Die Büchse der Pandora*, 1929); and the Fritz Lang films discussed above. For example, in the second part of *Dr. Mabuse, the Gambler*, a wavering shadow-pattern of prison bars dances over the face of Mabuse's incarcerated mistress, expressing both her panic and her crazed devotion; and in *The Last*

Laugh a huge shadow cast by the defrocked hotel doorman conveys his sense of self-inflation when he reclaims his status-enhancing uniform.

German expressionist cinema exerted a lasting influence on filmmaking all over the world, including the United States, where its distinctive elements were modified and absorbed into general Hollywood style. This influence was exerted both indirectly, through the exhibition of German films in foreign markets, and directly, through the large number of German film personnel (including Fritz Lang) who in the 1920s and 1930s emigrated to other countries, principally the United States.

One of the areas of moviemaking in which the influence of expressionism has been most relevant is the thriller. Expressionism emphasized specific visual codes that would be recycled throughout the history of the thriller, most obviously in film noir (see Chapter 4) but by no means confined to it: overdetermined chiaroscuro lighting, oppressive settings, exaggerated perspectives, intense compositional tension. More generally, expressionism provided a model for combining psychology and spectacle – for expressing internal psychological states through setting, lighting, camera movement, and other external cinematic means – that was quickly adapted, in more or less diluted form, to mainstream filmmaking practice. Expressionism is especially well suited to express such inner states as anxiety, tension, fear, and dread that have been central to the thriller. In addition, the expressionist concern with transforming the ordinary world into a heightened realm charged with extreme states of feeling is applicable to the heightened, intensified, sensationalized world of the thriller.

Harold Lloyd and the Comedy of Thrills

In the more prosperous and optimistic context of the United States in the 1920s, the major arena for thriller-related developments in the movies was comedy. Film comedy was at a peak of achievement during this period (sometimes referred to as the Golden Age of Movie Comedy or, in the title of a classic 1949 James Agee essay, "Comedy's Greatest Era"), reaping both commercial success and critical acclaim. Among the major figures of American silent comedy, the one with the most significant relationship to the thriller is Harold Lloyd.

Lloyd, an erstwhile dramatic actor who had drifted into movie comedy in 1914, spent three very busy years trying to perfect a clownish, eccentric character named Lonesome Luke. Lloyd's emergence as a major comedian began in late 1917, when he discarded Lonesome Luke's grotesque appearance for a more normal look whose salient feature was a pair of horn-rimmed glasses. In more than eighty short films made during the next four years, the tenacious Lloyd gradually developed a full-fledged character to go with his new appearance: an ordinary, all-American boy, aggressive but likable, immature but ultimately resourceful, who pursues (and almost always achieves) such conformist goals as popularity, financial success, and the girl of his dreams.

The other legendary comic stars of the era – the shabby, bowlegged Charlie Chaplin, the enigmatic, stone-faced Buster Keaton, the rotund Fatty Arbuckle, the infantile Harry Langdon, the cross-eyed Ben Turpin – flaunted an incongruous, even freakish quality in the very way they looked, dressed, moved, and behaved. However, there was nothing inherently outlandish or even comical about the Glass Character (as Lloyd called his spectacles-wearing persona). Lloyd said, "Everything about him was normal – his shoes, his clothes, the way he walked and talked. He could be the young man living next door. He was like anyone you passed on the street."[24]

Although the Glass Character might be too ordinary to be consistently funny in himself, Lloyd compensated by involving the character in extraordinary situations, so that the comedy would mostly happen to him rather than emanate from him. Such qualities give the Lloyd character much in common with many thriller heroes: He is a somewhat passive or reactive figure who is thrown into a series of extreme predicaments to which he must respond (see Chapter 1). One form this strategy took was what Lloyd called his "thrill pictures" and what Agee, more precisely, called "the comedy of thrills."[25] Lloyd's rationale was that, if audiences were scared or in suspense (that is, thrilled), they would also be more inclined to laugh. As Lloyd puts it in his 1928 autobiography, *An American Comedy,* "The recipe for thrill pictures is a laugh, a scream and a laugh. Combine screams of apprehension with stomach laughs of comedy and it is hard to fail."[26]

The purest form of Lloyd's comedy of thrills, derived in part from the cliff-hanger situations of serials, places his character in precarious suspension on the ledge of a high building. Lloyd first tried out the concept in a few of his short films, then made it the centerpiece of a full-length feature, *Safety Last* (1923), which has become his most famous film, featuring the legendary, often-reproduced image of Lloyd dangling from the minute hand of a large clock [see Fig. 3].

The plot of *Safety Last* sets up a situation in which the inexperienced and unwilling Harold (as Lloyd's character is called in almost all his silent features) must scale a twelve-story building in order to achieve both professional and romantic success. His upward progress is impeded by a number of perilous and amusing obstacles: Pigeons perch upon him, a net falls over his head, a dog snaps at him, and so on. A characteristic example of Lloyd's "a laugh, a scream and a laugh" method begins with Harold wearily hoisting himself onto the ledge of the eleventh story. An adventurous mouse crawls up his left pant leg. In an effort to dislodge the tiny intruder, Harold does an impromptu jig, legs shimmying, arms flailing, feet sliding toward the abyss. The spectators gathered below applaud mindlessly. Harold slips, falls, and catches hold of the ledge again. The rodent abandons Harold and lands atop a man poking his head out a window below. The man's toupee comes loose; he clutches his bald pate as mouse and hairpiece plummet together to an unknown fate.

An important factor in enhancing the thrill component of Lloyd's thrill comedies is the solidity of their usually urban settings. Although various tricks were used to ensure the star's safety, the climb up the building in *Safety Last* was filmed entirely on location, without any back projections or studio backgrounds. As several writers have pointed out, the film reinforces our awareness of this authenticity by using camera angles that nearly always show Harold (even in close shots) together with the busy street far below.[27] The film's forceful use of urban locations transforms everyday reality into a heightened, thrilleresque double world, as we see ordinary street traffic flow by in the distance, seemingly unaffected by the presence of this foolhardy adventurer risking his life high above.

Such realism caused some critics of the time to speculate that the film's tangible sense of danger would dampen its comedy – the audience members would be too busy biting their nails to laugh.[28] Indeed, there were newspaper reports of overthrilled patrons screaming and even passing out during the movie, and nurses were placed on duty in some theaters to attend to the faint of heart.[29] Despite these critical misgivings and alleged swoons, audiences then and now have had little trouble both screaming and laughing at Harold Lloyd's quintessential "thrill picture." *Safety Last* stands as an early and vivid example of the key thriller operation of sharply evoking combined and ambivalent emotions (see Chapter 1).

Although Lloyd applied the label "thrill picture" only to the three shorts and three features in which he grapples with tall buildings, film historians have reasonably expanded the category to include those Lloyd films that feature extended, hair-raising chase sequences. Among these are *Girl Shy* (1924), in which Harold races via fire engine, electric streetcar, motorcycle, horse-drawn wagon, horseback, and numerous automobiles to prevent his misguided sweetheart from marrying a two-timing cad, and *Speedy* (1928), Lloyd's last silent movie, which climaxes with a furious streetcar ride, filmed on location in New York City with only a few process shots.

The nonclownish, normalized persona of Lloyd's mature films was not without precedent in American silent comedy. Douglas Fairbanks, one of the biggest stars of the day, appeared in a number of popular feature-length comedies, made between 1915 and 1919, in which he typically portrays a modern young man who triumphs over wrongheadedness, in himself and/or others, through his qualities of enthusiasm, athleticism, and good-natured charm. In 1920, Fairbanks (who was a close friend of Lloyd's) switched his métier, specializing thereafter in period adventure films such as *The Mark of Zorro* (1920), *Robin Hood* (1922), and *The Black Pirate* (1926). From the early 1920s to the present day, film critics and historians have noted the resemblances between Lloyd's Glass Character and the brash, go-getting, all-American Fairbanks of the pre-1920 comedies.[30]

For the sake of tracking the evolution of the movie thriller, however, one can also point out a significant if less obvious relationship between Lloyd's Jazz Age go-getter and the Fairbanks of the post-1920 historical adventure films. At times, these associations take the form of specific gags and flashes of swashbuckling iconography. For example, in *Speedy* Harold brandishes a buggy whip like a pirate's cutlass in order to fend off a gang of thugs. In *Girl Shy* he dangles from the contact pole of an electric trolley, then drops into the front seat of a passing car, as efficiently if not as gracefully as Zorro or Robin Hood swinging from rafters or tree limbs. At the end of *Girl Shy*, Harold, prevented by his habitual stutter from explaining the situation to the would-be bride, simply slings her over his shoulder and carries her off in traditional buccaneering fashion [Fig. 13].

Even though Harold is often associated with such modern conveyances as the automobile and the trolley car, there is a certain lack of rapport implied in his tendency to part company with those mechanized vehicles. A frequently repeated gag in Lloyd's films has Harold running furiously to catch up with a train, trolley, or auto that has sped off, often driverless, without him. In addition, Lloyd's big chase scenes

Figure 13. *Girl Shy:* Modern-day swashbuckler (Harold Lloyd) and damsel in distress (Jobyna Ralston).

tend to describe a retrogression from modern-day conveyances to more primitive and traditionally heroic ones. For instance, the climactic chase in *Girl Shy,* with its multiple forms of transportation, follows a general pattern of devolution, beginning with automobiles and ending with Harold aboard a wagon drawn by a team of horses. Rising up out of his seat, he drives the wagon like a Roman chariot; when a wheel comes loose, he jumps on one of the horses and completes his journey riding bareback.

More generally, much of Lloyd's physical humor evokes the daredevil spirit of the swashbuckling Fairbanks of the historical adventures. Lloyd's archetypal comedy character can be seen as a descendant of such romantic adventure heroes as Robin Hood and Zorro, placed in a more ordinary, modern-day context. Similarly, Harold's edifice-scaling feats transport the mystiques of mountain climbing and tightrope walking into the concrete-and-steel regularity of urban architecture. As discussed in Chapter 2, the bringing of traditional romantic adventure into a "low-mimetic" modern world is a crucial operation in the thriller. Harold Lloyd's sunny, all-American "thrill pictures" have little sense of the exotic, and they largely lack the dimension of paranoia and conspiratorial menace that underlies most thrillers, but their fusion of mundane modernity and restored adventurousness, together with their laughing–screaming emotional dynamic, represent important contributions to the movie thriller.

Although Lloyd was the foremost practitioner of thrill comedy, the laughs-and-screams formula was employed by other silent-comedy stars, such as Charles Chaplin, whose classic *The Gold Rush* (1925) climaxes with a literal cliff-hanger in which Charlie and massive Mack Swain teeter in a cabin balanced on the edge of an icy precipice. Another example is Buster Keaton, whose imaginative masterpiece *Sherlock, Jr.* (1924) includes a hair-raising and strangely beautiful sequence in which his sleuth-hero sits unaware on the handlebars of a driverless motorcycle as it narrowly avoids oncoming cars, precipices, and other imminent disasters.

Thrill comedy declined in importance after the silent era; some commentators feel that the added realism of sound elevated the thrill component at the expense of the comedy.[31] However, the form still survives in latter-day variations, including the heist comedy *Quick Change* (1990), especially a nail-biting, laugh-getting scene in which fugitive bank robber Bill Murray frantically struggles to obtain the exact change for a departing bus as the police close in; *So I Married an Axe Murderer* (1993), a Mike Myers farce with its premise in its title and a Lloyd-like climax set on the ledges and rooftops of a multistory hotel; and several horror films that include heavy doses of slapstick violence and gory humor, such as Stuart Gordon's body-parts free-for-all *Re-Animator* (1985) and Sam Raimi's hyperkinetic *Evil Dead II* (1987).

Monsters of the Early 1930s

The early 1930s saw the flourishing of two generic movements – the Gothic-style horror film and the gangster film – that, although tangential to the mainstream of the thriller, exerted an important influence on later, more purely thrilleresque forms.

The horror cycle of the 1930s was in part a development of the thrill-comedy mode described in the previous section. In addition to dangerous heights and speeding vehicles, an often-used site for combining screams and laughs was the haunted house. Many silent-comedy stars explored the subject in their short films: Harold Lloyd inherited a ghost-infested mansion in *Haunted Spooks* (1920), Buster Keaton stumbled into *The Haunted House* (1921), Hal Roach's Our Gang were vexed by *Shivering Spooks* (1926), and so on. A number of feature-length films also mined this formula, several based on Broadway plays that had been spawned in the wake of Avery Hopgood and Mary Roberts Rinehart's smash comedy–thriller *The Bat* (1920, based on her 1908 novel *The Circular Staircase*). *The Bat* itself was filmed in 1926, to mixed commercial and critical response, but the major impetus came from *The Cat and the Canary,* a mixture of atmospheric chills and farcical laughs based on a 1922 play and released by Universal in 1927 to tremendous success. Paul Leni, the imported director of *The Cat and the Canary* and its 1929 follow-up *The Last Warning,* had been a leading figure in the German expressionist cinema; the expressionist influence at Universal was augmented by the arrival in 1930 of innovative German cinematographer Karl Freund.

Universal's leadership of the horror genre expanded in the early 1930s, again based on a combination of expressionist-derived atmospherics and theatrical literary sources, with humor a less central but still often vital ingredient. In 1931 Universal released the two most famous of all horror films, *Dracula* and *Frankenstein,* both derived primarily from recent stage adaptations rather than from the original novels by Bram Stoker and Mary Shelley, respectively. There had been successful and influential horror films before – such as the German-made *Nosferatu* (1922), considered the first major film treatment of the vampire theme, and *The Phantom of the Opera* (1925), in which grotesquerie specialist Lon Chaney gave the definitive interpretation of this often-filmed role – but the sensational successes of *Dracula* and *Frankenstein,* released less than ten months apart, spurred the first sustained cycle in the horror-film genre. This boom yielded such landmark horror movies as Rouben Mamoulian's flashy, innovatively sexualized *Dr. Jekyll and Mr. Hyde* (1932); Tod Browning's unsettling confrontation with the abnormal, *Freaks* (1932); Robert Florey's mad-doctor shocker, *Murders in the Rue Morgue* (1932); Karl Freund's solemn reincarnation tale, *The Mummy* (1932); James Whale's witty haunted-house movie, *The Old Dark House* (1932); Whale's inventive H. G. Wells adaptation, *The Invisible Man* (1933); Erle C. Kenton's Wells-based scientist-as-God parable, *Island of Lost Souls* (1933); Merian C. Cooper and Ernest B. Schoedsack's resonant ape-and-eros myth, *King Kong* (1933); Edgar G. Ulmer's mixture of Deco and diabolism, *The Black Cat* (1934); and Whale's *Bride of Frankenstein* (1935), an extravagantly stylized brew of offbeat visuals, black humor, and sexual innuendo that marks the culmination of the early thirties horror cycle.

These films are almost entirely set in hyperatmospheric, fantastic, already heightened environments, distant in time and/or place from the realm of familiar contemporary existence. For example, *Frankenstein* takes place in a temporally and geographically indeterminate setting that combines elements of Ruritanian operetta, Victorian manor house, modern electronic gadgetry, and traditional Gothic decay, centering on the ruined, crazily twisted tower that serves as Frankenstein's laboratory [Fig. 14]. Like its companion piece *Dracula* and most other films of the 1930s horror cycle, *Frankenstein* lacks the thriller's fundamental tension between the familiar and the exotic/adventurous.

In addition, these horror films are dominated by their dark eminences: villains, monsters, mad scientists. There is little sense of a vulnerable character drawn into a maze of danger and conspiracy. Possible candidates in this vein (such as the fiancée in *Frankenstein* or the young couple in *Dracula*) are peripheral and pallidly drawn, while center stage is monopolized by the compelling and repelling antics of the ruthless Count Dracula (Bela Lugosi), the demented Henry Frankenstein (Colin Clive), his monstrous creation (Boris Karloff), and power-crazed scientists such as Dr. Griffin (Claude Rains in *The Invisible Man*), Dr. Mirakle (Lugosi in *Murders in the Rue Morgue*), and Dr. Moreau (Charles Laughton in *Island of Lost Souls*).

A similar observation could be made about the concurrent upsurge of gangster films, which began in the late 1920s and was accelerated by the economic desperation of the early Depression. The gangster cycle produced a trio of definitive classics – Mervyn LeRoy's *Little Caesar* (1930) starring Edward G. Robinson, William A. Wellman's *The Public Enemy* (1931) starring James Cagney, and Howard Hawks's *Scarface* (1932) starring Paul Muni – with many less famous examples flooding movie screens in the peak years of 1930–2. The most characteristic of these films center on the rise and fall of a dynamic criminal, often monstrously fascinating in the manner of the horror-film cynosures and flanked by an equally grotesque collection of fellow hooligans, sporting such aptly uninviting monikers as Putty Nose, Fish Face, Snake Eyes, Bat, and Scabby. Much like in the horror films of the early 1930s, suspense is relatively slight, as more accessible and vulnerable identification figures are relegated to the sidelines, and we watch with mingled fascination and horror the ruthless rise and brutal demise of the vicious gangster.

Figure 14. *Frankenstein:* The Gothic environment.

Nevertheless, the early 1930s gangster cycle left an imprint on most subsequent forms of crime thriller, especially the mid-1930s "G-Man" cycle, the early 1940s detective film, the film-noir movement of the late 1940s, and the syndicate-gangster films of the 1950s (all covered in Chapter 4). In contrast to the horror films of the 1930s, the primary setting of the gangster film is emphatically urban and contemporary. The gangster film's most important contribution to the movie thriller was its investment of the modern urban environment with mythic, adventurous, and larger-than-life overtones. As cultural critic Robert Warshow wrote in his well-known 1948 essay, "The Gangster as Tragic Hero": "The gangster is the man of the city . . . not the real city, but that dangerous and sad city of the imagination which is so much more important, which is the modern world."[32]

The gangster metropolis is defined by such iconographic elements as lonely nighttime gas stations and warehouses, ripe for the robbing; glittering speakeasies and casinos, magnets for the same sort of decadent suckers upon whom Lang's Dr. Mabuse preyed; swanky apartment suites with plush white decor, representing the fleeting pinnacle of the gangster's climb and his illusory claims to whitewashed respectability; and flashing electric signs, signaling both the allure and the superficiality of the high life. It is a world of extreme highs and lows, both physical and social, as the gangster's trajectory yo-yos from the gutter to the penthouse and back to the gutter again. Gang wars turn neighborhood streets into literal battlefields, with automobiles spitting machine-gun fire and grenades shattering storefront windows. A frontier mythology of unbridled, self-made opportunity is squeezed into the pressure-cooker confines of city life, with inevitably explosive results. In this jungle of cities, gangsters are presented as atavisms, throwbacks to a more primitive and elemental phase of existence, and they are often given both simian and childlike qualities [Fig. 15].

In a manner similar to that described by G. K. Chesterton (see Chapter 2), the everyday features of the modern city become an adventurous landscape of caverns, peaks, and thickets. In *Little Caesar,* a neighborhood fruit store, presided over by a witchy crone, contains a false wall that springs open to disclose a burrowlike hideout where the fugitive Rico (Edward G. Robinson) is forced to hole up like an animal. In an ingenious heist in *The Public Enemy,* gangsters climb in through the roof to a warehouse's upper-story booze stash and snake a long siphon tube down the side of the building into the belly of a waiting gasoline truck far below. In *Scarface,* the camera twists through a dense jungle of potted palms and confetti streamers, following the path of an off-screen gunman (glimpsed only in apelike silhouette) as he stalks his prey.

The horror and gangster films of the era illustrate the impact of the coming of sound (ca. 1929) to motion pictures. This innovation was of particular relevance to the thriller in two contrasting though complementary ways. On the one hand, sound contributed greatly to the vis-

Figure 15. *Scarface:* The gangster (Paul Muni) as monster.

ceral immediacy of the thriller. The screeching of brakes and roar of automobile engines, the chatter of machine guns, the shattering of glass, and other acoustic outbursts boosted the sensational dimension of gangster films. The horror film was similarly enhanced by howling wind, crashing thunder, crackling electronic gizmos, creaking coffin lids, and screaming female voices (Fay Wray of *King Kong* and the 1933 *Mystery of the Wax Museum* was especially renowned for her piercing shrieks). In addition to sound effects, the quality of the spoken word was significant: Bela Lugosi's ripely accented intonations added immeasurably to the compelling strangeness of Count Dracula, and the citified patois of gangster films amplified their sense of urban immediacy.

On the other hand, the availability of offscreen sound contributed to the importance of the invisible – our anxious awareness of what we cannot see – that underlies critic Pascal Bonitzer's concept of partial vision in film suspense (see Chapter 2). In *Frankenstein,* the growls of the unseen monster announce to the distraught Henry Frankenstein that his botched creation is not only alive but within the creator's own home, although exactly where cannot be determined. In the opening scene of *Scarface,* the mournful whistling of hit man Tony Camonte (Paul Muni) increases the sense of menace as he advances out of frame toward his unsuspecting target. Similarly, a crucial scene in Fritz Lang's seminal crime film *M* depicts the capture of the hunted killer Hans Beckert (Peter Lorre) after he has hidden in the attic storeroom of a large office building. At the scene's climax, rather than crosscutting between the killer and his pursuers or showing them within the same frame, Lang keeps the camera fixed on the cowering Beckert [Fig. 16], unforgettably capturing his mounting panic as we hear the offscreen din of cracking wood and breaking glass, approaching footsteps and urgent voices, until a flashlight beam transfixes his terrified figure and a shout rings out, "Here! Here he is, the lousy cur!"

As noted above, the gangster films and horror films of the early 1930s, although lacking some key elements of the thriller, are important in its history because they lay the groundwork for later, purer forms in which these earlier models are constantly referenced. However, rather than the central classics, such as *Little Caesar, Scarface, Dracula,* and *Frankenstein,* it is some of the minor and peripheral films of these cycles that give us more direct anticipations of the future of the crime thriller and the horror thriller.

In 1931, the same year that he directed the gangster classic *The Public Enemy,* William A. Wellman made *The Star Witness,* a more modest (though still commercially successful) production. Gangsterism is also the mainspring of its plot, but, unlike in *The Public Enemy* and many other gangster films of the era, the gangsters themselves are not the film's central focus, which falls instead on an average American family named Leeds. They are tucking into their usual Sunday dinner when the city street outside their home erupts in an uproar of squealing brakes and crackling gunfire. Two men are being murdered, and the gangster responsible makes his getaway straight through the Leeds's

Figure 16. *M:* Cornered killer (Peter Lorre) hears doom approaching.

front door. As material witnesses, the family members now find themselves squeezed between a relentless district attorney and the gangster's murder-bent henchmen. Their home is besieged, their neighborhood streets and alleys a potential cover for kidnapping and murder. *The Star Witness* is a less ambitious and richly realized film than *The Public Enemy,* but its focus on vulnerable, identification-friendly characters, whose ordinary existences are suddenly plunged into adventure and danger, points more directly toward the future of the crime thriller – toward films such as *D.O.A.* (1950), in which a small-town accountant's inadvertent notarizing of an incriminating document leads to his being given a rare poison; *The Desperate Hours* (1955), in which a middle-class household is invaded by escaped convicts; and *Cape Fear* (1962), in which a respectable lawyer and his family become the targets of a vengeful ex-con.

In the horror genre, a comparable glimpse of things to come is provided by Michael Curtiz's *Mystery of the Wax Museum* (1933). Heavily indebted to *The Phantom of the Opera,* the story centers on Ivan Igor (Lionel Atwill), a brilliant wax sculptor whose treasured figures are destroyed in a fire that leaves him horribly scarred. Years later, his disfigured visage concealed beneath a lifelike mask, Igor resurfaces with a new wax museum, but his figures are now built upon corpses. His obsession fastens upon a young woman named Charlotte (Fay Wray), whom he traps in his underground workshop with the intention of immortalizing her beauty under boiling wax.

These elements align the film with the Gothic tradition and with most major horror films of the early 1930s, but *Mystery of the Wax Museum* departs from the norm in two important respects. First, Igor, although certainly a major presence in the film, is not allowed to dominate it to the extent that Henry Frankenstein, Count Dracula, and other monstrous figures do. More weight is given to the points of view of Igor's potential victims – not only Charlotte, but also Flo Dempsey (Glenda Farrell), an enterprising newspaper reporter who sets out to uncover the mystery of Igor's museum – with a resulting enhancement of the vulnerability and partial vision that produce suspense.

Second, after a prologue set in a heavily Gothicized and somewhat archaic London, Igor, along with all his Gothic/horror baggage, is transported to New York City, 1933 – in other words, to the same type of contemporary urban setting that might be found in a gangster film, populated with slang-slinging newspaper people, dissolute playboys and playgirls, Irish cops, and bootleggers. Although the join between the Gothic and modern sides of the film is sometimes clumsy, their coexistence creates the kind of double world, both ordinary and exotic, that epitomizes the thriller. In a similar manner, the key elements developed in the Gothic-style horror classics of the early 1930s would later become more powerfully thrilleresque when relocated into mundane modern-day contexts – as in *Cat People* (1942), which brings a medieval Serbian legend into contemporary Manhattan; *The Exorcist* (1973), in which an ancient Babylonian demon sets up camp in a Georgetown town house; *Martin* (1978), which mixes age-old vampire lore with supermarkets and talk radio; and countless others.

4

Classical Period

I n the mid-1930s, the movie thriller entered its classical period. This period was marked by the emergence of key, previously minor (sometimes even nonexistent) thriller genres, such as the spy film, the detective film, film noir, the police film, and the science-fiction thriller. A flamboyant visual style – characterized primarily by black-and-white cinematography, deep-focus lenses, low-key lighting, expressionist flourishes, and (especially after 1945) the increased use of location shooting – was evolved to convey the convoluted, charged world of the thriller. The period also witnessed the rise to prominence of the movie thriller's most famous practitioner, Alfred Hitchcock, discussions of whose work open and close this chapter.

Alfred Hitchcock and the Rise of the Spy Film

The popular appeal of horror films in the United States in the early 1930s (see Chapter 3), with their Europeanized settings and villains, can be attributed in part to a growing uneasiness regarding Europe – both as a source of the foreign "isms," such as communism and fascism, that were becoming increasingly prominent in the political life of Depression-blighted America, and also as the site of a deteriorating international situation that threatened to drag the United States into a widely dreaded war (the American public was overwhelmingly isolationist throughout the early and mid-1930s).[1] Horror films of the era present a mythic image of Europe as a source of decadence, rot, threat, madness – and, in the allegorical *The Black Cat* (1934), as a war-haunted powder keg about to blow sky high.

Such anxieties were more directly registered in the rise of the spy thriller, previously a marginal film genre, which was given increased relevance first by the ominous international tensions of the 1930s and then by the actual outbreak of World War II. The spy-movie boom represented a shift away from the isolationism that had informed early thirties horror films; nearly all spy movies of the period 1934–41 preach the inevitability of involvement and the necessity of commitment.

The spy-movie upsurge initially centered in Great Britain, where the genre dominated the midthirties output of Britain's leading filmmaker, Alfred Hitchcock. Between 1934 and 1938, Hitchcock directed five major spy thrillers: *The Man Who Knew Too Much* (1934), in which foreign agents kidnap a British couple's daughter in order to make them suppress their knowledge of a planned assassination; *The 39 Steps* (1935), about a London man who stumbles upon a plot to steal vital British military secrets; *Secret Agent* (1936), about a British spy (John Gielgud) trailing an enemy agent in Switzerland during World War I; *Sabotage* (1936), about a woman who discovers that her husband is involved in terrorist activities; and *The Lady Vanishes* (1938), in which passengers on a Continental train journey find themselves in the midst of a plot to kidnap a British agent. After relocating to the United States, Hitchcock continued his attachment to the spy genre with *Foreign Correspondent* (1940), about an American journalist (Joel McCrea) who uncovers the abduction of a peace-seeking Dutch diplomat, and *Saboteur* (1942), about a California munitions worker (Robert Cummings), wrongly accused of sabotage, who flees cross-country in search of the real culprits.

Hitchcock's quintet of British spy films secured his international reputation as a major director and cemented his identification with the movie thriller, a form in which he had worked only occasionally before – just four of the sixteen features Hitchcock made previous to *The Man Who Knew Too Much* could be considered thrillers. Hitchcock joined Fritz Lang in the top rank of filmmakers specializing in thrillers, and these two great directors' concerns both complemented and contrasted each other in ways that shaped the parameters of the classical movie thriller.

Hitchcock's approach to the spy genre and to the thriller in general is less abstract, less epic, less external than Lang's, with a greater emphasis on individual psychology and subjective points of view. (It should be noted that these differences are more a matter of relative emphasis than of stark opposition. The qualities foregrounded in Lang's films are by no means absent in Hitchcock's, and vice versa.) Whereas Lang's primary focus is on (as critic Andrew Sarris has said) "the structure of the trap," Hitchcock's is on the mental state of the entrapped.[2] Lang was the key figure in developing the thriller's architecture, its environmental exostructure, whereas Hitchcock performed a

Figure 17. *The Man Who Knew Too Much:* Low-key villain (Peter Lorre, center) and distraught father (Leslie Banks, right).

similar service for its psychological endostructure, through his development of techniques for emotional identification and intensification.

In Hitchcock's films, the villains are less awesome and otherly than those in the tradition of Fantômas, Dr. Mabuse, Haghi (*Spies*), Dracula, Tony Camonte (*Scarface*), and many of the American and European serials. Abbot (Peter Lorre), the leader of the spy group in *The Man Who Knew Too Much* [Fig. 17], projects an offhand, sardonic authority, broken by revealing moments when the mask of self-control slips; the terrorist Verloc (Oscar Homolka) in *Sabotage* is an awkward family man troubled by financial worries and a strained marriage. Both the villains and the protagonists in Hitchcock's thrillers are more individualized, psychologically detailed, and ordinary (as opposed to allegorically Everyman-like) than are those in the Langian tradition.

The viewer's emotional involvement with these more accessible characters is reinforced by the techniques of identification and point of view that have become widely associated with Hitchcock. In *Sabo-*

tage, after Mrs. Verloc (Sylvia Sidney) faints in the street at the news of her brother's death, a point-of-view (POV) shot shows a crowd of curious children peering down at her, with her brother's face appearing hallucinatorily among them. A similar configuration conjures up the vanished Miss Froy (Dame May Whitty) for the baffled traveler Iris (Margaret Lockwood) in *The Lady Vanishes.*

More crucial – if less overt than such heavily underlined, literal point-of-view configurations – is Hitchcock's use of the cinema's basic tool for indicating subjectivity: the reaction shot. Hitchcock became particularly adept at shifting between different conflicting, counterpointing, and coinciding perspectives in ways that complexify our response to the action and enrich it with dimensions only hinted at in the script. In the early sections of *The Man Who Knew Too Much,* reaction shots emphasize the effect of the kidnapping on the girl's mother (Edna Best), establishing the pivotal importance of her emotional conflict (climaxing in the assassination attempt at Albert Hall), even though the father (Leslie Banks) takes a more central and active role in the scenes that follow. Similarly, in *Secret Agent,* the emphasis on reaction shots of the initially flippant British agent Elsa (Madeleine Carroll) places her growing uneasiness at the center of the espionage maneuvers in whose action she has only a peripheral role. At the climax of *Sabotage,* the interplay of Verloc's and his wife's gazes around the deadly carving knife in her hand suggests a mysterious collusion between the two characters in his subsequent stabbing, as if he were inviting his own death.

Nearly all of Hitchcock's films from this period develop a strong tension between male and female points of view, with the villain's perspective occasionally invoked to complicate matters further. In *Sabotage,* Hitchcock encourages us to share Verloc's anxiety as he watches his wife confer with a nosy British undercover agent and as he impatiently waits for her dawdling kid brother to depart with a hidden time bomb. In *Saboteur,* the saboteur Frye (Norman Lloyd) is presented throughout as a remote and repellant figure; but in the famous Statue of Liberty climax, with Frye dangling helplessly from the top of the monument, the film details his terror with an immediacy that cannot help but arouse compassion for this ruthless killer. Such devices intensify the characteristic ambivalence of the thriller, pulling us in different directions and undermining our emotional stability.

Hitchcock at times uses Langian editing to convey a sense of abstract design and conspiratorial connection. Near the beginning of *The*

Man Who Knew Too Much, a circular array of pointing fingers indicates the hole left in a window by the assassin's bullet; this image is followed by a matching circular close shot of the distinctively brilliantined hair of the assassin himself. The opening montage of *Sabotage* shows electric lights flickering out throughout London, then a disabled power plant; a voice cries out, "Sabotage! Who did it?" – followed by a shot of the saboteur Verloc looming ominously into the foreground.

In Hitchcock's films, however, the underlying personal/psychological connections are ultimately more important than the conspiratorial ones. In the early scenes of both *The Man Who Knew Too Much* and *Sabotage,* the most essential elements are not those that indicate conspiracy but those that define the central family relationships in each case. In *The Man Who Knew Too Much,* the parents' flippant, seemingly callous references to adultery and unwanted children belie, with characteristic British reserve, an underlying affection and inner toughness that will enable this family to pull through their coming ordeal. In *Sabotage,* on the other hand, the intimations of deception, obligation, and insecurity beneath a surface of civility are already pointing toward that family's imminent disintegration.

Hitchcock's use of crosscutting between different locales operates in a similar manner (as does his cutting between reaction shots within a single locale). As in Lang's films, Hitchcock's crosscutting serves other functions while building suspense. Primarily, it elaborates not the structure of the trap (as in Lang) but the psychological dimensions of the event, drawing connections based on such elements as guilt, emotional involvement, and conflicted loyalties. An example is the agonizing scene in *Secret Agent* wherein the approaching doom of a suspected traitor is intercut with the mounting anxiety of his worried wife, his whining dog, and the guilt-ridden conspirator Elsa.

Another, even more resonant example is the Albert Hall sequence in *The Man Who Knew Too Much,* possibly the first great scene of Hitchcock's career. Although personal issues are foregrounded in Hitchcock's spy films, broader political dimensions are by no means lacking. Indeed, the spy genre provided him with an especially effective format for dramatizing the conflict between private and public spheres, the narrow and broad perspectives. The Albert Hall sequence is notable for the expressive way in which it employs point-of-view shots, focus changes, and linked camera movements to portray the dilemma of a mother who must choose between the safety of her kidnapped child and that of a politician whose imminent assassination will bring chaos to Europe. The intense intertwining of personal and public reaches a crescendo when a long shot of the concert hall slowly blurs, coloring the larger perspective of political conflict with the immediacy of a mother's tears.

Hitchcock's British spy thrillers developed some of the patterns that would be continued in the work of British and American filmmakers as the spy film moved from depictions of prewar maneuvering to the even deadlier game of wartime espionage. Hitchcock was the most active figure in bringing to the screen the literary fashion of the "amateur-spy story," pioneered by such early spy novels as *The Riddle of the Sands* (1903) and *The Thirty-Nine Steps* (1915) and refined by authors Graham Greene and Eric Ambler in the 1930s (see Chapter 8). With the exception of the offbeat *Secret Agent,* all of Hitchcock's pre-1945 spy films center on civilians accidentally caught up in the dirty business of espionage. This format places a greater emphasis on the disruption of ordinary existence by the intrusion of international intrigue, as opposed to business-as-usual maneuvers in the more insular, specialized world of diplomats and professional agents. The amateur-spy format was employed in Hitchcock's first two American spy films (*Foreign Correspondent* and *Saboteur*) and in several wartime film versions of Ambler and Greene novels, including *Journey into Fear* (1942), an Ambler adaptation in which a naïve American arms expert (Joseph Cotten) finds himself trapped on a ship with a porcine Nazi assassin, and *Ministry of Fear* (1944), a Fritz Lang journey into paranoia, based on Greene's tale of a released "mercy killer" (Ray Milland) who blunders straight into a Nazi spy ring operated under the auspices of a British mothers' charity.

The double world of the thriller metropolis – at once ordinary and exotic, humdrum and adventurous – was a central element of many of the era's spy films, which extended their scope beyond the boundaries previously established by the gangster film. The urban locus of the gangster film had been a fairly circumscribed one, centering on the ethnic working-class neighborhoods of New York and Chicago, fringed by a tawdry night world of speakeasies and gangster hangouts. The vaguer and more pervasive world of spying broadened the class and spatial boundaries of the thriller metropolis, placing its subversive activities not just in "those" neighborhoods but in every conceivable corner of the city, no matter how anomalous or seemingly innocuous.

Hitchcock was a master of such juxtapositions of the familiar and the sinister, and they became a central ingredient of the "Hitchcock touch." In *Sabotage,* a cozy pet shop filled with twittering birds is the front for a family-operated bomb factory, where explosives are packed into jam jars and share shelf space with a little girl's dolls. In *The Man Who Knew Too Much,* a church full of hymn-singing parishioners is actually a nest of ruthless conspirators. In *The 39 Steps* and *Saboteur,* urbane upper-class gatherings proceed smoothly while murder is pursued in their midst. Such convivial public functions as a concert (*The Man Who Knew Too Much*) and a music-hall performance (*The 39 Steps*) become covers for political violence. In both *Sabotage* and *Saboteur,* these disruptive activities take place in movie theaters, as if Hitchcock were trying to extend a sense of destabilizing menace to the very auditorium where we spectators are sitting.

In part, this dispersion of menace reflects the democratic spirit of these spy films – the idea that everyone is involved, everyone at risk, everyone a potential if unofficial soldier. It also conveys a more comprehensive paranoia, a sense of shadowy conspiracies whose reach extends far beyond that of even the most extensive gangster organizations, with their relatively crude and anarchic methods. In *Confessions of a Nazi Spy* (1939), the first major American spy thriller of the World War II era, a quaint Scottish village serves as the communications nexus of a Nazi espionage network that extends throughout the United States; spy plots are hatched at drugstore soda fountains; propaganda leaflets are slipped into schoolchildren's lunch boxes.

The spy films of this era not only broadened the thriller's concept of the city but also extended its scope beyond the city. A large number of spy films from this period involve travel to a significant degree. Most often, these excursions do not traverse the exotic locales – African jungles, Indian temples, Incan ruins – that were commonly visited in serials and series films such as *The Adventures of Kathlyn* and *The Spiders;* nor do they usually involve extraordinary methods of transportation, such as parachute drops, safaris, submarines, or even high-speed auto chases. Instead, they are most often explicitly connected to ordinary tourism. Michael Denning, in his excellent book on British spy fiction, details how the discourse of tourism pervades the James Bond novels.[3] However, the essential connection between tourists and spies can be dated much earlier than that, to the pioneer spy novels *The Riddle of the Sands* and *The Thirty-Nine Steps* (see Chapter 8) and to the spy-genre renaissance that began in the 1930s in both film and literature.

The period between the wars could be considered the first golden age of tourism, a time when travel became substantially domesticated and middle-class – a tamer version of the more expensive and/or exacting expeditions of earlier decades. The idea that one's cozy package tour to Scotland or Switzerland could suddenly become a flash point of life-threatening danger and world-shaking crisis restores a romantic/adventurous dimension to vacation travel, much as the car chase restores a romantic dimension to daily commuting. This attachment to the familiar forms of foreign travel centers on two areas in the spy thriller: (1) modes of transportation (typically the rail journey and the sea cruise) and (2) quintessentially touristic settings.

The Man Who Knew Too Much, Hitchcock's first major spy thriller, begins with images of travel folders; the initial action, involving murder and kidnapping, takes place during a British family's Alpine vacation at the resort of St. Moritz. A major sequence of *The 39 Steps* is set on the Flying Scotsman train run from London to Edinburgh; the innocent fugitive Hannay (Robert Donat) and his reluctant companion Pamela (Madeleine Carroll) spend the night at a quaint Scottish inn. The events of *Secret Agent* are centered at a Swiss resort hotel, with a chase scene set during a tour of a chocolate factory. *The Lady Vanishes* opens with a group of stranded tourists at an Alpine inn; the rest of the film is set on a passenger train [Fig. 18]. Carol Reed's *Night Train to Munich* (1940) involves another intrigue-laden train journey; the final shoot-out takes place on a ski-resort cable car. The major portions of both *Journey into Fear* and *Across the Pacific* (1942) are set on sea cruises, which cloak Nazi assassination and Japanese sabotage, respectively.

The spy genre, by its very nature, centrally involves the key thriller theme of the intrusion of exotic and foreign elements into the familiar and domestic. In the late 1930s and early 1940s, this theme took such forms as the disruption of comfortable modern tourism into a more primitive, vulnerable, and exciting state; the revelation of the familiar modern metropolis as a center of espionage and conspiracy; the entanglement of ordinary citizens and their ordinary lives in the perils of international intrigue; and the transformation of modern mass warfare into an arena of old-fashioned individual heroism. The last issue, along with the spy story's literary background, is discussed at greater length in Chapter 8.

Detective Films of the 1940s

Other major developments in the forties thriller centered around various forms and phases of the crime film. The early and mid-1940s saw

Figure 18. *The Lady Vanishes:* Embattled train passengers discover the thrilling side of tourism.

a rise in the popularity and importance of the detective film. B-movie detective series flourished during the period, including those featuring the relatively gritty Michael Shayne (1940–7), the debonair Gay (later Tom) Laurence a.k.a. "The Falcon" (1941–9), the reformed thief Boston Blackie (1941–9), the psychologist-sleuth Robert Ordway a.k.a. "Crime Doctor" (1943–9), and the updated adventures of Sherlock Holmes (1942–6), with Holmes battling Nazi spies as well as more mythic opponents such as the Spider Woman and the Creeper.

Of special relevance to the development of the thriller was a smaller but enduringly influential group of detective films that were major productions (involving top-rank personnel, commercial success, and critical attention) and reflected the hard-boiled style developed by such authors as Dashiell Hammett and Raymond Chandler. The first important entry in this movement was John Huston's *The Maltese Falcon* (1941), featuring Humphrey Bogart as Dashiell Hammett's adamantly unsentimental, dubiously ethical Sam Spade, challenged by an alluring woman (Mary Astor), corrupt father figure (Sydney Greenstreet), and elusive treasure. On its initial release, *The Maltese Falcon* was a respectable but not remarkable success whose reputation and influence soared as the hard-boiled detective-film cycle gained ground in the next few years.[4]

The Glass Key (1942), another Hammett adaptation, told a complicated tale of a murder frame-up during a political campaign. The most esteemed hard-boiled dick, Raymond Chandler's cynical but gallant Philip Marlowe, was introduced to the screen in *Murder, My Sweet* (1944), with former musical star Dick Powell transforming himself into a credibly tough private eye, hired by an intimidating goon (Mike Mazurki) to find his long-lost love amid a web of upper-class decadence and deception. Marlowe appeared again in *The Big Sleep* (1946), centered on the romantic chemistry of Humphrey Bogart and Lauren Bacall (see Chapter 6), and *Lady in the Lake* (1947), noted for director-star Robert Montgomery's heavy use of subjective-camera techniques. Other notable hard-boiled mysteries of the era include the elegant *Laura* (1944), in which a taciturn police detective (Dana Andrews) develops an obsession for the fashionable young woman (Gene Tierney) whose murder he is investigating; and the soft-edged *The Dark Corner* (1946), in which an embittered gumshoe (Mark Stevens) is helped out of a jam by his devoted secretary (Lucille Ball).

These hard-boiled detective films drew upon elements from previous thriller and thriller-related genres: thick nocturnal atmosphere and semiexpressionist style from the Gothic-style horror film; tough-guy dialogue, seedy urban demimonde, and stock criminal characters from the gangster film; and, from the spy film, the use of lone-wolf heroes, the frequent location of villainy among decadent upper-class types, and a sense of large-scale intrigue and conspiracy. As with the spy film, the enhanced popularity and status of the detective film were largely war-generated phenomena. Similarly though less overtly, the detective film can be seen as a response to the regimentation and deindividualized conflict of the war. Like the typical spy-film hero of the period, the detective is often a neutral who becomes personally committed in the course of the action, working out a private accommodation between self-reliance and social responsibility. However, unlike the spy-film hero, the hard-boiled detective is usually neither an amateur nor an organization man. Instead, he is a free-lance professional (albeit a marginal one), typically operating out of a small office in a less-than-fashionable part of town, working for hire but ultimately answerable to no one but himself. (Exceptions include *The Glass Key,* in which the primary investigator is a political boss's loyal henchman, and *Laura,* in which he is a plainclothes police detective.)

Many commentators have pointed out the kinship between the individualistic private detective and more traditional adventure heroes such as the gunslinger of westerns and the questing knight of medieval romances. In Chandler's novels, Marlowe is referred to, with more than a touch of irony, as "a knight in dark armor rescuing a lady," a "shop-soiled Galahad," and "Two-Gun Marlowe, the kid from Cyanide Gulch."[5] However, in characteristic thriller fashion, the detective operates not in the more romantic and adventurous realms of the Wild West or the enchanted forest, but in the mean, low-mimetic streets of the modern city. Los Angeles (despite strong contention from New York and San Francisco) is the capital of the forties detective film. Its assets include its boomtown atmosphere, premature decadence, "exotic" Latino and Asian enclaves, and proximity to Hollywood, polestar of bewitching and easily frustrated dreams. Also crucial is the city's sprawling, varied topography, extending from the wharfs of Long Beach to the foothills of Hollywood and calling for exploration by automobile, an accessory as essential to the 1940s detective as the cowboy's or knight's steed.

A central accomplishment of these hard-boiled detective films was to develop a more complex thriller hero – more sexualized, morally ambiguous, and, despite his hard-boiled label, vulnerable on a number of levels: emotional, moral, and, perhaps most vividly, physical (see Chapter 6). A striking but by no means unrepresentative example is provided by Dick Powell's Marlowe in *Murder, My Sweet* [Fig. 19]: brained by a blackjack, subjected to bone-crushing grasps from his gargantuan client, clubbed with a pistol, pumped full of drugs, blinded by an eye-scorching gun blast, and repeatedly sinking into a deep black pool of velvet oblivion. The numerous beatings and other forms of bodily harm suffered by these private eyes indicate the detective film's contribution to a general escalation of screen violence in the 1940s – an enhancement of the thriller's visceral and sadomasochistic aspects (see Chapter 1), which, although tame by later standards, generated considerable controversy at the time.

Film Noir

The hard-boiled detective film fed directly into – and often overlapped with – film noir. A phase of the crime film, strongly mixed with elements

Figure 19. *Murder, My Sweet:* Battered and drugged detective (Dick Powell) confronts sinister doctor (Ralf Harolde).

of melodrama, film noir arose in the mid-1940s, as World War II was coming to an end. After the movement was well under way, it was identified and labeled by French critics and film enthusiasts, who coined the term *film noir* (literally, "black film") in late 1946. The first book devoted to the subject, Raymond Borde and Étienne Chaumeton's *Panorama du film noir américain,* appeared in France in 1955. However, the film-noir phenomenon was not formally recognized by American filmmakers, critics, or audiences while it was actually taking place; neither the term nor the concept behind it received wide circulation in English-language film criticism until ca. 1970. The term was derived from "Série noire," a French series of black-covered crime novels (many of them translations of American hard-boiled fiction), and it aptly expresses the darkness at the heart of film noir, encompassing both its shadowy visual style and its bitter view of American society. Film noir was the most pessimistic general movement in Hollywood history, portraying a dark world riddled with corruption, deceit, neurosis, and victimization.

Film noir caught a powerful undercurrent of letdown and confusion beneath the bright surface of war's-end optimism. With the war ending, there was no longer a clear-cut enemy to focus upon (although the Soviet Union was soon to provide one), and the forces troubling people seemed vague and difficult to pin down. The incomplete reintegration of the wartime female work force into the domestic sphere expanded this sense of confusion to the areas of sexuality and gender roles, as reflected indirectly in the central film-noir figure of the femme fatale. Film noir plugged into the nebulous sense of insecurity that loomed at the time – and that would eventually be given more concrete form by the exaggerated fear of communist subversion, UFOs, and vast criminal syndicates found in many films of the 1950s. A few noir-related films – such as *The Blue Dahlia* (1946), *Crossfire* (1947), and *Act of Violence* (1949) – dealt explicitly with war-generated traumas and the maladjustment of returning soldiers. However, the film-noir movement, arising out of the war's-end vacuum, was oriented more toward expressing generalized anxiety, realized in abstract and mythic terms. This abstract dimension is one reason why the noir style and worldview have been able to detach themselves so easily from their original context and migrate to other eras and cultures, as in the French New Wave of the early 1960s and the neo-noir movement that began in the 1980s and is still going strong.

Because the film-noir phenomenon was largely overlooked during its initial heyday and recognized only later by film critics, film historians, filmgoers, and filmmakers, the boundaries of the movement are highly provisional, with a considerable gray area of more or less noirish films orbiting around a dark nucleus of widely acknowledged core classics. Fritz Lang's doom-laden couple-on-the-run tale *You Only Live Once* (1937), the nightmarish B movie *Stranger on the Third Floor* (1940), and the obsession-shaded Broadway mystery *I Wake Up Screaming* (1941) are frequently cited as harbingers of the movement. The earliest movie universally accepted as a major film noir is probably Billy Wilder's *Double Indemnity* (1944), based on James M. Cain's often-imitated story of an insurance agent (Fred MacMurray) who conspires with a faithless wife (Barbara Stanwyck) to murder her husband. By 1945–6, the film-noir movement, although unacknowledged and unlabeled, was in full swing, generating an array of retrospectively recognized noir classics: Fritz Lang's tense, rigorous *The Woman in the*

Figure 20. *The Maltese Falcon:* The hard-boiled detective (Humphrey Bogart) in control . . .

Window (1945) and *Scarlet Street* (1945), both concerning Milquetoast husbands (played by Edward G. Robinson in both films) who slowly sink into a quagmire of sexual temptation and murder; the low-budget wonder *Detour* (1945), in which a weak-willed hitchhiker (Tom Neal) is taken for a fate-filled ride; *Mildred Pierce* (1945), a James M. Cain adaptation in which a stirring melodrama about a self-made woman (Joan Crawford) is placed within a constraining film-noir framework of murder and guilt; *The Killers* (1946), whose famously complex flashback structure inserts a film-noir robbery-and-betrayal story within a detective-film framework; and *The Postman Always Rings Twice* (1946), based on another archetypal James M. Cain tale of lovers (John Garfield, Lana Turner) conspiring to kill the husband, with bracingly ironic results.

Many critics and historians have placed hard-boiled detective films such as *The Maltese Falcon* and *The Big Sleep* within the hazy borders of film noir. A possible basis for differentiating between the hard-boiled

Figure 21. . . . and the film-noir detective (Robert Mitchum, center) entrapped: *Out of the Past.*

detective film and purer forms of film noir – drawn more in terms of a continuous spectrum than a clearly marked dividing-line – might focus on the relative degree of control exercised by the detective hero. At one end of the spectrum would be the predominantly masterful Sam Spade (Humphrey Bogart) of *The Maltese Falcon* (1941) [Fig. 20], while at the other end would be more noir-shaded gumshoes such as Jeff Markham (Robert Mitchum) of the moodily masochistic *Out of the Past* (1947) [Fig. 21], bedazzled and ultimately doomed by a femme fatale, and Mike Hammer (Ralph Meeker) of the demythicizing *Kiss Me Deadly* (1955), whose Spade-like control and cockiness are ultimately revealed to be pathetic and even contemptible forms of self-delusion.

Although the extent to which hard-boiled detective films and films noirs overlap is open to question, there is general agreement that the primary literary influence on the film-noir movement was the hard-boiled detective movement spearheaded by Hammett and Chandler (see Chapter 6), along with the work of authors such as W. R. Burnett,

James M. Cain, and Cornell Woolrich, who extended the hard-boiled style into areas beyond the detective genre. Film noir took from the hard-boiled detective story its caustic, ironic tone (particularly in the dialogue); its colorful use of slang; its frequent use of the femme-fatale figure; its depiction of a decadent, seductive world; and its sense of widespread corruption extending through all levels of society, especially the upper ones. Film noir differs from the hard-boiled detective story in these ways: A detective protagonist is not necessary; there is even more emphasis on atmosphere and style; and the hero, whether a detective or not, is more of a victim and less in control than hard-boiled pros like Sam Spade or Philip Marlowe usually are.

Unlike the typical hard-boiled detective hero, who fights a lonely but usually efficacious battle against corruption, the film-noir hero is often crushed by a bewildering web of conspiracy, compounded by his own inner weaknesses. Like the detective, the film-noir hero is usually an outsider, but his ineffectuality functions more as a cautionary critique than as a glamorization of the lone-wolf hero. Such concerns locate film noir at the threshold of an era that would be characterized by an intense consciousness of conformity and its discontents, as reflected in such classic sociological studies as David Riesman's *The Lonely Crowd* (1950) and William H. Whyte's *The Organization Man* (1956).

As noted previously, a central element of the thriller is vulnerability. This encompasses both the sense of vulnerability that is created in the audience through emotional ambivalence and instability (see Chapter 1) and the vulnerability that frequently characterizes the thriller protagonist. In the spectrum of thriller protagonists, the film-noir hero is one of the most profoundly vulnerable, with a passive or susceptible personality that combines with hostile outside forces to overwhelm him and sweep him away.

Thrillers enhance vulnerability by suspending us between conflicting emotional responses, such as comedy–fright, curiosity–repulsion, sadistic superiority–masochistic identification. In film noir, the basic suspension is often between deterministic tragedy and black comedy. On the one hand, what happens to the victimized noir hero seems very grim and relentless; he is like a Greek tragic hero at the mercy of the Fates. On the other hand, the way he plays the fool, stumbling into one excruciating situation after another, makes him into something of a comic butt. To paraphrase Oscar Wilde, one must have a heart of stone not to laugh – or at least crack a mordant smile – when Tom Roberts (Tom Neal), the petulant protagonist of *Detour,* impulsively picks up a raspy-voiced shrew who happens to be the one person in the world who can guess his incriminating secret; or when Frank Chambers (John Garfield) and Cora Smith (Lana Turner), the none-too-clever conspirators of *The Postman Always Rings Twice,* find the glutinous district attorney hovering over their shoulders every time they try to bump off Cora's husband; or when Michael O'Hara (Orson Welles), the self-described "fathead" of Welles's *The Lady from Shanghai* (1948), gullibly agrees to fake a man's murder . . . and then watches open-mouthed as the police parade the "fake" victim's real corpse in front of him. The folly of the hero is underscored by the sardonic tone of many films noirs, to which the hero himself frequently contributes, through the use of first-person narration expressing an ironic, self-mocking attitude toward his own plight. The noir hero falls somewhere between a tragic victim and a hapless fool, and it is often difficult to decide whether he is a sympathetic or a ridiculous figure.

Film noir centrally involves a certain *look* as well as a certain type of tone, hero, and story. No other generic movement in Hollywood history has been so strongly characterized by its distinctive visual style. Although other influences are relevant (French crime films in the "poetic realism" vein of the late 1930s, the early twentieth-century "Ashcan" school of American painting, and individual artists such as George Bellows, Reginald Marsh, and Edward Hopper), the main source for noir style is the German expressionist cinema of the 1920s and early 1930s. As noted in Chapter 3, expressionist style breaks down a sense of ordinary visible reality to create a world shaped and even bizarrely distorted by subjective forces such as anxiety and terror.

Nearly all films noirs contain a marked degree of visual stylization, ranging from the highly atmospheric to the outright eccentric. At its most intense, film noir's renowned visual style is characterized by hyperatmospheric chiaroscuro lighting, ominously elongated shadows, nightmarishly extreme angles, and precipitously unbalanced compositions. The crucial "partial vision" aspect of the movie thriller (see Chapter 2) is greatly enhanced by this visual style, whose overriding functions often seem to be obscurity and disorientation rather than clarity and stability. Film noir provides a stylistic equivalent for the concept of the labyrinth, based on obliqueness, murkiness, splayed compositional lines, deep convoluted spaces, and foregrounds blocked by objects that limit our view. The labyrinthine dimension of the thriller is also reflected in film noir's penchant for complex, convoluted plots, their complexity sometimes enhanced by elaborate flashback structures. These elements of noir style, in toned-down and specifically applied forms, have entered into the general vocabulary of thriller movies as means of connoting menace, anxiety, and a general intensification of the ordinary world.

More than a genre or a type of story or even a distinctive look, film noir is perhaps most of all a general mood, evoked by such elements as sultry city nights, cool torch songs, walls striped by venetian-blind shadows, and streets splashed with rain and neon, evoking such feelings as hard-boiled cynicism, alienation, unfocused discontent, melancholy, and romantic yearning. The film-noir atmosphere is bluesy, shadowy, and predominantly urban. As the vital American cities of the early twentieth century began to rot at their underfinanced cores and dissipate into the regularity of suburbs and shopping centers, film noir represented a twilight efflorescence of the modern metropolis as a still glamorous and mythic place, where alluring decadence was about to fall into a sordid decay whose most suitable vehicle would be the police thriller.

Semidocumentary Crime Films

In recent years, film noir has become one of the most celebrated and influential forms of the movie thriller. However, as noted in the previous section, it was not perceived that way in the films' original context of the late 1940s, when the coherence of the movement was unrecognized and the individual films often dismissed by critics as trashy and lurid. At the time, much more significance was attached to another variety of crime film: the semidocumentary. The most distinctive and heavily promoted (though often exaggerated) aspects of these films were their reliance on factual story material and their extensive use of nonstudio locations. Location shooting had been a rarity in previous Hollywood sound films – for instance, the classic hard-boiled detective films of the early 1940s, such as *The Maltese Falcon* and *The Big Sleep,* were almost entirely studio-bound. Several factors created a receptive climate for the more extensive use of factual stories and authentic settings:

1. a number of Hollywood filmmakers' participation in making war documentaries,
2. the audience's growing familiarity with such documentaries and with relatively gritty and fact-based fictional war movies,

3. technical advances in lightweight equipment and fast film stocks,
4. spiraling production costs and labor disputes at Hollywood studios, and
5. the influence of the Italian neorealist film movement, which created a worldwide sensation in the mid-1940s with its striking use of location shooting and slice-of-life story material.

The semidocumentary movement began with *The House on 92nd Street* (1945), a tale of the FBI rooting out a nest of Nazi spies ensconced behind a swanky Manhattan dress shop; the movie was produced by *March of Time* newsreel veteran Louis de Rochemont and filmed in a choppy, newsreellike style. The more accomplished *Call Northside 777* (1947), in which a reporter (James Stewart) fights to clear a decent man framed for murder, makes especially effective use of the many-tiered rotunda of the Illinois State Penitentiary and the seedy, train-rattled neighborhoods around the Chicago stockyards. *The Naked City* (1948), the most acclaimed film of the movement, re-creates a Manhattan police manhunt for a brutal killer, with an exciting final chase through the crowded thoroughfares and Byzantine back ways of the Lower East Side.

Authenticity-connoting conventions of semidocumentary films include the use of a typewriterlike font in the opening credits, a newsreel-style voice-of-authority narrator, and an introductory statement asserting that this is a true story (usually taken from law-enforcement files), photographed "wherever possible" in the actual locales where the events had taken place. It wasn't long before films announcing themselves in these terms as semidocumentaries were toning down their factuality to accommodate more conventional story patterns and combining their documentary aspects with selectively applied noir stylistics. Films of this type include *Kiss of Death* (1947), an old-fashioned criminal-trying-to-go-straight melodrama garnished with New York locations, and *The Street with No Name* (1948), the story of an FBI agent (Mark Stevens) who goes undercover to befriend a mobster, harking back to the late-1930s "G-Man" cycle pioneered by its director, William Keighley. One of the most noteworthy of these hybrids is *He Walked by Night* (1949), in which the rational world of the police, presented in prosaic semidocumentary style, is sharply contrasted with the id-dominated realm of the cryptic killer (Richard Basehart), photographed in deep shadows and steep angles by the most distinc-

tive noir cinematographer, John Alton. By the early 1950s, noir elements and semidocumentary elements, despite their stylistic differences, had both been absorbed into the prevailing style of the era's
crime films.

Rather than diminishing the transformative aspect of thrillers (see
Chapter 2), the use of locations provided additional opportunities for
articulating the frisson – the tension between the ordinary world and
its adventure-heightened state – that stirs the thriller's feverish pulse.
For example, the richly textured cinematography of *The Naked City*
makes nighttime El trains glitter like strings of jewels on jet-black
bands of moving steel, and the climax of *He Walked by Night* transforms
Los Angeles's utilitarian storm drains into a *Phantom of the Opera* neth-
erworld of concrete caverns and rippling shadows.

Location shooting also made more accessible the types of vast labyrinthine spaces so amenable to the thriller but difficult to create within the limited confines of a studio or back lot. In the climax of *The
Naked City,* the high towers, crisscrossing girders, rushing trains, and
seemingly endless stairs and platforms of New York's Williamsburg
Bridge [Fig. 22] express the disorientation and exhaustion of the cornered killer to such an extent that (much as in the climax of Hitchcock's *Saboteur*) he compels unexpected sympathy. In *The Street with
No Name,* the final chase sends the participants clambering over the
catwalks and silent machinery of a dark, deserted factory, its dormant
dynamos suggesting a power struggle between the forces of law and
criminality for control of America's future might. Most spectacularly,
the far-flung network of underground storm drains in *He Walked by
Night* becomes both an extension of the killer's subterranean power
and a manifestation of the overwhelming immensity of modern Los Angeles, which eventually defeats even this cold-blooded superman.

The heroes of semidocumentary crime films are generally well-
adjusted insiders and organization men, happily married (and hence
femme fatale–proof), working diligently for newspapers, police depart-
ments, and government agencies such as the FBI. This represents a
turning away from the lone-wolf, socially marginal protagonists of the
detective film and film noir. The semidocumentary heroes are successful in their battles against crime while remaining relatively untainted
by their contact with it. Such qualities, together with the films' en-
dorsement of technology, teamwork, and the legal system, position
them as a rational and affirmative alternative to the paranoia and pessi-
mism of the contemporaneous film noir.

Figure 22. *The Naked City:* Exhausted killer (Ted de Corsia) atop the Williamsburg Bridge. (The Museum of Modern Art Film Stills Archive)

The rationalist and institutional dimensions of semidocumentary crime thrillers are reinforced by their extensive use of scientific crime-detection procedures, presented in elaborate and sometimes stupefying detail [Fig. 23]. The climax of *Call Northside 777* hinges upon the use of a newfangled method of photo enlargement and its transmission over a news wire. The dead center of *He Walked by Night* is a lengthy sequence in which witnesses gradually reconstruct an image of the suspect from an assortment of slides. Most semidocumentary films also prominently feature spectrography, fingerprint data banks, microscopic analysis, polygraph tests, and similar technocriminological marvels.

Authority figures, such as judges, police chiefs, political leaders, and newspaper publishers, are generally benign in these films. Flags, official buildings, and government plaques figure heavily and unironically in their iconography. Patriotic airs, such as "America the Beautiful" and "Battle Hymn of the Republic," are often woven into their musical

Figure 23. *The Street with No Name:* FBI agents (Mark Stevens, John McIntire, Lloyd Nolan) approach crime scientifically.

scores. The preceding cycles of spy films and detective films can be seen as individualistic alternatives to the war film. In contrast, the semidocumentary crime films of the late 1940s, with their patriotic trappings, vaunting of authority, and emphasis on cooperation, seem more like an extension of the war-film spirit into postwar civilian life. The films also feature frequent appearances by the FBI (including reverent invocations of its arch Red-hunter, J. Edgar Hoover) and a general atmosphere of relentless surveillance, widespread suspicion, and virtuous informing. All of these ingredients brought the crime thriller into the grim arena of the cold war.

Anticommunist Spy Films

The semidocumentary movement had begun with an anti-Nazi spy film, *The House on 92nd Street,* and it now encompassed the anticommunist spy cycle (inaugurated by *The Iron Curtain* in 1948), often with minimal adjustment of its basic ingredients. Like their domestic-set World War II counterparts, many of these early cold-war spy thrillers drew heavily upon the conventions of thirties gangster films. The American branch of the Communist Party was often fancifully depicted as a gangster organization, its members more likely to operate protection rackets, wear loud clothes, smoke big black cigars, drive big black cars, and take enemies for one-way rides than to circulate petitions or discuss Marxist theory. Also carried over from the gangster film were such conventional plot devices as the undercover agent infiltrating the gang (*I Was a Communist for the FBI*, 1951; and its offshoot TV series *I Led Three Lives*, 1953–6) and the reformed wrongdoer trying to go straight (*The Red Menace*, 1949; *The Woman on Pier 13*, 1950).

The anticommunist cycle has been interpreted (perhaps too wishfully) by historians as a half-hearted sop used by Hollywood to defuse criticism from political pressure groups such as the House Un-American Activities Committee (HUAC). Whatever one's opinion of their political content, as thrillers these films are usually deficient in action and suspense. Instead, much time is expended on declarations of contempt for communism, lending a distinctively rhetorical and querulous tone to many of the anticommunist spy films.

In addition, movie communists of the era were too limited and contrived to live up to their billing as major conspiratorial threats. Despite the political hysteria of the era and the rhetoric of the films themselves, Hollywood's version of the domestic Red Menace rarely added up to more than a few isolated groups of stereotyped goons from old gangster and anti-Nazi movies, sprinkled with some priggish intellectuals of the "striped-pants snob" variety vilified by Senator Joseph McCarthy and his supporters.[6] The sense of a sinister force invading and infecting all aspects of decent American life was much more effectively conveyed in syndicate-gangster films and in conspiracy-themed science-fiction films such as *Invaders from Mars* (1953) and *Invasion of the Body Snatchers* (1956).

In 1953 the anticommunist spy cycle produced its lone masterpiece, Samuel Fuller's *Pickup on South Street,* the story of a cynical pickpocket (Richard Widmark) who comes into possession of a top-secret microfilm. The limitations of the subgenre were transcended by the film's dynamic style and its vivid depiction of a seedy but vital subculture of grifters, bimbos, and stool pigeons. Otherwise, cold-war espionage remained a minor film subject until cultural perception of it had evolved to the point where it could be viewed with more ironic distance, for purposes of either spoof-inflected fantasy (as in the James Bond movies and their many imitations) or downbeat demythologizing (as in the anti-Bond spy films of the late 1960s and early 1970s).

The Flawed-Cop Cycle

Crime continued to be a significant focus of the thriller in the 1950s. Merging elements of film noir and semidocumentary, the police thrillers of the early 1950s combined the organizational heroes of the latter with the social and spiritual malaise of the former. Unlike the clean-cut, well-adjusted lawmen of semidocumentary films, these police heroes are often deeply flawed and morally compromised in the noir tradition. One group of films, dealing with corrupt cops led astray by greed and/or sexual desire, are basically extensions of film noir, with police protagonists traveling down the same dark road previously navigated by such noir antiheroes as insurance agent Walter Neff (Fred MacMurray) in *Double Indemnity* and private detective Jeff Markham (Robert Mitchum) in *Out of the Past*. Films in this vein include *The Man Who Cheated Himself* (1951), in which a veteran San Francisco cop (Lee J. Cobb) covers up a killing committed by his manipulative mistress (Jane Wyatt); *The Prowler* (1951), about a frustrated policeman (Van Heflin) who murders an innocent man in order to get both his money and his beautiful wife (Evelyn Keyes); and *Pushover* (1954), a melancholy, rainy-streeted romance in which a cop (Fred MacMurray) on a stakeout falls hard for the woman (Kim Novak) on the other side of his binoculars.

A smaller but more significant group of 1950s police thrillers deal with cops whose failings spring not from moral weakness but from rigidity and excessive zeal. These protagonists are anguished renegades whose neurotic obsession with justice alienates them from society and ultimately drives them to either self-destruction or a painful catharsis. The opportunities for moral and psychological complexity provided by this framework produced peaks of achievement for several of the directors and actors involved.

The first major film of this type was *Where the Sidewalk Ends* (1950), in which a notoriously brutal police detective named Mark Dixon (Dana Andrews) accidentally kills a suspect and then tries to pin the crime on the mobster (Gary Merrill) against whom he has a long-standing personal vendetta. Setting a pattern for other films in this vein, *Where*

Figure 24. *Where the Sidewalk Ends:* "Half-cop and half-killer" (Dana Andrews).

the Sidewalk Ends depicts a war waged on two parallel fronts, one against the criminal-infested city and the other inside the hero's tormented head. Dixon is split in two directions, so that he resembles both his victim and his nemesis (Merrill), but this is just one of several intricate moral conflicts explored by Otto Preminger's tense, subtle film. The tangled ambiguities of *Where the Sidewalk Ends* are grounded by the great stone face of Dana Andrews [Fig. 24], who delivers a superbly suggestive deadpan performance as the divided detective – "half-cop and half-killer," as his gangster antagonist says.

Less concentrated than *Where the Sidewalk Ends* but often equally intense is *On Dangerous Ground* (1952), the story of a burnt-out big-city cop, Jim Wilson (Robert Ryan, in one of the era's most moving portrayals of alienation and loneliness), whose uncontrollable violence causes him to be exiled to a backcountry murder case. Going well beyond semidocumentary, the use of locations here is thoroughly expressive; the heart of the film is its poetic contrast between the feverishly dark city that defines the hero's despair and the chill snow-white countryside that catalyzes his rebirth. Nicholas Ray, a director known for his kinetic vision of an unstable universe, makes especially effective use of views from moving automobiles as a destabilizing vantage point to present the two rhyming environments of the film. *On Dangerous Ground* also features two electrifying chases through the snow, with the out-of-place policeman a dark, awkward figure in a white world, his city-slicker shoes slipping and skidding across the icy terrain.

That the deeply flawed heroes of these films are policemen, rather than the marginal men of detective films and film noir, conveys a more urgent sense of crisis, closer to the heart of the social order. However, both Mark Dixon and Jim Wilson are maladjusted loners, initially without family or loved ones, alienated from their fellow policemen as well as from the civilian world. The next major film in the cycle, *The Big Heat* (1953), provided a significant shift in emphasis. The hero, Dave Bannion (Glenn Ford, giving a powerful interpretation of cold fury), is initially more like the heroes of semidocumentary crime films: normal, mentally sound, blessed with a loving wife and daughter, generally satisfied if occasionally frustrated with his job as a policeman. Rather than quickly plunging us into the dark side, as do *Where the Sidewalk Ends* and *On Dangerous Ground, The Big Heat* begins with a lengthy, careful exposition of Bannion's job routine and happy home life – until his wife's gangland murder sends him over the edge into a revenge-obsessed crusade against the criminal syndicate. The film thus gives increased emphasis to the disruption of ordinary middle-class life by sinister forces – a theme central to many later crime films and other forms of the thriller.

In contrast to the eccentric, high-contrast world of film noir and the other major flawed-cop films, *The Big Heat* is filmed in a crisp, austere style, for the most part only lightly shadowed. The film depicts a homogeneous, deceptively antiseptic world, keyed on stark walls and hard glass surfaces. Even the odious Mob boss Lagana (Alexander Scourby) presents a facade of impeccable respectability, complete with a portrait of his sainted mother and jitterbug parties for his doted-upon teenage daughter. Rather than the starkly divided world forged by Ray in *On Dangerous Ground,* director Fritz Lang here creates a treacherous double world, poised between icy detachment and searing violence.

Another major thriller related to the flawed-cop cycle is Orson Welles's *Touch of Evil* (1958). Although the ostensible hero is a clean-cut drug-enforcement agent played by Charlton Heston, the film is dominated by Welles's showy performance as the villainous cop Hank Quinlan, corrupt in the name of justice (unhinged by the unavenged murder of his wife, he frames suspects who, he asserts, are always guilty). One of the most baroquely stylized Hollywood films ever made, *Touch of Evil* represents a climactic explosion of high noir style, transforming a seedy border town into a bewildering labyrinth of sleaze and industrial decay, and a drab motel into a chamber of perverse horrors.

Intensified by tortured McCarthy-era liberalism, expressive late-noir stylistics, and postwar Hollywood's obsessive preoccupation with masculine vulnerability, the major flawed-cop films of the 1950s collectively represent a peak of character development and moral complexity in the history of the movie thriller. Their strong interior dimension links them perhaps more closely to the Hitchcockian psychological crime thriller (see Chapter 7) than to more action- and mystery-oriented forms of the police thriller.

The relentless exploitation of the law-and-order issue in American politics during the last quarter-century has caused police thrillers to take a simpler and more indulgent attitude toward their protagonists' moral fallibility, psychological vulnerability, and use of violence. The culmination of this trend is Mel Gibson's popular portrayal of the psychotic cop as a lovable clown in the *Lethal Weapon* series (1987, 1989, 1992, 1998). Occasional efforts have been made, however, to treat the subject with a complexity that recalls (though rarely equals) the best police thrillers of the 1950s. Examples include *Tightrope* (1984), in which a kinky New Orleans cop (Clint Eastwood) is both shadowed and mirrored by the sex maniac he is hunting; *Q & A* (1990), in which a green assistant district attorney (Timothy Hutton) struggles to bring down a corrupt veteran policeman (Nick Nolte); *The Glass Shield* (1995), in which an idealistic black rookie (Michael Boatman) allows himself to become involved in an LAPD cover-up; and *L.A. Confidential* (1997), in which the deceptively clear moral positions of three fifties cops – a thug (Russell Crowe), an opportunist (Kevin Spacey), and a reformer (Guy Pearce) – become scrambled into Premingerian ambiguity.

Syndicate-Gangster Films

Flourishing around the same time as the flawed-cop cycle were the syndicate-gangster films, which place their protagonists in conflict with vast, shadowy criminal organizations that seem to reach into every corner of American life. This theme is sometimes combined with that of the neurotic cop, as in *The Big Heat* (described in the previous section) and *The Big Combo* (1955), the latter a stylish mix of perverse sexuality and spectacular low-key lighting, about an embittered police detective (Cornel Wilde) who is obsessed with both destroying a Mob boss (Richard Conte) and possessing the mobster's mistress (Jean Wallace), a high-class blonde with a yen for down-and-dirty sex.

Like the era's anticommunist spy films and alien-invasion science-fiction films, the syndicate-gangster films reflect a mood of generalized cold-war paranoia – the pervasive sense that a hostile organized force is invading everyday life and threatening American security. They were also directly inspired by a specific current event: the Kefauver hearings. Beginning in 1950, a congressional committee headed by Senator Estes Kefauver made a headline-generating circuit of major American cities in order to establish its premise that crime in the United States was controlled by an organized national syndicate. The Kefauver committee's notion of an all-powerful, monolithic syndicate is considered by crime historians to have been exaggerated (organized crime is not *that* organized, tending more toward anarchy and fragmentation); but, like such contemporaneous preoccupations as UFO sightings and domestic communist subversion, it exerted a powerful pull on the popular imagination and produced a cycle of films to accompany it.[7] In 1957 the waning syndicate-gangster cycle received a double boost, first from the McClellan committee's Senate investigation of underworld ties to labor unions, and then from the Apalachin Conference, a secret confab of top mobsters in upstate New York that was accidentally discovered by local police and given sensationalized coverage in the national press.

The first film in the syndicate-gangster cycle was *The Enforcer* (1951), released in the wake of the Kefauver hearings but based on an earlier investigation: the exposure in 1940 of the notorious Murder, Inc., a criminal organization dedicated to the business of murder-for-hire. The film presents a chilling vision of crime as an impersonal and institutionalized business, similar in many respects to legitimate businesses, with contracts, accounts, and deliveries. This vision contrasts with the more emotional and personalized criminal style of earlier crime-film cycles, such as gangster and film noir, and introduces one of the distinctive themes of the emerging syndicate-gangster cycle, with its emphasis on the thin line between the criminal world and the normal world.

Although *The Enforcer* represents a major step in the evolution of the syndicate-gangster film, it lacks an important ingredient that would be supplied by later entries, including *The Big Heat.* The central character of *The Enforcer* is a public prosecutor (Humphrey Bogart) working to expose the murder racket. We learn absolutely nothing about his personal life – family, romantic, or otherwise – and the film begins on a note of extreme, shadow-drenched paranoia that never lets up. On the other hand, *The Big Heat,* as noted in the preceding section, begins with a lengthy establishment of the hero's normal routine and happy home life, which are subsequently shattered by the disruptive force of the criminal world.

The Big Heat places its primary emphasis not on the war against the criminal syndicate (as does *The Enforcer*), nor on the obsession of the hero (as do *Where the Sidewalk Ends* and *On Dangerous Ground*), but on the violation of ordinary life and decent institutions, particularly the home and the family. The most resonant syndicate-gangster films of the period are centrally concerned with families being terrorized, wives blown up, brothers bumped off, children slaughtered, and sacred domestic sanctuaries invaded, assaulted, contaminated. This emphasis moves the syndicate-gangster film closer to the key thriller dynamic of ordinary modern life being transformed by the incursion of forces that are more primitive, dangerous, and violent.

The Phenix City Story (1955) was the first of two crucial but markedly different syndicate-gangster films (the second was *The Brothers Rico* in 1957) directed by low-budget specialist Phil Karlson. Based on recent events and shot in a raw, visceral style, it tells of an Alabama lawyer (Richard Kiley) who is driven to lead the fight against a syndicate that has turned his hometown into an infamous Sin City [Fig. 25]. More briefly than *The Big Heat,* the film establishes the hero's family life and typical suburban neighborhood. It then plunges Hometown, USA, into an orgy of violence that features women and children slapped silly in the middle of Main Street, a crippled old man shot point-blank in the face, a paper boy mowed down by an automobile, and, most appalling, a little girl's corpse heaved into the hero's front yard with a note pinned to her dress: "THIS WILL HAPPEN TO YOUR KIDS TOO."

A blunt variation on the theme of the underworld invading the domestic world occurs in *Murder, Inc.* (1960), a late, post-Apalachin entry in the cycle. The weak-willed hero (Stuart Whitman) is a struggling singer in debt to the Mob. Needing a place to hide out, the infamous ganglord Louis Lepke (David J. Stewart) peremptorily commandeers the singer's apartment. The idea of mobsterism violating the family's sacred space is nightmarishly literalized by having the gangsters actually move into the hero's home and intrude themselves into his daily routine: Lepke takes over one of the bedrooms, pries into the sexual habits of the hero and his wife, orders two-minute eggs every morning, plans murders in the living room.

The breakdown of the borderline between the criminal world and the lawful world is a major theme of fifties syndicate-gangster films. Earlier forms of the gangster film had drawn a strong distinction between the two worlds: Gangsters inhabited a clearly demarcated milieu of speakeasies, pool halls, back rooms, and lower-class ethnic neighborhoods; their appearance and behavior set them apart from the respectable world, and they looked painfully out of place whenever they tried to enter it. In the syndicate-gangster films of the 1950s, this sharp division is radically undermined: Organized crime comes right into your living room (as in *Murder, Inc.*) and your front yard (as in *The Phenix City Story*).

The appearance and environment of the movie gangster thus become less distinct. This tendency is evident in *The Big Heat,* as discussed in the previous section. The Mob boss Lagana behaves in a sophisticated and civilized manner, lives in the best part of town, and associates with the best kind of people. Although Lagana's underlings are less refined, they, too, adopt styles of dress and decor that are more mainstream than those traditionally associated with gangsters. *The Phenix City Story* draws a sharper distinction between goonish gangsters and spick-and-span suburbanites, but Karlson's later syndicate-gangster classic, *The Brothers Rico* (1957), takes the process of homogenization to its furthest extent. In this eerie, understated film, whose aura of invisible menace invites comparison with the science-fiction classic *Invasion of the Body Snatchers,* the criminal and normal worlds have become virtually indistinguishable. The film's gangsters, from the kingpin down to the lowliest henchman, do not resemble conventional criminals in appearance, manner, or life-style. They dress casually, with yachting caps and cowboy hats in place of the traditional fedoras; their manner is bland and nonconfrontational; even their violence is muted,

Figure 25. *The Phenix City Story:* The Mob comes to Main Street.

causing hardly a ripple in the placid surface of American society. In *The Brothers Rico,* the syndicate has become so ordinary, so ubiquitous and invisible, so thoroughly woven into the fabric of American life, that it is like the very air one breathes – a vision of crime that is in some ways more disturbing than the graphic and outrageous violence of *The Phenix City Story.*

Science-Fiction Thrillers and Monster Movies

The 1950s saw the first major movement in the movie science-fiction thriller. Even though it had been flourishing throughout the 1930s and 1940s as a form of specialized popular literature, science fiction before 1950 was an occasional and minor movie genre, its rare ambitious works, such as *Metropolis* (1926) and *Things to Come* (1936), having at best a tangential relationship to the thriller.

Reflecting anxiety over nuclear war, communist subversion, and, more subtly, the era's conformist values, science-fiction films enjoyed their first golden age in the 1950s. However, unlike previous science-fiction films, these do not center on speculative futures (in contrast to *Metropolis* and *Things to Come*) or mad scientists (such as the transparent protagonist of 1933's *The Invisible Man* and the people-shrinker of 1940's *Dr. Cyclops*). With a few notable exceptions, such as producer George Pal's nuts-and-bolts space-travel tales *Destination Moon* (1950) and *Conquest of Space* (1955), science-fiction films of the 1950s concentrate on the more thriller-oriented theme of the alien invasion. This theme has an obvious kinship to the contemporaneous anticommunist and syndicate-gangster cycles, with a similar emphasis on sinister outside forces subverting American normalcy.

The alien-invasion theme took four basic forms in the 1950s. The first, with strong connections to the war film, depicted a full-scale assault, complete with flying saucers and massive destruction. Examples include the pattern-setting George Pal production *The War of the Worlds* (1953), in which reptilian Martians blast Earth into near-submission; the less prestigious *Earth vs. the Flying Saucers* (1956), in which Ray Harryhausen's special effects wreak exhilarating havoc on Washington landmarks; and the chamber-drama variation *The Thing from Another World* (a.k.a. *The Thing,* 1951), in which the invading force consists of a single but very dangerous vegetable creature at large in an Antarctic compound.

In a less common, liberal variant on the alien-invasion scenario, the visiting aliens are actually benign (though they may possess great destructive powers) but are perceived as monstrous by small-minded humans. Examples are *The Day the Earth Stood Still* (1951), in which the space-federation emissary Klaatu (Michael Rennie) comes to Earth with a message of nonviolence, only to be greeted with hysteria and bullets, and *It Came from Outer Space* (1953), in which crash-landed aliens race to repair their spaceship before a lynch mob of unenlightened Arizonians closes in.

More prevalent was a hybrid of science fiction and horror that is sometimes referred to as the "monster movie." In this type of film, the invading force consists not of aliens from outer space but of ordinary (if creepy) Earth species bloated to monstrous proportions by nuclear testing or some other form of bad science. Humankind was threatened on screen by a remarkable assortment of king-sized creatures – such as ants, coming out of the desert and giving the L.A. storm drains another workout (*Them!*, 1954); a furry arachnid, devouring livestock and menacing a desert community (*Tarantula,* 1955); grasshoppers, bouncing into Chicago (*Beginning of the End,* 1957); a lizard, flicking its forked tongue at small-town teenagers (*The Giant Gila Monster,* 1959); ravenous rodents, gnawing the inhabitants of a remote island (*The Killer Shrews,* 1959); and even *Homo sapiens,* stomping through gaudy Las Vegas (*The Amazing Colossal Man,* 1957). Some monster movies involve an aberration of the time factor rather than the size factor, as in *The Beast from 20,000 Fathoms* (1953), best known for its spectacular Harryhausen climax in which a nuclear-thawed dinosaur tangles with a Coney Island roller coaster. A very effective reversal of the gigantism theme is provided by the metaphysically tinged *The Incredible Shrinking Man* (1957), in which the hero dwindles incessantly and the familiar world around him becomes perilously large.

In the most resonantly thrilleresque version of the alien-invasion theme, the aliens proceed by stealth rather than overt force, taking over the planet via mind-control and replication, so that "They" are nearly indistinguishable from "Us." This theme produced the quintessential science-fiction film of the 1950s, *Invasion of the Body Snatchers* (1956), in which the inhabitants of a California town are transformed into emotionless replicas by "pods" from another world. The theme had been explored earlier in *Invaders from Mars* (1953), visualized in a striking storybook-expressionist style by director and production designer William Cameron Menzies [Fig. 26]. The story is told from the point of view of a small boy who, one stormy night, sees a flying saucer land virtually in his backyard. The aliens, hidden underground, use brain-embedded devices to transform ordinary citizens into zombies bent on sabotage. In a dark reversal of Ozzie-and-Harriet domesticity, Dad becomes an abusive tyrant, Mom turns into a coldhearted dragon lady, and the nice little girl next door grins maliciously as she burns down her family's home. The second half of *Invaders from Mars* concentrates on the less provocative spectacle of U.S. military might being deployed against the aliens. On the other hand, *Invasion of the Body Snatchers,* filmed by director Don Siegel in a style precisely poised between science-fiction mundaneness and film-noir moodiness, maintains its focus on the growing estrangement of the desperate hero (Kevin McCarthy) from his Norman Rockwell small-town world. The pipe-puffing grandfather mowing his lawn, the chatty antique-store proprietress, the reassuring psychiatrist, the gruff policeman, the operator at the other end of the phone line – any one of them could be one of Them.

Figure 26. *Invaders from Mars:* Storybook expressionism.

Despite their bizarre content, the most effective of these fifties science-fiction thrillers are set not on distant planets or in faraway futures but in familiar present-day locales. *Invaders from Mars* and *Invasion of the Body Snatchers* take place in picture-perfect small towns. Several of the films (especially *It Came from Outer Space*) make effective use of desert locations, with the small town perched precariously on the edge of the desert providing an evocative analogue for our small planet wheeling at the edge of the universe. The purest statement of the familiarity theme occurs in *The Incredible Shrinking Man.* The most ordinary domestic settings become the stuff of high adventure through the simple device of the hero's diminution: A basement floor becomes a vast plain, a workbench a lofty precipice, a spider a fearsome dragon, and a needle the sword with which the beast is slain [Fig. 27]. In a variation on the central thriller principle of the transformation of the mundane, these films employ characteristic science-fiction strategies of plausible abnormality (or "cognitive estrangement," as genre theo-

Figure 27. *The Incredible Shrinking Man:* Sword and dragon.

rist Darko Suvin terms it) to reinforce their central theme that the most alien of all worlds is the planet Earth.[8]

Hitchcock's Golden Period

The 1950s launched a run of Hitchcock masterpieces that represent the most impressive sustained individual achievement in the history of the movie thriller. After a period of unevenly achieved and received experimentation in the late 1940s, Hitchcock hit his stride with *Strangers on a Train* (1951), centered on the ambiguous relationship between a clean-cut tennis star and the ingratiating psychotic who embroils him in a bizarre murder pact. *Rear Window* (1954), another major success, evokes the voyeuristic nature of cinema through its tale of an immobilized New York apartment dweller who peeps at his neighbors, one of whom may be a murderer. *Vertigo* (1958), initially received as a failure, is now widely considered the American cinema's supreme treatment of romantic obsession, wherein a psychologically crippled San Francisco detective develops a doomed passion for the mysterious blonde he is following. In *North by Northwest* (1959), the most spectacular of Hitchcock's spy thrillers, a complacent Madison Avenue advertising executive is chased halfway across the country when he is mistaken for a secret agent. *Psycho* (1960), a sensationally successful foray into the horror genre, follows an embezzling Phoenix secretary to her fateful encounter with a strange young man at a remote motel. *The Birds* (1963), Hitchcock's most technically ambitious film, demonstrates the precarious security of everyday life by depicting a California seaside town inexplicably besieged by avian hordes.

This period saw an enrichment of Hitchcock's already formidable tactics of identification and point of view, more boldly undermining the spectator's stability and evoking conflicting responses to the action, while still largely maintaining the basic drive of suspense. *Strangers on a Train* (see Chapter 7) deftly juggles several points of view, with the fascination and desperation of the villain (Robert Walker) threatening at times to steal the film from its blander hero (Farley Granger). This ambivalence is taken even further in *Psycho*. The film initially fosters our strong attachment to the fugitive thief (Janet Leigh), but this is abruptly severed in the famous shower scene. The vacuum is then filled by a *Strangers on a Train*–like configuration wherein our allegiance is split between a disturbingly sympathetic psychopath (Anthony Perkins) and the less compelling normality represented by the missing woman's suspicious sister (Vera Miles) and boyfriend (John Gavin).

The complex treatment of viewer identification in late Hitchcock involves not just the mixture of different, often conflicting points of view but also the presentation of individual points of view in a more critical and contradictory manner. *Rear Window* links the viewer to the hero's perspective in a strong, even overdetermined way. The camera remains at all times with L. B. Jeffries (James Stewart), a photographer whose broken leg has confined him to his apartment, from which he observes the sometimes amusing, sometimes disturbing activities of his neighbors. This constriction of point of view, underlined by the distance from which we are forced to view the crucial events across the courtyard and by Jeffries's frequent use of binoculars and telephoto lenses to do so [Fig. 28], has the effect of making our identification with the hero more self-conscious, less natural seeming. The film capitalizes on this self-consciousness by periodically calling into question Jeffries's motives – the dubious ethics of his spying, his somewhat bloodthirsty

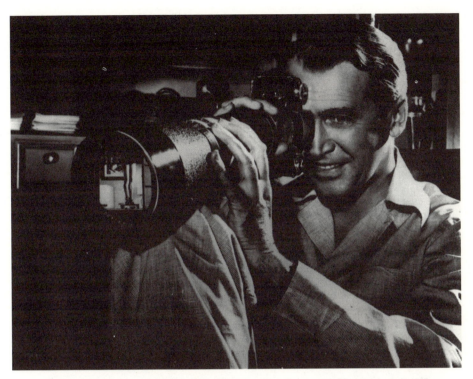

Figure 28. Self-conscious identification: Inquisitive spectator (James Stewart) in *Rear Window*.

eagerness to discover a murder, his use of the murder mystery as an escape from emotional commitment – and, by extension, our own motives as spectators.

The hero of *Rear Window,* though open to question, is ultimately an attractive and stable identification figure. *Vertigo* takes the questioning of its protagonist, Scottie Ferguson (James Stewart again), to a more disturbing extreme. Although generally sympathetic, Scottie is also pathetic. His condition of vertigo is an emblem of his crippling guilt, first over the accidental death of a fellow policeman, then over the suicide of the woman (Kim Novak) whom he was hired to follow and with whom he fell in love. Scottie's traumas draw him into the dark regions of delusion, domination, and fetishism, as he attempts to reconstruct his lost love-object [Fig. 29]. After submerging us in his increasingly oppressive and befogged perspective, the film proceeds to undermine that perspective in various ways: temporarily blocking it by sending

Scottie into a catatonic trance, switching briefly to the point of view of his torch-carrying friend Midge (Barbara Bel Geddes), and then, in a stunning stroke, bringing forward another, unexpected point of view that hopelessly confuses the positions of object and subject, victim and victimizer, with tragic results. Among these late Hitchcock classics, only *North by Northwest* and *The Birds* establish a relatively straightforward focus on a central protagonist, in both cases an initially superficial person (the flippant advertising executive played by Cary Grant in *North by Northwest,* the spoiled rich girl played by Tippi Hedren in *The Birds*) whose complacency is then severely shaken.

In addition, Hitchcock's films from this period function as critiques and commentaries on the specific genres to which they relate, and on the general natures of filmmaking, film watching, and art itself. As most writers on the film have noted, *Rear Window* is a highly self-reflexive work that examines its own status. The position of the wheelchair-bound Jeffries at his apartment window reflects that of the spectators in the movie theater, immobilized in their seats, with the windows across the courtyard resembling a series of screens or shots, combined in various montagelike arrangements. Jeffries functions as author as well as spectator, piecing together (and possibly inventing) the story of the murder, a process compared to a songwriter's simultaneous struggle to compose a tune in a neighboring apartment (where arch-author Hitchcock can be glimpsed, in his ritual cameo).

Similarly, *Vertigo* has been interpreted as a darker commentary on the processes of image making from both sides of the fence. Scottie is at first the victimized spectator of an illusion, when he becomes entranced by the mysterious Madeleine, and then the ruthless creator of one, when he tries to mold the plebeian look-alike Judy into a replica of his dead beloved. The concept of the femme fatale, central to the hard-boiled detective and film-noir traditions on which *Vertigo* draws, is examined and undercut – the film is explicitly about how men, out of their own anxieties and for their own convenience, create mythic images of women.

Although Anglo-American critics of the time continued to prefer the director's lighter-hearted British classics of the 1930s, these more ambitious and mature works became the focus of a major reevaluation of Hitchcock's artistic stature. This reevaluation, led by the auteurist (i.e., director-oriented) school of French film criticism, included the first book-length study of the director, *Hitchcock* (1957), by future New Wave filmmakers Eric Rohmer and Claude Chabrol, and the first important

Figure 29. Oppressive identification: Mystery woman (Kim Novak) and obsessed detective (James Stewart) in *Vertigo*.

English-language assessment, Robin Wood's still invaluable *Hitchcock's Films* (1965). Such attitudes, initially derided by many mainstream critics, had become gospel by the early 1970s. Hitchcock's films (especially from his post-1950 "golden period") – endlessly revived, written about, and taught to film students – were enshrined as cultural monuments that exerted a continuing influence on young filmmakers. The plots, techniques, and general themes of these later Hitchcock classics were frequently reworked by thriller specialists such as Jonathan Demme, Brian De Palma, Curtis Hanson, and Tobe Hooper. For example, elements of *Psycho* resurface in *The Texas Chain Saw Massacre* (Hooper, 1974) and *Dressed to Kill* (De Palma, 1980); *Rear Window* clearly influenced *Body Double* (De Palma, 1984) and *The Bedroom Window* (Hanson, 1987); and strong traces of *Vertigo* can be seen in *Obsession* (De Palma, 1976) and *Last Embrace* (Demme, 1979).

More generally, the major films of Hitchcock's late period, because of his preeminence and persistent influence, have a Janus-headed relationship toward the development of the movie thriller, both drawing upon previous generic movements and pointing the way toward future ones. For example:

Strangers on a Train builds upon some aspects of film noir, such as the persecuted and somewhat complicit protagonist. It also looks forward to "intimate-enemy" thrillers, such as *Play Misty for Me* (1971), *Fatal Attraction* (1987), *Unlawful Entry* (1992), and *Single White Female* (1992), because of the clinging, insinuating emotional bond forged by the nemesis character who bedevils the hero.[9]

Rear Window evokes the detective film, with the hero initially possessing the godlike detachment and seeming invulnerability of the amateur sleuth (see Chapter 6). It also paves the way for a group of self-reflexive thrillers that explicitly comment upon filmmaking and film watching, such as *Peeping Tom* (1960), Michael Powell's disturbing study of a filmmaker-psychopath; *Blowup* (1966), Michelangelo Antonioni's enigmatic account of a photographer whose camera witnesses a murder; *Blow Out* (1981), Brian De Palma's sound-track-centered homage to *Blowup;* and *Strange Days* (1995), Kathryn Bigelow's slightly futuristic tale of the thrills and perils of virtual reality.

North by Northwest is an obvious successor to similarly plotted pre-cold-war spy thrillers such as *The 39 Steps* and *Saboteur.* It also anticipates in some ways (such as its apolitical villain and extravagant action scenes) the upcoming series of James Bond films and, in other ways (such as the U.S. intelligence establishment's initially callous disregard for the safety of the hero), the slightly later cycle of pessimistic anti-Bond spy films.

Psycho, in an effort to reach the growing youth market, was partially patterned after the popular low-budget horror films of American International Pictures and gimmick-happy producer-director William Castle.[10] It is also a widely acknowledged influence on the stalker/slasher cycle catalyzed in 1978 by *Halloween.*

The Birds clearly derives from the science-fiction monster movies of the 1950s, but its emphasis on ecological payback rather than cold-war paranoia (the birds are neither aliens nor scientifically created mutations) prefigures such angry-critter movies as *Frogs* (1972), *Jaws* (1975), *Day of the Animals* (1977), and *The Swarm* (1978). In addition, the birds' reliance on sheer numbers rather than abnormal size or powers links *The Birds* to George A. Romero's "Living Dead" films (1968, 1978, 1985) and their many imitators.

5

Modern Period

Whereas the classical period of the movie thriller had been characterized by the entrenchment of most of the central thriller genres, the period beginning around 1960 was marked primarily by reconceptions of those genres. Key thriller categories underwent major overhauls, ranging from subversive debunking that virtually closed the door on the genre (the detective film), to neoclassical revival that recontextualized an earlier generic movement (neo-noir), to revitalization that greatly enhanced the popularity of a genre, whether on a short-term basis (the spy film) or a long-term one (the police film, the horror film). Among the factors contributing to these new directions were the decline of the old Hollywood studio system (symbolized by the content-controlling Production Code) and the vogue of imported foreign films, which achieved unprecedented success and influence in the 1950s and 1960s.

European Influences, American Censorship, and Heist Films

The postwar expansion of foreign-film exhibition in the United States popularized a number of highly regarded imported thrillers that provided both an alternative to American thrillers and an influence on their future development. In the early 1950s, this impact was centered largely on the level of subject matter. The content of Hollywood movies was still subject to the Production Code, written in 1930 and effectively enforced since 1934, though its strictures were being increasingly criticized and challenged. The Code's authority had been weakened by the government's severance (announced in 1948 and enforced gradually over the next decade) of the monopolistic link between the Hollywood studios and their theater chains. In addition, a number of landmark court decisions began to undermine local censorship of movies in the 1950s, including decisions that extended First Amendment protection to motion pictures (*Burstyn* v. *Wilson,* 1952), separated sex from obscenity, and protected works with "redeeming social importance" (*Roth* v. *United States, Alberts* v. *California, 1957*). Several of these key decisions involved foreign films (*The Miracle [Il miracolo]*, 1948; *La Ronde*, 1950; *The Game of Love [Le Blé en herbe]*, 1954; *Lady Chatterley's Lover [L'Amant de Lady Chatterley]*, 1955; *The Lovers [Les Amants]*, 1958); moreover, the distributors and theaters that handled foreign films were often not under the waning but still formidable authority of the Production Code Administration that enforced Hollywood's private Code. American film audiences, filmmakers, and film critics were increasingly exposed to foreign-made films – including thrillers – whose moral ambivalence, cynical tone, lack of uplift, and more explicit presentation of sex and violence distinguished them from their homegrown equivalents. It should be pointed out, however, that the passage of influence between American and foreign films has always been reciprocal, and one should beware of drawing too sharp or simplistic distinctions between them. For example, film noir (as noted in Chapter 4) constituted an unusually lurid and pessimistic cycle of Hollywood filmmaking, which had been noted and named and emulated in Europe long before it gained recognition in its native land.

One of the earliest postwar foreign thrillers to create a stir in the United States was *The Wages of Fear (Le Salaire de la peur*, 1953), directed by the French crime-film specialist Henri-Georges Clouzot. The anonymous *Time* magazine reviewer, both repelled and fascinated by the film, called it "a picture that is surely one of the most evil ever made."[1] Opening in a stagnant, squalid South American backwater (with this initially exotic setting moving the film into the borderland between thriller and adventure), the story centers on four stranded expatriates who take the suicidal job of driving a pair of nitroglycerin-loaded trucks over nondescript but hazardous mountain roads. Given a successful American release in 1955, the film's hair-raising suspense sequences created a sensation. Even after being extensively pruned for U.S. consumption, it treated American audiences to a number of ingredients not likely to be found in Hollywood films of the era, such as the sordid atmosphere of the opening scenes, the beyond-buddiness bonding of the male characters, the dim view taken of American corporate imperialism, and the stark presentation of sudden death and drawn-out violence (including an agonizing scene in which a man's leg is crushed by a truck). Clouzot scored another international success with *Diabolique (Les Diaboliques*, 1955), a stony-cold shocker in which the wife and the mistress of a hateful schoolmaster join forces to murder him, leading to a legendary twist ending.

Another French thriller to register strongly in the United States was *Rififi (Du Rififi chez les hommes,* 1955). Directed by expatriate Jules Dassin (the blacklisted director of *The Naked City* and other notable American crime films), *Rififi* details a daring Parisian jewel robbery and its grim aftermath. The emotional emphasis of the film is on issues of honor and loyalty among the thieves, and its centerpiece is a wordless thirty-one-minute sequence leading up to and through the robbery. The "heist-film" (a.k.a. "caper-film") format, given a lighter treatment, was the basis of two other popular imports: Britain's *The Lavender Hill Mob* (1951), in which a gray little bank employee (Alec Guinness) masterminds a calamity-filled bullion robbery, and Italy's *Big Deal on Madonna Street (I soliti ignoti,* 1958), about a gang of petty crooks who bungle their way through a "scientifically" planned burglary.

The heist film, centering on the preparation and execution of an elaborate robbery, had already accumulated a small history in the United States. In still embryonic form, it was represented by such films as *High Sierra* (1941), an elegiac gangster movie with Humphrey Bogart as an old-timer directing the holdup of a resort hotel, and *The Killers* (1946), a film-noir classic with a spectacular payroll robbery nested inside its complex flashback structure. In 1950 John Huston (who had contributed to the scripts of both *High Sierra* and *The Killers*) directed the first full-fledged masterpiece of the heist-film form, *The Asphalt Jungle,* concerning a jewelry-store job plotted by a group of ill-starred outcasts. *The Asphalt Jungle* was a critical but not a commercial success, and the heist film did not establish itself in the American cinema until the latter half of the decade. Examples include *The Killing* (1956), a hard-edged racetrack-robbery tale with a time-stuttering flashback structure; *Odds against Tomorrow* (1959), the wintry account of a small-town bank job that goes sour; and the sentimental *Seven Thieves* (1960), in which a disgraced old man (Edward G. Robinson) turns a Monte Carlo casino heist into his last chance for glory.

The heist film, on either side of the Atlantic, did not fully jell until after World War II. In fact, many of its early examples can be interpreted as peacetime transpositions of certain war-film motifs, with a platoonlike group of well-trained men working together to plan and execute a dangerous mission. The war-film connection is made especially explicit in the Rat Pack convocation *Ocean's Eleven* (1960), in which a group of ex-paratroopers reunite on a mission to "liberate" millions of dollars from five Las Vegas casinos, robbed simultaneously on New Year's Eve; and in the British-made *The League of Gentlemen* (1960), in which eight former soldiers pool their skills to pull off a London bank robbery that is planned "like a textbook military operation." The incursion of war-film elements into an ordinary peacetime context reflects the transformative aspect of thrillers noted throughout this book.

The early heist films exerted pressure on the Production Code in several ways, including their presentation of criminal activity in morally neutral terms. Crime is viewed mainly as a profession ("a left-handed form of human endeavor," as it is described in a famous line from *The Asphalt Jungle* [Fig. 30]), basically similar to, if more disreputable and dangerous than, other ways of making a living. Whereas syndicate-gangster films often equate their brand of crime with corporate big business, crime in the heist film comes more under the heading of craft: skilled, labor-intensive, and somewhat anachronistic. The pièce de résistance of the heist film is often an elaborate presentation of the heist itself, at great length and detail, in order to display its intricacy, precision, and fine workmanship.

The Production Code contained a prohibition against showing criminal methods in explicit detail, with specific mentions of theft, robbery, and safecracking, among others. It also warned in several places against creating sympathy for "the side of crime." Besides showing criminal procedures in great detail and shifting crime from a moral to a professional dimension, the heist-film format evoked sympathy for criminal characters to an extent unusual in Code-dominated Hollywood. *High Sierra* was probably the most sympathetic gangster portrait of its era; Roy Earle, the nobly named hero, towers above the punks and hypocrites he encounters on both sides of the law. Similarly, the thieves of *The Asphalt Jungle,* from the genial mastermind (Sam Jaffe) to the troubled thug (Sterling Hayden), are predominantly figures of integrity and sympathy.

Irony is a central ingredient of the heist film, with the protagonists defeated more often by twists of fate than by the forces of justice. This ironic tone can easily shade into wry farce, as demonstrated by *The Lavender Hill Mob* and *Big Deal on Madonna Street,* and into wry romantic comedy, as exemplified by later heist films such as *Topkapi* (1964), Jules Dassin's candy-colored variation on *Rififi; How to Steal a Million* (1966), in which Audrey Hepburn and Peter O'Toole smooch their way through a Paris art-gallery caper; and *Gambit* (1966), about an overly rigid thief (Michael Caine) whose dream-perfect heist is undermined by rude reality and an unpredictable accomplice (Shirley MacLaine).

The American heist films of the 1950s and early 1960s had much in common with some of the less moralistic products of the contempora-

Figure 30. *The Asphalt Jungle:* Professional thieves (Sterling Hayden, Anthony Caruso, Sam Jaffe) practice their craft.

neous European cinema, and they chipped away at the crumbling Production Code. The Code specified that kidnappers and real-life criminals could not be depicted on screen unless they were punished for their misdeeds; apparently this restriction was extended into a de facto policy that all movie lawbreakers must be caught and punished. Heist films provided some of the first major American-made exceptions to this legendary interdiction. In both *Seven Thieves* and *Ocean's Eleven,* the thieves get away (though not with the money); in *Dead Heat on a Merry-Go-Round* (1966), the mastermind (James Coburn) of an airport heist gets the loot but not the girl. By the time of Sam Peckinpah's *The Getaway* (1972), which ends with the larcenous hero (Steve McQueen) and heroine (Ali McGraw) driving into Mexico with a blessing ("Vaya con Dios!") and a satchel full of stolen money, the Code was long gone, and it was clear that, in Hollywood films, crime could indeed pay handsomely.

Latter-day variations on the heist film include *Thief* (1981), about a fanatically professional safecracker (James Caan) planning his last big job; *Reservoir Dogs* (1992), which perversely deletes the heist itself, concentrating instead on the bloody aftermath of an ill-fated diamond robbery; and *Out of Sight* (1998), which updates the romantic-heist vein of the 1960s by depicting the dangerous liaison between a dedicated law officer (Jennifer Lopez) and a daring thief (George Clooney). The heist-film format (and some of its accompanying moral slipperiness) also translates easily into the spy genre, with vital secrets rather than money or jewels as the object of the heist. Examples include *Five Fingers* (1952), about a mercenary British-embassy employee (James Mason) pilfering crucial Allied documents for the Nazis in Turkey, and *Mission: Impossible* (1996), with its dangling-from-the-ceiling robbery of CIA headquarters.

The French New Wave

Another example of cross-fertilization between American and European thrillers is the French New Wave (or *nouvelle vague*), a highly influential film movement that arose in the late 1950s. One of the most distinctive aspects of the *nouvelle vague* was the high proportion of film critics among its leading directors, including Claude Chabrol, Jean-Luc Godard, Jacques Rivette, Eric Rohmer, and François Truffaut. As critics, these future filmmakers subscribed to the same general attitudes that had identified the film-noir movement and championed the work of Alfred Hitchcock, along with that of numerous other American genre filmmakers. Accordingly, several distinguished New Wave films were strongly influenced by American thrillers and, in turn, exerted their own influence on American thrillers of the 1960s and after.

As noted in the previous section, the distinctiveness and influence of European thrillers of the early 1950s, such as *The Wages of Fear* and *Rififi*, primarily concerned subject matter. Although this dimension was certainly not absent from the French New Wave, the movement's most significant impact occurred on the levels of style and structure. The style of New Wave films was generally more self-conscious and intrusive than that of Hollywood films. Again, one should beware of overstating the contrast: The postwar period produced some of the most flamboyantly stylized work in American film history, especially in certain areas, such as the film-noir movement, and in the work of certain directors, such as Robert Aldrich, Samuel Fuller, Nicholas Ray, and

Orson Welles, all of whom were greatly admired by the French critic-filmmakers. The most striking New Wave films took this development further than their American models (with the possible exception of Welles's work) had done. They pursued styles that were overtly eclectic, fragmentary, and collagelike, with the hand of the director more visibly inscribed within the films, manipulating and interpreting the material. New Wave directors freely made use of such illusion-disrupting devices as *jump cuts* (i.e., chunks of footage excised within an otherwise unchanged camera setup), actors directly addressing the camera, blatant references to other movies, and jarring asides and digressions.

Godard's *Breathless* (À *bout de souffle,* 1959), perhaps the most innovative New Wave film, uses such techniques to remold a story similar to those of classic heist films and criminal-on-the-run films such as *High Sierra, The Killers,* and *The Asphalt Jungle:* A small-time crook (Jean-Paul Belmondo) steals a car, shoots a motorcycle cop, and hides out in Paris with his fickle girlfriend (Jean Seberg) while a police dragnet closes in. Chabrol's dazzling though less renowned *Web of Passion* (À *double tour,* 1959) relates a *Laura*-like tale about a much-desired young woman (Antonella Lualdi) who is mysteriously murdered, with suspicion falling upon various inhabitants of a country château. Truffaut's popular *Shoot the Piano Player* (*Tirez sur le pianiste,* 1960) is the noirish account of a tragedy-haunted concert pianist (Charles Aznavour) who tries to bury himself in a cheap honky-tonk, only to be put at risk by the misdeeds of his criminal brothers.

The difference of these films from their Hollywood prototypes is not just a matter of style but also of narrative emphasis. The prime thriller aspects of the story are often treated in a shorthand and seemingly perfunctory manner. In *Breathless,* the initial theft and murder have an abrupt, throwaway quality, and the police manhunt occurs almost entirely offscreen, whereas a memorable twenty-four-minute scene (over a quarter of the entire film) is devoted to the hero's persistent attempts to make love to his lukewarm paramour in the course of a lazy morning [Fig. 31]. Although *Web of Passion* is less fragmentary, the murder occurs late in the story and is solved fairly quickly; much of the film is devoted to digressive displays of the characters' boorishness and perversity, punctuated by bursts of ravishing lyricism. *Shoot the Piano Player* begins in high noir style, with a desperate man being pursued through dark, twisting streets. Then the fugitive runs smack into a lamppost and is aided by a total stranger, who strikes up a lengthy conversation on such topics as the joys of marriage and the propor-

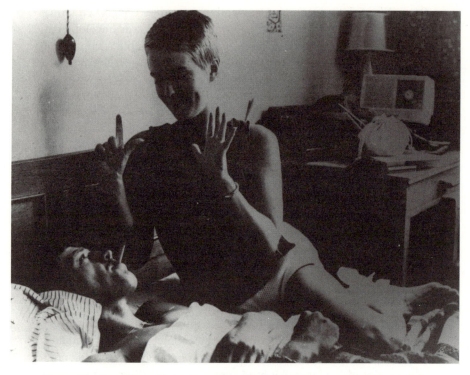

Figure 31. *Breathless:* Wanted murderer (Jean-Paul Belmondo) and fickle girl-friend (Jean Seberg) dally in the midst of a manhunt.

tion of virgins in Paris. A few minutes later, the narrative is interrupted again for a jaunty music-hall ballad about a love-hungry dame who tried plastic surgery, to no avail; a subsequent kidnapping scene consists mainly of the kidnappers and their victims chatting about the stimulating effects of women's underwear.

Such skits and digressions often illuminate the central themes of these films: in *Breathless,* the separate continents of Male and Female, and the existentialist ideal of "living in the moment"; in *Web of Passion,* the coexistence of beauty and ugliness in a paradoxical world; in *Shoot the Piano Player,* the elusiveness of romantic love, and the difficulty of establishing emotional contact with another human being. However, they deviate from the main plot line to a degree that is virtually un-thinkable in a classical Hollywood thriller and seems more character-istic of a hipster/modernist novel (such as *On the Road,* 1957; *Naked Lunch,* 1959; *Zazie dans le métro,* 1959) or a bebop jazz improvisation, twisting around the melody line.

In the 1960s, these innovations of the *nouvelle vague* (and other related foreign-film movements) were incorporated into such European-influenced American thrillers as *Mickey One* (1965), the highly stylized and allegorical account of a nightclub comedian (Warren Beatty) on the run from a faceless Mob; *Point Blank* (1967), a gangland vengeance tale whose fluid juggling of time and memory evokes the work of New Wave filmmaker Alain Resnais; and the epoch-defining *Bonnie and Clyde* (1967), a couple-on-the-run crime film whose script was originally offered to Godard and Truffaut and whose jarring tone shifts and flamboyant stylistic flourishes reflect the New Wave influence. More recently, that influence has endured in the thrillers of Brian De Palma (*Sisters*, 1973; *The Fury*, 1978), Martin Scorsese *(Taxi Driver*, 1976; *Cape Fear*, 1991), David Lynch *(Blue Velvet*, 1986; *Lost Highway*, 1997), and Quentin Tarantino *(Reservoir Dogs*, 1992; *Pulp Fiction*, 1994), with their eclectic stylization, antirealistic manipulations, freewheeling digressions ("Do you know what they call a Quarter Pounder with Cheese in Paris?"), and conspicuous references to other movies.

James Bond in the 1960s

A European influence of a very different sort sparked another new direction in the movie thriller. After enjoying a productive period ca. 1935–46, the spy movie had been stagnating for several years, its development hindered by the limitations of the postwar anticommunist films: their dour and undiversified tone, their excess of rhetoric at the expense of action and suspense, and their hackneyed and unimpressive portrayals of the Red Menace.

In 1962–3, the spy movie was dramatically revitalized by the surprise success of *Dr. No.* This American-financed (United Artists), British-based production introduced one of the screen's most durable and popular heroes, the superspy James Bond, derived from a series of novels (at that time, only modestly successful) by the former Royal Navy intelligence officer Ian Fleming. The profitability of *Dr. No* led to a series of increasingly expensive and lucrative sequels, and the James Bond films spearheaded a 1960s spy craze in the movies and other mass media.

Dr. No, in which Bond (Sean Connery) journeys to Jamaica to investigate the mysterious disruption of Cape Canaveral missile launches, quickly corrected the limitations that had plagued the anticommunist spy cycle. The film was conceived as an episodic series of action set pieces (called "bumps" by series coproducer Albert R. Broccoli), from the brutal opening assassination of a British agent by three "blind" men to the explosive final destruction of the villain's elaborate island citadel.[2] In a departure from its more straight-faced literary source, the film's action and violence (considered unusually strong for its day) are mixed with generous doses of humor, such as Bond's postbloodshed quips and his sexual banter with various females. A sense of the exotic is conveyed by the colorful Jamaican locations, production designer Ken Adam's Mod/expressionist decors, and the presence of an Asian seductress and a half-Chinese villain. The sexualized dimension of hard-boiled detective films, film noir, and European thrillers resurfaces in *Dr. No*'s double-entendre dialogue, mild sadism, and cutting-edge cheesecake – the Botticellian emergence of statuesque Ursula Andress from the Jamaican surf in a clinging white bikini was a defining moment in the sixties liberalization of screen eroticism [Fig. 32]. As for the villainous Dr. No (Joseph Wiseman), he may not have been less hackneyed than the screen communists of the 1950s, but he was a good deal more flamboyant, with his black rubber-gloved claws, adventurous taste in interior decoration, and cockeyed scheme for sabotaging the American space program.

Like the anticommunist spy films, the Bond films were products of the cold war, rising out of strained USA–USSR relations in the early sixties. In the previous decade, anticommunist anxieties had focused substantially on domestic subversion – the specter of spies and traitors infiltrating the American heartland. Such concerns had become less pressing by 1960, and apprehension centered instead on increased tensions in the international arena, as evidenced by the U-2 spy-plane incident (May 1960), the abortive Bay of Pigs invasion (April 1961), the erection of the Berlin Wall (August 1961), the first significant increases of U.S. military presence in Vietnam (November–December 1961), and, most unnervingly, the Cuban missile crisis (October 1962 – the same month *Dr. No* premiered in Britain).

Although *Dr. No* was completed before the Cuban missile crisis, there are some curious general similarities in their central ingredients: a Caribbean island setting, a conspiracy involving missiles, a perceived small-time tyrant becoming a thorn in Uncle Sam's side. The lingering reverberations of the Cuban crisis possibly contributed to the unexpected popularity of *Dr. No* when it was released in the United States in May 1963. However, close parallels to contemporary political crises are not pursued in subsequent Bond movies, which work more to de-

Figure 32. *Dr. No:* Nature girl (Ursula Andress) and cool spy (Sean Connery) warm up the cold-war espionage thriller.

flect than to confront such issues. A remarkable aspect of the Bond movies is the extent to which these most celebrated of cold-war spy thrillers marginalize the cold war itself.

Nearly all Bond-movie villains, starting with Dr. No, are individualistic, apolitical megalomaniacs, motivated not by ideology but by greed, pique, sexual inadequacy, an abstract lust for power, and a sheer delight in spreading worldwide chaos. The Bond villains represent a throwback to such earlier movie malefactors as Feuillade's Fantômas, Lang's Dr. Mabuse and Haghi (*Spies*), and Emperor Ming of the 1930s Flash Gordon serials. At times, the Bond films seem like they might as well be taking place on the Planet Mongo, for all the substantive relationship they have to the contemporary global struggle between capitalism and communism. In the Fleming novel, free-lancer Dr. No's missile-toppling scheme is financed by the Russians. In the movie version, even this tangential Red connection is deleted: No's motives are explicitly depoliticized (as he says, "East, West: just points of the compass, each as stupid as the other") and attributed to wounded pride (his brilliant ideas were rejected by both sides).

The second Bond film, *From Russia with Love* (1963), is based on the 1957 Fleming novel that is generally considered the most cold war–conscious of the series. The book's plot concerns a Soviet plan to damage the prestige of the British Secret Service by discrediting James Bond; a Russian beauty is recruited to set up his "suicide" under lurid circumstances. In the movie adaptation, the conspiracy is taken out of Russian hands and transferred to Fleming's later invention, SPECTRE, an international organization that combines elements of a Vampires-like secret society and a 1950s gangster syndicate. The eponymous villain of the third Bond movie, *Goldfinger* (1964), is another apolitical kingpin, whose plan to break into Fort Knox is motivated by greed and hubris. SPECTRE, led by the nefarious, kitty-stroking Blofeld and devoted to extortion and mischief-making on a grand scale, is the chief opponent in the next four Bond films: *Thunderball* (1965), another Caribbean holiday, with stolen A-bombs the source of trouble; the atypically politicized *You Only Live Twice* (1967), sending Bond to Japan on the trail of missing space capsules; *On Her Majesty's Secret Service* (1969), an Alpine adventure with the world's agriculture at stake; and *Diamonds Are Forever* (1971), centered on Las Vegas and a satellite-borne laser-gun.

James Bond discreetly avoids the true hot spots of the cold war, such as Cuba, Berlin, Israel, and Vietnam, gravitating instead to peripheral tourist meccas like Jamaica, Istanbul, Venice, Miami, the Bahamas, Japan, Switzerland, Amsterdam, and Las Vegas. In contrast to the grim spy thrillers of the 1950s, the Bond films give the cold war a friendlier, less threatening aspect, displacing the conflict and containing it within a series of picturesque sideshows. This containment idea is often literalized in the climaxes of the Bond films, which present a pitched battle within an isolated, sealed-off environment: the subterranean fortress of *Dr. No*, the Fort Knox vault of *Goldfinger*, the underwater reef of *Thunderball*, the hollowed-out volcano of *You Only Live Twice*, the mountaintop clinic of *On Her Majesty's Secret Service*, the offshore oil rig of *Diamonds Are Forever*.

Although the Bond films are historically important in the development of the movie thriller, their thrilleresque dimension is limited. Their diminished sense of the familiar weakens the tension between the ordinary and the exotic/adventurous that activates the double world of the thriller, and the Bonds gravitate toward the realm of the epic adventure. Suspense sequences are usually moderate, the tensions simple (especially in comparison to Hitchcock or Lang) and quickly discharged. The Bond films greatly reduce the characteristic vulnerability of the thriller hero, which had become especially intense in the postwar period. Bond is involved in a great deal of violent action, but the sense of danger is weak – he is typically seen wading calmly through a scene of mass carnage. With the notable exception of the laser scene in *Goldfinger* (one of the few times we see Bond squirm and sweat), the physical ordeals – tortures, beatings, immersions – endured by Bond are also diluted, much less grueling than they are in the Fleming novels. Emotionally, Bond is even more invulnerable. His demeanor is cool, even cold; friendships are not strongly developed; women are used and discarded, and the ones who get killed on his behalf are rarely accorded more than fleeting regret. As he admits in *Thunderball,* "I'm not what you'd call a passionate man."

The glaring exception to this general tendency is *On Her Majesty's Secret Service* (1969), the great oddity of the Bond series, in which a fed-up Sean Connery was unsuccessfully replaced by the one-shot misfire George Lazenby. A cheerful, self-deprecating bloke lacking Connery's ruthless elegance, Lazenby's Bond is easily the most vulnerable of the series (a quality enhanced by the actor's lack of authority in the role). Bond's relationship to the father-figure intelligence chief "M" is exceptionally strained in this film, and his faith in his profession is at times seriously shaken. He falls deeply in love with Tracy di Vicenzo (Diana Rigg), a self-assertive, self-destructive jet-setter who is the most fully developed female character in the Bond films. The predominant tone is romantic – broodingly (the opening suicide attempt on a dawn-lit beach [Fig. 33]), mushily (a song montage of the lovers frolicking), warmly (their first night together in a stable), and exhilaratingly (as they soar down ski slopes the morning after). In place of the usual Bond-film structure of strung-out set pieces, the film is more cohesively divided into a leisurely, even sluggish first half that is mostly build-up, and an intense second half that is a nearly unbroken series of credible romantic scenes and spectacular action scenes, the latter given an additional edge by the emotional involvement of the characters.

Though flawed (and at times uneasily suspended between the old Bond formulas and these new directions), *On Her Majesty's Secret Service* is the most substantial film of the Bond series – emotionally, dra-

Figure 33. *On Her Majesty's Secret Service:* Vulnerable Bond (George Lazenby) rescues suicidal jet-setter (Diana Rigg).

matically, artistically. It was also, unsurprisingly, a disappointment at the box office. The next Bond movie, *Diamonds Are Forever,* took a spoofy, gimmick-laden approach that turned the series in a more juvenile-oriented direction and moved it further away from the central concerns of the thriller.

Mock-Bond and Anti-Bond

Spurred by the success of James Bond, the spy film enjoyed its most active period in the 1960s. The Bond movies dominated the genre, conceptually as well as commercially. As Tony Bennett and Janet Woollacott observe in their cultural-studies analysis *Bond and Beyond* (1987), James Bond became the standard by which all other spy heroes of the era were defined, whether in terms of their similarities or dissimilarities to Agent 007.[3]

As in the Bond movies, a certain cynicism and irreverent detachment characterized the spy films of the 1960s (in contrast to the urgent and committed temper of most 1935–60 spy films), with the world of espionage seen more as a cool, dangerous game than as a fervent moral-political struggle. The suave hero, colorful locations, pretty girls, flamboyant decors, and apolitical supervillains of the Bond films were recycled in a number of largely undistinguished derivatives. Many of these sought to differentiate themselves marginally from their Bondian model by flaunting the element of self-parody.

Although humor and parody had always been important ingredients of the Bond movies and became increasingly prominent as time went on, the pre-1970 Bonds could still be described as spy films punctuated with comic relief. However, the Bond-derived "spy spoofs" are predominantly comedies with spy-movie trimmings. Among them are two big-budget American attempts to close the spy-hero gap with Great Britain: *Our Man Flint* (1966, followed by a 1967 sequel), starring James Coburn as Derek Flint; and *The Silencers* (1966, followed by three sequels through 1969), featuring Dean Martin as Matt Helm. Both series are facetious and weightless to an extent that makes the Bond films look positively Langian by comparison. These American contributions to the spy-movie boom are loath to conceive of their heroes as organization men (even loose-cannon organization men like James Bond) working for large government agencies. Both Flint and Helm are freelancers (when not spying, Helm is a girlie-magazine photographer, and Flint is a leisured dilettante in the tradition of literary sleuths Lord Peter Wimsey and Philo Vance), at liberty to work for the government or not, as they choose.

Another group of spy films sought to differentiate themselves from the Bonds by depicting espionage in a grimmer and more realistic light, although with a sense of irony and a lack of moral/patriotic certitude that distinguished them from the earlier anti-Nazi and anticommunist spy films. These "anti-Bond" spy movies, predominantly British in origin, reflected the treason scandals that had recently rocked the British spy establishment, culminating with the defection to Russia of highly placed double-agent Kim Philby in early 1963. There was a parallel movement toward deglamorization in spy literature, led by such authors as Len Deighton, Brian Freemantle, John Gardner, and, preeminently, John le Carré. The primary model for this new direction was le Carré's breakthrough novel *The Spy Who Came in from the Cold* (1963), which dominated the best-seller list in 1964 and received an unusually faithful film adaptation the following year. In the film version, an aging British agent named Leamas (Richard Burton) pretends to defect to East Germany in order to frame their ruthless security chief (Peter Van Eyck). Leamas eventually learns that he has been duped by his own side; the "filthy operation" is rigged so that it ends up strengthening those whom he aimed to destroy and destroying those whom he aimed to help. As the trap springs shut, Leamas dourly informs his bewildered lover (Claire Bloom), "Spies are just a bunch of squalid, seedy little bastards like me."

Although *The Spy Who Came in from the Cold* contains many of the key elements of the anti-Bond spy thrillers (bleak settings, disenchanted hero, grim irony, East–West mirroring), it is more a psychological drama than a thriller; much of this static film is devoted to conversational exposition, with a lengthy trial scene as its centerpiece. Four months earlier, the first full-fledged spy thriller in the anti-Bond vein had been released – *The Ipcress File* (1965), whose "squalid, seedy little bastard" was Harry Palmer (Michael Caine), an insolent British intelligence agent derived from a series of novels by Len Deighton. The film involved a number of top collaborators from the James Bond movies (including coproducer Harry Saltzman, editor Peter Hunt, production designer Ken Adam, and composer John Barry), and the result strongly suggests a deliberate effort to go against the Bondian grain. Under the credits, we see not a flashy Maurice Binder girls-and-guns design, but a groggy Palmer shuffling through his morning routine in a grubby flat: making coffee [Fig. 34], reading the paper, getting dressed. He could be any ordinary civil servant preparing for the day's work, were it not for the black pistol he tucks into his belt just before heading out the door. Palmer, a low-ranking operative with a petty-criminal past, is bullied and manipulated by his superiors – tactics which he himself employs, albeit more ingratiatingly, as he slogs through drab London locales in search of a communist conspiracy to brainwash British scientists.

The Ipcress File was followed by several spy thrillers that similarly explored the dark side of espionage. Harry Palmer returned for *Funeral in Berlin* (1966), a defection drama in which British intelligence is shown routinely employing ex-Nazis and ordering cold-blooded executions. *The Defector* (1966) features an American physicist (Montgomery Clift) blackmailed by the CIA into an ultimately pointless mission to fetch scientific secrets from East Germany. *The Quiller Memorandum* (1966), a Berlin tale concerning a neo-Nazi conspiracy, is notable for

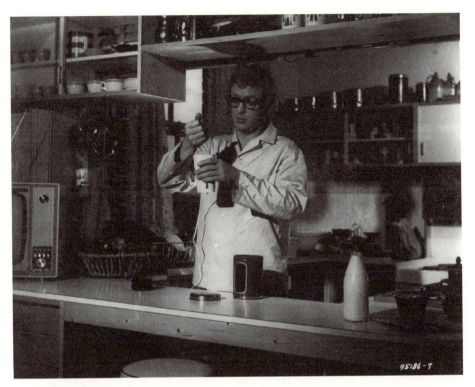

95186-7

Figure 34. *The Ipcress File:* Deglamorized spy (Michael Caine) goes through his wake-up routine.

screenwriter Harold Pinter's barbed dialogue, which reflects the duplicity of espionage by charging the most banal utterances with layers of unspoken irony and menace. *The Deadly Affair* (1967), based on an early le Carré novel, tangles the unhappy marriage of a British civil servant (James Mason) with his investigation of an espionage-tainted "suicide." *A Dandy in Aspic* (1968) goes from London to Berlin to track the desperate maneuvers of a British intelligence official (Laurence Harvey) assigned to eliminate a Russian "mole," who is, in fact, himself.

Besides being generally more substantial than the Bond films and their spoofy offshoots, the anti-Bond films are also closer to the central concerns of the thriller. In contrast to the flippant invincibility of James Bond, Matt Helm, and other superspies, the more vulnerable anti-Bond protagonists endure truly punishing ordeals (such as Palmer's grueling regimen of physical and mental torture in *The Ipcress File*), experience messy emotional entanglements (upon discovering the identity of his wife's lover, the hero of *The Deadly Affair* bolts to the nearest bathroom and vomits), and occasionally are left lying dead on the unmarked battlefields of the cold war.

In addition, the anti-Bond spy films develop a sharper paranoid edge. The field of anxiety is widened: The agent usually has to contend with dangers emanating not only from the other side but also from his own, which is riddled with traitors and/or is using him as an expendable pawn in a dirty game. In *The Ipcress File* Palmer finds his well-being threatened by communist thugs, by the CIA (because he has mistakenly killed one of their agents), and by his two rival superiors, one of whom is a double agent. The spy hero becomes a man in the middle, caught between two or more sides, with his top priority not finding the secret or winning the cold war but simply staying alive. In an eloquent passage of *The Quiller Memorandum,* the British spy chief Pol (Alec Guinness) uses two ashtrays and a peanut to illustrate the situation: two opposing armies, obscured by fog, with the agent Quiller (George Segal) alone in the gap between them. Pol then impassively pops the peanut into his mouth and swallows it.

In contrast to the free-floating, fantasy-oriented world of Bond & Co., the anti-Bond films develop a more thrilleresque sense of a solidly ordinary world transformed by paranoia and danger. There is greater attention given to the routine, less glamorous aspects of the spy's profession – paperwork, leg work, office politics, bureaucratic squabbling. Michael Denning in his book *Cover Stories* interprets professional-spy stories, with their civil-servant heroes, as a romanticized version of the routine of white-collar office work.[4] This dimension is more strongly realized through the relatively tangible drudgery of the anti-Bond protagonists than through James Bond's leisure-class life-style.

The colorful vacation spots that dominate the Bond movies are avoided in their anti-Bond counterparts. The twin capitals of these films are London and Berlin: two gray, history-shrouded cities reflecting and blurring into each other at the center of what le Carré, in the title of one of his finest novels, called *The Looking Glass War* (1965; film version, 1970). The settings are painted with a somber palette: overcast skies, desolate corners, dingy flats, rain-drizzled streets, chilly winterscapes, leafless trees. The most memorable segment of *The Deadly Affair* is set in a dreary Battersea waterfront area. In *A Dandy in Aspic,* the two sides coldly bargain for the hero's life in a wintry Berlin park. The climactic scenes of *Funeral in Berlin* take place on a rusting bridge and in a series of dark, bombed-out buildings. In *The Ipcress File,* Palmer, after weeks of torture in the depths of a dank Albanian prison, staggers out to the street, where he is greeted by the familiar sight of a red double-decker bus: He has been in London the whole time. The cold war never seemed colder or more viciously circular than in these downbeat dramas of disillusion and deceit.

Supercops

Thriving in the wake of the spy-movie boom was another genre that featured organizational heroes: the police thriller. Its resurgent popularity stemmed from a growing sense of urban crisis, a foregrounding of law-and-order issues in the 1968 and 1972 presidential campaigns, and a general (though still transitional and deeply conflicted) swing to the right in American politics. After reaching an artistic peak in the early 1950s, the police-centered crime film had been in decline, with the crime genre dominated by gangster films, heist films, and films spotlighting romanticized outlaws from the Hell's Angels to Bonnie and Clyde. The ascendant police thriller incorporated elements from previously hot but at the time declining genres, such as the spy film, the war film, and especially the western, all of which suffered from the controversy and nationalistic confusion engendered by the Vietnam War. Like such fifties flawed-cop films as *Where the Sidewalk Ends* and *The Big Heat,* the post-1967 police thrillers center on policemen bucking the system and taking the law into their own hands. However, these later films are generally much less critical in their treatment of the justice-obsessed lawman, who is often built up into a virtual superhero fighting to protect society where official institutions have failed.

The comeback of the police thriller began in 1967 with the multi-Oscar-winning *In the Heat of the Night,* in which a black police detective (Sidney Poitier) and a redneck sheriff (Rod Steiger) reluctantly join forces to solve a Mississippi homicide. The film is a small-town murder mystery rather than a big-city police story, and it was perceived more as a social-problem film than as a thriller. Nevertheless, the Steiger character, not averse to using racial epithets or strong-arm methods, helped pave the way for such urban rednecks as Dirty Harry and Popeye Doyle in the upcoming police cycle. The groundswell gathered force in 1968 with such films as *Madigan,* a morally gray study of the contrasting pressures facing a rigid New York City Police Commissioner (Henry Fonda) and an unorthodox street cop (Richard Widmark);

The Detective, a static, set-bound account of a rebel New York police-man (Frank Sinatra) whose investigation of a gory homosexual mur-der leads him to a high-level cover-up; *Coogan's Bluff,* the first of five collaborations between top cowboy star Clint Eastwood and ace ac-tion director Don Siegel; and *Bullitt,* a Steve McQueen vehicle that was more successful at the box office than any previous police thriller had been.

These last two films highlight different key elements of the evolving modern police thriller. Frank Bullitt (McQueen), a top San Francisco cop assigned to protect a Mob informer, appropriated much of the mystique of James Bond. Like Bond, Bullitt is a stylesetter [Fig. 35], leading a chic life-style undreamed of by the more plebeian coppers of previous eras. He lives in a stylishly decorated residence, complete with a stylish, decorative girlfriend (Jacqueline Bisset), dines at styl-ish, upscale cafés, and dresses in stylish, tasteful ensembles. Like Bond, Bullitt is an elite specialist working within a large organization, granted considerable autonomy in the course of his assignment. In ef-fect, Bullitt enjoys the best of both worlds, combining a private eye's independence with a policeman's institutional clout. Also like Bond, and unlike the tough but tormented cops of the 1950s, Bullitt is emo-tionally impassive to the point of anesthesia. Although not all movie (and television) cops of the coming decades would be as elegant as Bullitt, most would share his independence, his stoical manner, and his sense of eliteness and apartness.

The superspy thus began to give way to the supercop. *Bullitt* fea-tures a prime demonstration of the supercop's power: the extended set-piece car chase (another derivation from the James Bond films). Al-though relatively decorous by later screen standards of automotive mayhem, the chase in *Bullitt* set a new high in terms of length, non-back-projected realism, and exhilarating sense of power, with Bullitt's sporty black coupe flying over the dips and crests of hilly San Francis-co. *Bullitt* producer Philip D'Antoni featured even more elaborate vari-ations in his later productions *The French Connection* (1971) and *The Seven-Ups* (1973), and car chases became, in ever escalating form, a staple of the modern police thriller (see Chapter 9).

Although the emerging supercop had much in common with James Bond and other superspies of the sixties, he operated in a harsher, more conflict-riddled world, closer to that of the anti-Bond spy films. As in the anti-Bond films, the resolutions were often downbeat, espe-

Figure 35. *Bullitt:* The supercop (Steve McQueen) as stylesetter.

cially in the early years of the cycle, with many of the police protagonists either being killed, quitting the force, or getting demoted while their criminal antagonists run free. The predominant tone is less the grim irony of the anti-Bond films than a powerful, often sarcastic sense of disgust, directed at both the criminal vermin who pollute society and the bureaucratic weasels who enable them to flourish.

One of the most significant aspects of modern police thrillers is their hellish vision of the modern metropolis, presented in lurid and violent terms made possible by the demise of the Production Code. These films maximize the police genre's tendency to moralize the urban environment, fashioning it into a battleground of good and evil, with evil usually in the ascendancy (see Chapter 9). It is in this respect that *Bullitt* fails to anticipate the future course of the police thriller. Shot in a smooth, glossy style, the movie is characterized by vague and neutral environments. Although filmed at the height of the hippie phenomenon, *Bullitt* contains virtually no signs of the city's renowned bohemian counterculture or of the sordid sex industry that would figure so prominently in other San Francisco–set police thrillers, such as the Dirty Harry series and *The Laughing Policeman* (1973). Instead, the film depicts a clean, posh, weightless world, filled with wide spaces and light colors.

Coogan's Bluff, released almost simultaneously with *Bullitt,* develops a more detailed, dystopian vision of the modern metropolis, while also foregrounding the modern police thriller's significant relationship to the western genre. The story concerns an Arizona small-town deputy, Walt Coogan (Eastwood), sent to New York City to extradite a prisoner, who quickly escapes from his custody. The core of the film is the often comic culture clash between the Stetson-hatted, straightforward Coogan and the devious urban environment he encounters [Fig. 36]. Although *Coogan's Bluff* avoids a sentimentalized, Capraesque opposition between the virtuous hick and the vicious city (neither the opportunistic Coogan nor the mean-spirited West seen in the prologue are so virtuous), the New York of the film, viewed through Coogan's glowering eyes, typifies the urban nightmares found in later police thrillers, with its garbage-strewn streets, dingy buildings, overcrowded offices, overworked policemen, and rich assortment of swindlers, hookers, pimps, perverts, nuts, and nasties.

The film's central plot device of The Cowboy Goes East, along with Eastwood's status at the time as the hottest new western star (following his roles in Sergio Leone's 1964–6 "Dollars" trilogy), underscored the fact that the police thriller was about to displace the western as the most essential form of the American action film. Although subsequent police thrillers rarely make their connection to the western so explicit, the connotations are always present in more or less implicit form. The gunslinger is supplanted by the plainclothes policeman, the frontier by the urban jungle, the six-shooter by the .44 Magnum, and the horse by the motorcycle or automobile. In thrilleresque fashion, the grandly adventurous dimensions of these traditional elements are

Figure 36. *Coogan's Bluff:* Straightforward cowboy (Clint Eastwood) encounters devious urban environment.

problematically transposed into a diminished, modern, low-mimetic context. At one point, Coogan looks out over the smog-shrouded city and tries to picture it the way it was, just trees and river, "before people came along and fouled it all up." The action of *Coogan's Bluff* eventually gravitates toward the relatively wide-open spaces of Riverside Park and its medieval-style museum, The Cloisters, evoking the more elemental worlds of the Wild West and the Age of Chivalry. In the final chase, motorcycles substitute for horses, charging awkwardly but excitingly over the narrow paths and stone steps of this modern-day reduction of the wilderness and enchanted forest.

The ascendance of the police thriller was confirmed by the success of two influential films released in late 1971. The first was William Friedkin's prestigious, award-winning *The French Connection,* the fact-based story of two New York police detectives (Gene Hackman, Roy Scheider) struggling to block a massive heroin shipment (see Chapter 9). The second was Don Siegel's controversial *Dirty Harry,* starring Clint Eastwood as Harry Callahan, a rogue San Francisco police detective who uses illegal but effective methods to track down the psychotic "Zodiac Killer" (Andy Robinson). Both of these landmark films crystallized central elements of the modern police thriller, including the heroic isolation of the police protagonist and the spectacular decay of the urban environment.

Harry's hard-bitten wisecracks and extraordinary powers link him to James Bond, but he lacks the elegance and insider status of both Bond and Bullitt. Harry is an anarchic, embittered loner, closer in this respect to such neurotic fifties cops as Mark Dixon (*Where the Sidewalk Ends*) and Jim Wilson (*On Dangerous Ground*). However, in those earlier films, the loner cop's alienation is his curse, whereas for Harry Callahan and many of his successors it is primarily their glory, granting them an awesome purity in relation to the corrupt world around them. The police hero's old-fashioned sense of individualism and simple justice gives him great power but also isolates him from the very society he strives to protect. Although often a figure of strength and durability, the supercop is not as invulnerable as the superspy. Like the anti-Bond spy hero, he is caught between hostile forces on both sides of the struggle. His emotional vulnerability may be limited, especially in comparison with fifties police heroes, but he is subject to frustration, ostracism, and constant contact with society's worst horrors, as well as to considerable physical harm.

Following the lead of the earlier Siegel–Eastwood police thriller *Coogan's Bluff, Dirty Harry* articulates its San Francisco setting into a charged urban inferno that barely resembles the antiseptic city of *Bullitt.* Siegel's film portrays a multileveled metropolis in which a precarious Sky City of helicopters, hilltops, rooftops, glassed-in skyscrapers, and enveloping fog is perched over a primitive underworld of burrows, tunnels, alleys, and quarries. A series of oddly sinister religious icons suggests a fallen world: In a rooftop shoot-out, a neon JESUS SAVES sign [Fig. 37] spits electric brimstone onto the police; in another scene, a massive stone cross

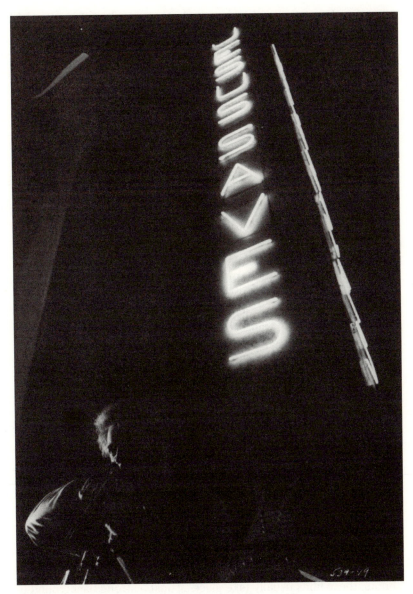

Figure 37. *Dirty Harry:* Religious icons in a fallen world.

looms ominously over the bleeding Harry. The deserted arena of Kezar Stadium is used to evoke a perverse gladiatorial combat between policeman and psychopath. *Dirty Harry* presents a labyrinthine, thrilleresque environment that must be fought through and twisted through – most vividly in the tour-de-force sequence in which the killer runs Harry ragged from one end of town to the other as part of an evasive scheme to receive a bundle of ransom money. Although few subsequent police thrillers worked out their urban milieus as rigorously or resonantly as did *Dirty Harry* and *The French Connection*, most of them employed similar combinations of color and bleakness, decadence and desolation, to convey the dark allure of urban decay.

In part because the political issues fueling it have remained prominent, the modern police thriller (whose basic form was set ca. 1970) has proven to be a remarkably durable movement, continuing through the immensely popular *Die Hard* and *Lethal Weapon* series and still flourishing in such recent hits as *Speed* (1994) and *Seven* (1995). The booming police thriller has also attached itself to other genres – including science fiction (*Mad Max*, 1979; *Blade Runner*, 1982; *RoboCop*, 1987; *Demolition Man*, 1993), horror (*Assault on Precinct 13*, 1976; *Wolfen*, 1981), and comedy (*48 Hrs.*, 1982; *Beverly Hills Cop*, 1984).

An offshoot of the modern police thriller is the vigilante film, in which the urban avenger throws off even the nominal restraints of the supercop and operates as a loner without badge or uniform, usually with a motivation that transcends personal revenge and encompasses a general desire to cleanse society of its evildoers. Examples include the simplistic but popular *Death Wish* (1974; followed by four sequels), in which a New Yorker (Charles Bronson) whose family was attacked conducts a one-man war against street criminals; the complex, ironic *Taxi Driver* (1976), in which violent misfit Travis Bickle (Robert De Niro) sees himself as the scourge of a corrupt society; and the disturbing, intensely subjective *Ms. 45* (1981), in which an unhinged rape victim (Zoe Tamerlis) pursues a bloody vendetta against the male sex.

Black Action Films

Related to both the modern police thriller and the vigilante film was the short-lived heyday of the so-called blaxploitation (more accurately, 1970s black action-film) cycle. Like the police thriller and its offshoots, these films usually take place against a strong background of urban conflict and decay, but seen from the other side of the fence, the side that is often the target of police surveillance and vigilante action. With the notable exceptions of *In the Heat of the Night*'s Virgil Tibbs (Sidney Poitier), who returned for two sequels (*They Call Me MISTER Tibbs!*, 1970; *The Organization*, 1971), and novelist Chester Himes's Harlem cops Gravedigger Jones (Godfrey Cambridge) and Coffin Ed Johnson (Raymond St. Jacques), who appeared in two films (*Cotton Comes to*

Figure 38. *Shaft:* The unaffiliated, supercool black action hero (Richard Round-tree).

Harlem, 1970; *Come Back, Charleston Blue,* 1972), there are few orga-nizational heroes, even of the loose-cannon variety, in these films. In-stead, the focus is on individualists: private eyes, as in *Shaft* (1971) [Fig. 38] and *Sheba, Baby* (1975); vigilantes, as in *Slaughter* (1972) and *Coffy* (1973); and illicit hustlers, as in *Superfly* (1972) and *The Mack* (1973).

In comparison with police films and vigilante films of the same era, these black action films tend to place greater emphasis on threats posed by the corrupt establishment and large criminal organizations than by psychopaths and street criminals. Several black action films feature supercool superheroes in the James Bond mold; some of the most distinctive center on beleaguered (though almost mythically in-vincible) outcasts who are assailed from all sides – e.g., *Sweet Sweet-*

back's Baad Asssss Song (1971), a feverish blend of chase film and art film in which the fugitive hero (director-star Melvin Van Peebles) runs a gauntlet of sex-hungry women and bloodthirsty cops, and Superfly, in which a cocaine kingpin (Ron O'Neal) trying to quit the racket faces heat from desperate junkies, black militants, his longtime business partner, and corrupt policemen.

Black action films were often derivations of earlier films and formulas – such as Cool Breeze (1972), a remake of the classic 1950 heist film The Asphalt Jungle; Hit Man (1972), a Watts-set remake of the 1970 British crime thriller Get Carter; Black Mama, White Mama (1973), a distaff version of the 1958 prison-escape drama The Defiant Ones; Abby (1974), a demonic-possession tale riding the wake of 1973's The Exorcist; and Black Shampoo (1976), an action-enhanced variation on the 1975 sex comedy Shampoo. The cycle was derailed by political pressures in the mid-1970s before it could develop a more distinct identity. More recently, such noteworthy films as Fresh (1994), an offbeat vigilante tale centered on a 12-year-old drug courier; Clockers (1995), a powerful social vision that combines a police murder-investigation story with a Superfly-like drug-dealing drama; and Set It Off (1996), a noirish saga of four women who would rather be bank robbers than janitorial workers, have demonstrated the extent to which established thriller forms can by enriched by black-oriented social themes.

Revisionist Thrillers

The late 1960s and early 1970s were an extremely turbulent period in the American film industry, shaped by a massive financial crisis, a shift in the composition and viewing habits of the movie audience, the breakdown and eventual realignment of the old studio system, and the general political and cultural turmoil of the era. One result of these upheavals was a strong "revisionist" movement in which the traditional assumptions of Hollywood genres were viewed as questionable and outdated. This skepticism produced an unusually pronounced impulse to criticize such assumptions and reinterpret them in a less reverent (though not necessarily parodic) manner. The revisionist impulse received its most spectacular application in the western genre, as exemplified by such films as The Wild Bunch (1968), Little Big Man (1970), McCabe and Mrs. Miller (1971), and Dirty Little Billy (1972), all of which present the Winning of the West as a brutal process of violence and exploitation.

Figure 39. *Chinatown:* Revisionist detective hero (Jack Nicholson) after getting too nosy.

The type of thriller most strongly affected by revisionism was that bastion of romanticized individualism, the detective genre. Anticipated by Robert Aldrich's remarkably iconoclastic *Kiss Me Deadly* (1955), revisionist detective movies of the early 1970s include *Hickey & Boggs* (1972), in which two destitute L.A. detectives (Bill Cosby, Robert Culp) stumble wearily through a bloody battle over a stolen bankroll; *The Long Goodbye* (1973, directed by Robert Altman, the leading revisionist filmmaker of the period), a tour de force of fluid camerawork in which Raymond Chandler's idealized Philip Marlowe (Elliott Gould) becomes a clownish wise guy amid amoral Angelenos; *Chinatown* (1974), an elegant, pessimistic portrait of a slick thirties bedroom dick (Jack Nicholson) [Fig. 39] caught up in a massive Southern California land grab; and *Night Moves* (1975), a melancholy tale of an unsuccessful L.A. private eye (Gene Hackman) who goes to the Florida Keys on a dubious quest for a runaway girl.

These films variously but resoundingly undermine the traditional detective hero's ability to function as an idealized moral champion who fights a lonely but necessary battle against the forces of darkness, his isolation and nonconformity enabling him to succeed where the official machinery of justice fails. Instead, these revisionist detective heroes are more often duped and deluded, leaving them unable to enforce moral justice, or else able to enforce it only in a questionable way. The private eye's vaunted sense of honor comes to seem self-righteous, irrelevant, and even destructive. His anachronistic qualities are not viewed nostalgically in these films, nor do they give him an aura of lonely but awesome power, as they do to many police heroes of the same era. The displaced detective is seen as a diehard in a dying profession, ineffectual and out-of-date in a world increasingly dominated by media saturation and institutional power. He is both enfeebled and dangerous – on the one hand, misjudging the case and failing to protect the innocent; on the other hand, leaving a trail of pain and blood everywhere he goes. The films typically end either with vivid images of futility (e.g., *Chinatown,* in which the handcuffed detective is powerless to avert the grim outcome, and *Night Moves,* in which the hero helplessly watches a drowning man through the glass bottom of a boat) or with exercises of power that leave a sour taste (e.g., *The Long Goodbye,* in which Marlowe's final posture as self-appointed executioner rings false, and *Hickey & Boggs,* in which the two partners trudge off into an ironic sunset, leaving behind a beach littered with bleeding and burning corpses).

Other forms of thriller were influenced, though not so strikingly, by the revisionist tendencies of the era. Examples include the police film *Serpico* (1973), in which the hero's primary (and primarily futile) battle is not with criminals but with other, corrupt policemen; the science-fiction film *The Man Who Fell to Earth* (1976), in which the alien "invader" (David Bowie) is corrupted and absorbed by his new world; the horror film *Martin* (1978), which demystifies traditional vampire lore; and several of the anti-Bond spy films mentioned above.

Conspiracies and Other Disasters

A related movement of the period was the conspiracy thriller, fueled by such contemporaneous phenomena as the Watergate scandal, post-

Vietnam disillusionment, and increasing public skepticism toward the Warren Commission report. Anticipated by *The Manchurian Candidate* (1962), which links Chinese communists and American politicians in a bizarre assassination plot, and closely related to the anti-Bond spy films of the late 1960s, these thrillers locate conspiratorial evil at the heart of the governmental and corporate establishments. Films in this cycle include *Executive Action* (1973), a speculative reconstruction of President Kennedy's assassination by a right-wing cabal; *The Parallax View* (1974), in which an investigative reporter (Warren Beatty) ties a sinister corporation to a series of political murders; *The Conversation* (1974), a complex character study of a reclusive surveillance expert (Gene Hackman) embroiled in corporate chicanery; *Three Days of the Condor* (1975), in which a minor CIA employee (Robert Redford) finds himself marked for death by "another CIA inside the CIA"; and *Winter Kills* (1979), in which the half-brother (Jeff Bridges) of a Kennedy-like president follows the tangled threads behind the latter's assassination.

The conspiracy-thriller cycle reflected the period's tendency to turn the focus of political paranoia strongly inward, toward America's own fundamental institutions, rather than toward external threats (such as communism or gangsterism) to those institutions. This inward focus helped shape the bewildering, hall-of-mirrors atmosphere of the most effective of these films, such as *The Parallax View* and *The Conversation,* whose heroes end up helplessly entangled in the webs of their own investigations, and *Winter Kills,* which mischievously rolls up numerous Kennedy-assassination theories into a single convoluted ball.

Another thriller-related movement of the 1970s, briefly very popular, was the cycle of disaster movies. This cycle was germinated by the tremendous success of *Airport* (1969), an extended Boeing commercial about a bomb-crippled airliner's struggle to land in a snowstorm. It blossomed into a trend with the equally successful *The Poseidon Adventure* (1972), produced by Irwin Allen (the acknowledged master of the disaster-movie form), about a motley group of survivors attempting to escape from a capsized ocean liner. The disaster cycle produced two more major hits – *The Towering Inferno* (1974), another imaginatively designed Allen production, concerning a runaway fire in a San Francisco skyscraper, and *Earthquake* (1974), about a bunch of troubled Los Angelenos shaken by a major quake – before drifting off into a diminuendo of sequels, TV movies, fiascos, and parodies.

Big-budget productions with all-star casts, these disaster movies employ a so-called *Grand Hotel* structure (after the omnibus 1932 melodrama), usually highlighting a leader figure but also spreading the dramatic emphasis among a large group of characters. In his definitive essay on the subject, "Only the Stars Survive," film scholar Nick Roddick points out that, although disasters had been a common ingredient in previous Hollywood films, the disaster-movie cycle of the 1970s was distinguished by the fact that the disaster itself nearly always occurs early or midway in the story, rather than at the climax.[5] The narrative's major weight falls on the *reaction* to the disaster, involving a formerly secure and ordinary modern environment that has been transformed by the cataclysm into something more dangerous, adventurous, primitive, labyrinthine, and resonantly thrilleresque. In *The Poseidon Adventure,* the simple but resonant device of turning everything upside down converts the plush refuge of a luxury liner into a strange new world of peril and excitement [Fig. 40]. In *The Towering Inferno,* a fire-blasted stairwell becomes both an Alpine precipice and a jungle of twisted metal vines; the building's top-floor restaurant evokes the main deck of the *Titanic,* with elevators as sky-high lifeboats. Like the police thriller, the disaster film centrally involves moral judgments of modern society, albeit in milder and more optimistic form, indicting a soft and decadent society that is punished but ultimately strengthened by the disaster. The disaster movie has recently experienced a revival, sparked by the success of the science fiction–disaster hybrid *Independence Day* (1996) and encompassing both theatrical features (*Dante's Peak, Volcano, Titanic* – all 1997) and TV movies (*Asteroid, Robin Cook's Invasion, Tidal Wave: No Escape* – all 1997).

Splatter

Along with the police film, the most active area in the development of the movie thriller over the past twenty-five years has been the horror film. After the spate of Gothic-style horror classics in the 1930s and the low-budget but richly atmospheric series of horror films produced by Val Lewton in the early 1940s (including *Cat People, I Walked with a Zombie, The Seventh Victim*), the horror genre had been stagnant since the war, its major new creative directions occurring in hybrid forms of the flourishing science-fiction film, such as *The Thing from Another World* and *Invasion of the Body Snatchers.*

Catering to the increasingly important teenage/young-adult audience (for whom horror movies have functioned much as Disney films do for younger viewers), the horror film experienced a limited revival in the late 1950s and early 1960s, spearheaded by two small companies, Hammer Film Productions in Great Britain and American International

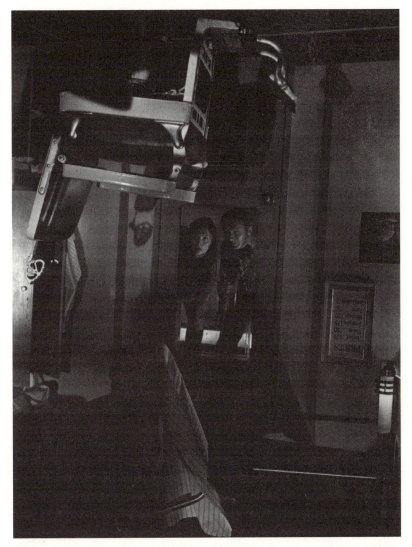

Figure 40. *The Poseidon Adventure:* Capsized luxury liner transformed into adventurous new world.

Pictures in the United States. With a few exceptions (such as AIP's 1957 drive-in hit *I Was a Teen-age Werewolf*), these films represented an extension rather than a major reconception of the Gothic-style format that had previously dominated screen horror. Hammer, led by director Terence Fisher, specialized in stately, bitter reworkings of established horror classics, such as *The Curse of Frankenstein* (1957), *Dracula*

Figure 41. *Pit and the Pendulum:* In the Gothic tradition.

(a.k.a. *Horror of Dracula,* 1958), and *The Curse of the Werewolf* (1960). AIP, led by director Roger Corman, specialized in colorful expansions of Edgar Allan Poe stories, such as *The House of Usher* (1960) and *Pit and the Pendulum* (1961) [Fig. 41]. Much like the Gothic-style classics of the 1930s, these films take place primarily in isolated, antiquated settings (castles, manor houses, remote villages), and they are usually dominated by awesomely monstrous or Faustian figures (typically Peter Cushing's arrogant Baron Frankenstein and Christopher Lee's sexually magnetic Count Dracula in the Hammer films, and Vincent Price's assortment of flamboyant eccentrics in the AIP films), while more ordinary and vulnerable identification figures remain pallid, peripheral, or unappealing.

The dawn of the modern horror-film era is widely acknowledged to be 1968, which saw the successful releases of two crucial films: *Rosemary's Baby,* adapted from Ira Levin's novel of a pregnant young woman (Mia Farrow) whose baby becomes the target of a satanic cult, and *Night of the Living Dead,* the grisly account of a farmhouse besieged by flesh-eating zombies. Roman Polanski's glossy summertime hit and George A. Romero's gritty midnight cult movie were worlds apart in

Figure 42. *Rosemary's Baby:* Filmed in the manner of a sophisticated romantic comedy. (The Museum of Modern Art Film Stills Archive)

terms of budget, marketing, and general appearance, but they shared two characteristics that would be central to the development of the modern horror movie: the familiarity of their settings and the visceral explicitness of their horrific content.

Although their subject matter (witchcraft, zombies) links them to traditional, Gothic-style horror, both films are strongly contemporary in period, and they juxtapose their supernatural elements with predominantly nonexotic locations. *Rosemary's Baby* carefully develops the bohemian-bourgeois life-style of its central couple as they set up house in an imposing but still characteristic apartment building in the heart of Manhattan. *Night of the Living Dead* takes place in and around an ordinary farmhouse in the Pennsylvania countryside.

The two films also represent a departure from the heavily atmospheric, Gothicized visual style of classical horror films, which had been adapted to color cinematography by both the Hammer and AIP series. *Rosemary's Baby* is filmed mostly in the manner of a sophisticated romantic comedy, keyed on pastel colors and spacious long takes, with little sense of the looming shadows and oppressive compositions of Gothic-style horror [Fig. 42]. This bright and airy style is subtly undermined by an unsettling deployment of restricted vision and offscreen space, most strikingly when the camera remains fixed for several minutes on the terrified Rosemary as she frantically calls for help from a telephone booth. *Night of the Living Dead* is more of a hybrid in its visual style. Dollops of low-key lighting and tilted angles hark back to the James Whale tradition, but the predominant effect – and a major source of the film's initial impact – is the sense of newsreellike immediacy conveyed by its vigorously unpolished, jaggedly edited style. Certain passages of *Night of the Living Dead* seem designed both to evoke and to oppose the classical horror-film tradition. For example, the opening scene in a nondescript cemetery contrasts the Gothicized graveyard that begins Whale's 1931 *Frankenstein,* and the frenzied, torch-carrying mob at *Frankenstein*'s finale finds its mundane counterpart in *Night of the Living Dead*'s hunting party of nonchalant rednecks.

Hollywood's crumbling system of self-censorship, centered upon the Production Code, broke down in 1966, leading to two years of virtual deregulation until the Code was replaced by the more permissive MPAA ratings system, which took effect in November 1968. The horror genre was especially affected by the relaxing of restrictions on screen content. As discussed in Chapter 2 (see the section on Pascal Bonitzer), the concept of partial or blocked vision is central to such key thriller elements as the labyrinth and suspense. This concept is given a particular inflection in horror movies, which tend to foreground issues of seeing in very explicit ways. Several writers have pointed out that the horror film is essentially based on a tension between fascination and repulsion, between wanting to see and not wanting to see. One of these writers, Dennis Giles, epitomizes the situation with an image of his squeamish girlfriend who, while watching a horror movie, put her hands over her eyes but peeked through her fingers at the same time.[6]

The horrific content of earlier horror films had been conveyed primarily through suggestiveness. Even the early Hammer horror classics, such as *The Curse of Frankenstein* and *Dracula,* which were virulently attacked in the British press for their supposed sadism and explicitness, seem discreet by later standards. In the post-Code horror film, much less – indeed, often very little – is left to the viewer's imagination. The opportunity to include more graphic material has produced a corresponding increase in the visceral, sadomasochistic, "jolt" component of the horror thriller (see Chapter 1). It also intensified the attraction–repulsion dynamic that lies at the heart of this richly ambivalent genre. By making the horrific elements shown on the screen much more explicit, post-Code horror films made those elements both more repulsive *and* more fascinating, because much of the films' creativity and cost was often invested in spectacularly gory special effects. This led to the rise of "splatter films" – that is, films making heavy use of explicit gore and violence.

Released during the interval between the demise of the Code and the advent of the ratings system, *Rosemary's Baby* and especially *Night of the Living Dead* capitalized on this new permissiveness. *Night*'s gruesome depictions of ghouls munching severed limbs and extracted viscera, as well as its horrifying spectacle of a bloody-mouthed little girl dining on her dad and then hacking her mom to death with a garden trowel, established the film as the first full-fledged example of splatter (a.k.a. "gross-out") cinema. The violence in the more restrained *Rosemary's Baby,* except for a bloody corpse glimpsed near the beginning, occurs offscreen. The film's explicitness is concentrated on the embattled body of its heroine – the representations of Rosemary's ritualistic rape and grueling pregnancy, though perhaps mild by later standards, are considerably franker than previously would have been possible in a mainstream Hollywood movie.

Despite the impact of *Rosemary's Baby* and *Night of the Living Dead,* the modern horror-film movement did not attain full momentum until the mid-1970s. Once again, the way was led by a pair of influential films, one expensive and prestigious, the other cheap and less reputable. The first was *The Exorcist* (1973), the most successful (inflation-adjusted) horror film ever, depicting the demonic possession of a twelve-year-old girl (Linda Blair). It was followed by *The Texas Chain Saw Massacre* (1974), a low-budget nightmare laced with brutal poetry, in which a vanload of young travelers encounter a grotesque family that makes no distinction between humans and livestock.

For approximately the next dozen years, the post-Gothic, splatter-dominated, thriller-oriented horror film enjoyed a period of unprecedented richness and innovation, encompassing both mainstream and low-budget productions. Less attached now to its Gothic tradition, horror fed easily upon other genres. Much of what used to be labeled science fiction was absorbed into the horror genre (for instance, *Night of the Living Dead,* which attributes the zombie plague to radiation brought back by a Venus satellite probe). Horror also incorporated the conspiracy thriller, as in *The Fury* (1978) and *Scanners* (1981), which deal with secret government/corporate schemes to exploit paranormals for sinister ends; the disaster film, as in *Shivers* (a.k.a. *The Parasite Murders* and *They Came from Within,* 1975) and *Dawn of the Dead* (1978), which center on confined groups dealing with massively catastrophic situations; and the vigilante film, as in *The Hills Have Eyes* (1977), which pits a vacationing family against a pack of desert-dwelling cannibals, and *I Spit on Your Grave* (1978), a notoriously brutal rape-and-revenge drama.

These post-Code horror films lived up to the splatter designation by indulging heavily in blood, mayhem, mutilation, physical deformity, and repellent imagery. Canada's David Cronenberg, one of the leading directors to emerge from the modern horror-film movement, specialized in potent mixtures of the cerebral and the visceral, often centered on an insidious breakdown of the individual's psychological and physiological integrity. In his *Scanners,* telepaths with extraordinary mind-invasion powers make their opponents' heads bulge, pulsate, and explode into bloody geysers. In *Videodrome* (1983), a mind-altering videotape cassette is inserted directly into a slimy cavity in the subject's abdomen. *The Fly* (1986) deals graphically and gooily with its hero's physical disintegration as he metamorphoses from human to insect. Most spectacularly, *The Brood* (1979) climaxes with a hideous perversion of childbirth: A woman (Samantha Eggar) exposes her belly to reveal an external birth sac; she tears it open with her teeth and brings forth a blood-covered pseudochild (generated by her own inner rage), which she licks like an animal.

Such gory spectacles were by no means limited to offbeat, low-budget films. *The Exorcist,* nominated for ten Academy Awards, became profitably notorious for the ravages inflicted upon the possessed girl's body by both the medical profession and her demonic intruder. *The Omen* (1976), a big-budget, big-star production in which a well-heeled couple unwittingly adopt the infant Antichrist, features a gruesome tableau in which an inquisitive reporter is decapitated by a sheet of plate glass, across whose smooth surface the severed head tumbles like a football. *Damien – Omen II* (1978), the first of two sequels, tops that with a cross-sectional view of another overzealous investigator, who has been sliced in half at the waist by a snapped elevator cable. Even *Poltergeist* (1982), a PG-rated, Steven Spielberg-produced homogenization of *The Exorcist,* includes a scene in which a horrified researcher watches his face decompose in a bathroom mirror, bloody chunks of flesh spattering into the sink below.

Following the direction indicated by *Rosemary's Baby* and *Night of the Living Dead*, these grotesque visions are usually incorporated into familiar contemporary settings (often shot on location), making possible a more thrilleresque sense of a double world than had generally been possible in the traditional Gothic-style format. *The Exorcist* opens amid ancient Iraqi ruins but soon relocates to the posh Georgetown residence that becomes the primary site of the devil's mischief. *Carrie* (1978), adapted from Stephen King's debut novel about a teenage wallflower (Sissy Spacek) with telekinetic powers, is more baroquely stylized than most horror films of the era, but it locates its fantastic elements within a very recognizable context of high-school humiliation and pettiness. The haunted house of *The Amityville Horror* (1979), set in a gracious Long Island neighborhood, converts familiar fixer-upper problems like faulty phone lines and backed-up toilets into occult phenomena. The spook-infested dwelling of *Poltergeist* is nestled in an immaculate whitebread suburb; the evil spirits enter the house through the upstairs television set. The Gothic heritage of the genre, though not eliminated, is pushed further toward the background in many modern horror films, functioning as a shading or a contrapuntal element – as in *Carrie,* in which the commonplaces of high school and suburbia are offset by the musty, candlelit decor of the home where the heroine is held thrall by her religious-fanatic mother.

No filmmaker of the era was more adept at transposing traditional horror themes into contemporary contexts than George A. Romero. His trend-setting *Night of the Living Dead* links its zombies with such modern-day associations as civil-defense procedures, obtuse TV-news reports, Vietnam-style "pacification" of the countryside, and, in the final images of corpses being stacked and burned, Nazi genocide. *Martin* (1978), Romero's ingenious updating of vampire themes, places its alienated teenage antihero (who may also be an eighty-four-year-old vampire) [Fig. 43] in a Rust Belt environment of industrial decay, auto junkyards, and modest ethnic neighborhoods. The most evocative double world of the modern horror film was created by Romero in *Dawn of the Dead* (the 1978 sequel to *Night of the Living Dead*), in which four survivors seek refuge from the zombie plague in a vast shopping mall. The resonances of this archetypal late twentieth-century setting are brilliantly mined by the film. The brutal barbarities of zombie hunting (along with associations from lost-patrol war films, cavalry-outpost westerns, and tropical-paradise adventures like *Mutiny on the Bounty*)

Figure 43. *Martin:* Rust Belt vampire (John Amplas) uses razor blades and hypodermics rather than fangs and hypnotic gazes.

are placed within a screamingly ordinary context of chirping Muzak, fluorescent lighting, plastic greenery, and "Attention, all shoppers!" announcements. In between bouts of carnage, the refugees go on uninhibited shopping sprees, and a familiar form of consumption ("Looks like a free lunch!" one of the characters exults before setting out for the stores) is slyly paralleled with the more exotic variety practiced by the flesh-eating zombies.

Figure 44. *Dawn of the Dead:* "They're us, that's all."

Much like the settings, the monsters of many modern horror films are more familiar in appearance – less grotesque, less awesome, less otherly – than are those in the traditional Gothic-style classics. The quintessence of this idea is embodied by Romero's Living Dead, especially in *Dawn of the Dead.* The persistent cadavers shuffle and stumble through the shopping mall in forms that are both horrifyingly grotesque and comically familiar [Fig. 44]: nurse zombie, nun zombie, baseball player zombie, polyester housewife zombie, handyman zombie (perforated by his own screwdriver), and everybody's favorite, the shaven-headed, saffron-robed Hare Krishna zombie, complete with jingling tambourine. As one of the film's protagonists observes of these monsters, "They're us, that's all."

The presence of the familiar can also be extended to encompass the territory indicated by its Latin root *familia*. This association is certainly not a new development in the horror genre, which has always dealt centrally with family relationships. In traditional Gothic forms, however, that relationship is usually allegorized, one step removed: the witch as surrogate mother, Frankenstein as surrogate father, the haunted castle as surrogate home. Many modern horror films deal with the familial theme more literally and directly. Demon-infested fathers menace their families in the haunted-house thrillers *The Amityville Horror* and *The Shining* (1980); a neurotic woman in *The Brood* sets her monstrous progeny upon her own mother and daughter.

Especially common in post-Code horror films is the presence of children as monsters – ranging from infancy to adolescence, from vicious demons to victimized freaks. The title character of *Rosemary's Baby* may be none other than the Antichrist – who also appears as a five year old in *The Omen* and a twelve year old in *Damien – Omen II.* A minor but memorable character in *Night of the Living Dead* is the little girl who eats her father and makes mincemeat out of her mother. *The Exorcist*'s demon-possessed Regan, spewing vomit and breaking necks, is the most famous of the era's monstrous children, whose roster includes the murderous twin of *The Other* (1972); the telekinetic young heroines of *Carrie, The Fury,* and *Firestarter* (1984); and, most precocious, the monster infant of *It's Alive* (1974), who is lethal at birth and leaves the delivery room a corpse-strewn shambles.

Moving closest to home, the protagonists of modern horror films may be assaulted by malignant forces emanating from within their own bodies: the creature inside the heroine's womb in *Rosemary's Baby,* the video-generated tumor inside the hero's brain in *Videodrome,* the voices that invade the telepath's head in *Scanners,* the slimy monster that erupts from a spaceman's chest in the horror–science fiction hybrid *Alien* (1979). *They Came from Within,* the American-release title of a 1975 David Cronenberg film (*Shivers*) dealing with sexually transmitted parasites, could be applied to the modern horror film in general. They came from within . . . my hometown . . . my neighborhood . . . my house . . . my family . . . my bedroom . . . my body . . . my womb . . . my brain . . . my dreams. This interiorization contrasts with earlier Gothic-style strains of the genre, where horror comes more from without – a configuration that was largely revived in the next major development in horror thrillers: the stalker film.

Stalkers

The popularity of the horror genre was solidified in the late 1970s by the advent of the "stalker" film, also known by the sobriquets "slasher" (for the killers' fondness for machetes, cleavers, kitchen knives, and similarly sharp-edged implements of mayhem), "slice-and-dice" (for the same reason), "body-count" (for the escalating number of victims in the course of the story), and "teenie-kill" (for the preponderance of teenagers among those victims). The stalker film typically depicts a group of adolescents or young adults being menaced and systematically slaughtered by a prowling offscreen psychopath.

An important predecessor was *Jaws* (1975). A genre-straddling film that combines elements of disaster, adventure, and splatter/horror movies, Steven Spielberg's popular tale of a great white shark terrorizing a New England beach community also contains a number of ingredients that would be crucial to the upcoming stalker-film cycle. These include the opening tableau of frivolous, promiscuous, booze-swilling young people to provide the shark's first victim, the staging of pranks and false alarms to complicate suspense, the setting of the action during a holiday or special occasion (Fourth of July weekend), and the strategic use of "gross-out" gore. Most influential was the presentation of the monster itself: relentless, remorseless, inhuman, seemingly ubiquitous and omniscient, bridging the border between naturalistic and supernatural, and evoked via gliding underwater point-of-view shots that allow us to share the shark's perspective as it browses through the dangling limbs of unwary bathers, searching for its next snack.

The first bona fide stalker film was the Canadian production *Black Christmas* (1975), in which the shark of *Jaws* is paralleled by a murderous intruder who decimates a sorority house during the yuletide season. Opening with swaying wide-angle camera movements that represent the point of view of the heavy-breathing killer as he prowls past cozily lit windows, *Black Christmas* contains virtually all the key elements of the characteristic stalker film. However, the film's commercial success and critical recognition were limited, and it did not register enough of an impact to ignite the stalker-film cycle.

That impact was provided three years later by John Carpenter's *Halloween* (1978), concerning a superhuman psychopath named Michael Myers who escapes from an asylum and returns to terrorize the Illinois community where he had committed his first murder fifteen years earlier. An unheralded low-budget production from an obscure distributor (Compass International), *Halloween* generated tremendous word of mouth, becoming a major box-office success and winning critical acclaim for its visual precision and its resonant theme of middle-class insecurity. Still more lucrative was *Friday the 13th* (1980), a major-studio (Paramount) release in which an unknown killer preys upon young counselors at a lakeside summer camp. A blandly directed, crudely acted movie, *Friday the 13th* was perhaps more instrumental than *Halloween* in establishing the stalker-film cycle, because it demonstrated the bedrock commercial strength of the basic formula, irrespective of such unpredictable factors as inventiveness and skill. These two films spawned numerous sequels and imitations, and throughout the early 1980s stalker films flooded multiplexes and VCRs.

Like the splatter films of the 1970s, stalker films deal heavily in visceral violence [Fig. 45], their narratives often functioning as little more than a perfunctory framework for an episodic series of conversation-piece murder scenes. Examples of flamboyant stalker-film carnage include a boy pinned to a closet door with an arrow through his eye socket (*Friday the 13th*), a nurse flayed to a pulp in a boiling hydrotherapy tub (*Halloween II,* 1981), the entwined bodies of an amorous young couple shish-kebabbed by a spear (*Friday the 13th, Part 2,* 1981), a severed head mounted in a blood-filled toilet bowl (*The House on Sorority Row,* 1982), and, perhaps most brazen, a popped-out eyeball, propelled (via 3-D) into the faces of the appreciatively sickened audience (*Friday the 13th, Part III,* 1982).

Stalker films also carry on the modern horror film's preference for contemporary, commonplace settings. However, stalker films are less apt to use urban, crowded, or gritty locations (in contrast to seventies horror films such as *Rosemary's Baby, Martin,* and *The Fury*), tending instead toward settings with a sequestered, tranquil quality: the small town, the leafy neighborhood, the college campus, the summer camp. Such settings reinforce an isolated vulnerability that enables the killer to cut off (and cut up) his victims without detection. Some of the most effective stalker films, such as *Halloween, The Slumber Party Massacre* (1982), and *A Nightmare on Elm Street* (1984), play up the insularity of the nonurban household, with victims being slaughtered while the people next door remain obliviously glued to their television sets.

Although the stalker-film cycle is in some respects a continuation of the post-1970 horror-film renaissance, it departs from that tradition (as well as from pattern-setting psychopath movies such as *M, Psycho,* and

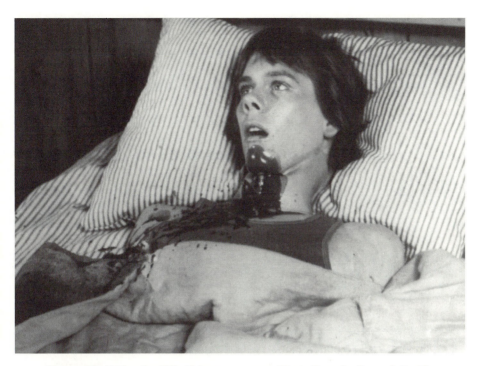

Figure 45. *Friday the 13th:* Unhappy camper (Kevin Bacon) after splatterific skewering.

Peeping Tom) in one especially important area: the characterization of the monster/murderer – or, rather, the lack thereof. As noted above (see "Splatter"), a major accomplishment of many modern horror films was to make their monsters less otherly, more familiar, less awesome, more vulnerable, less grotesque, more recognizably human – to the extent that in some cases (such as *Carrie* and *Martin*) the monsters become our primary identification figures. This type of ambivalence is largely lost in the stalker-film cycle, whose monsters are depersonalized, devoid of psychological detail, and faceless (often literally).

This distancing of the monster is accomplished in two basic ways. The first is to employ a whodunit format, wherein the killer is unidentified until the final moments of the film. Examples of this approach occur mainly at the opposite extremes of the cycle, in early stalkers such as *Black Christmas, Friday the 13th, Terror Train* (1980), *Prom Night* (1980), and *My Bloody Valentine* (1981), and in recent hits such as *Scream* (1996), *Scream 2* (1997), and *I Know What You Did Last Summer*

(1997). The other method is to reveal the killer's identity right away but to present him (much like the shark in *Jaws*) as an impassive cipher, more animal than human, more machinelike than animal, more of an abstract force than a physical form. This approach is the one taken with the two most durable stalker-film monsters, Michael Myers of the *Halloween* series and Jason Voorhees of the *Friday the 13th* series (the latter of which made an important move toward sequels-generated riches by switching from the whodunit format to the cipher format after the first film). Indeed, these two rudimentary characters are nearly identical: lumbering, implacable, featureless. In both the whodunit and cipher formats, the facelessness of the killer is often underlined by having him masked. Michael Myers wears a blank white mask (the face behind it is scarcely more expressive); Jason sports a hockey-goalie's headgear [Fig. 46]. Other stalker guises include a ski mask (*Prom Night*), gas mask (*My Bloody Valentine*), jester's makeup (*The House on Sorority Row*), and Groucho glasses (*Terror Train*).

There is, however, a well-known complication to this distancing of the stalker-film monster. Although identification is blocked on the levels of personality and sympathy, it is strikingly evoked in the form of moving-camera point-of-view shots that compel us to look through the unseen killer's eyes as he advances toward his victims. As mentioned above, the inaugural stalker film *Black Christmas* employs such shots, which are similarly used in several early whodunit-format stalker films, partly for the purpose of keeping the killer's identity hidden. However, even in stalker films that do not use the whodunit format and that reveal the killer from the start to be Michael or Jason or whoever, a mobile camera is often used to indicate the killer's prowling presence and to depict the vulnerability of the victims from his perspective.

This apparent identification of the spectator with the point of view of a vicious killer – especially a killer who is unseen or uncharacterized and thus becomes a blank screen onto which the audience can freely project all its pent-up hostilities – aroused a great deal of moralistic furor (most famously from celebrity critic Roger Ebert).[7] It is debatable, however, whether a disembodied POV shot is the best vehicle for creating identification with a movie character. The technique might even have an opposite, alienating effect – a point several critics have made in dismissing the claims ("YOU get socked in the jaw by a murder suspect!") of Hollywood's most extended subjective-camera experiment, the 1947 detective film *Lady in the Lake*.[8] A more effective tool for building identification is the shot–reaction shot technique, in which we see

Figure 46. *Friday the 13th [Part 5] – A New Beginning* (1985): Faceless cipher "Jason Voorhees."

what a character is looking at (not necessarily from her or his literal point of view) and then see her or his reaction to it. The use of this technique has been noted earlier in the climaxes of Hitchcock's *Saboteur* and Dassin's *The Naked City*, which employ reaction shots to evoke a disturbing empathy for those films' ruthless killers as they face their dooms high atop the Statue of Liberty and the Williamsburg Bridge, respectively [see Fig. 22]. In stalker films, the identification evoked by the killer's point-of-view shots might be more accurately described as a generalized identification with power – not simply the power of the monstrous, but also the power of the wide-ranging camera eye, and, self-reflexively, the power of the spectator/voyeur, enthroned outside the window of the movie screen.

Carol J. Clover and Vera Dika, two of the leading analysts of the stalker film, have pointed out that these films create situations in which our identification is split between the aggressor and the victim – Dika proposes that we identify with the killer's look but with the heroine's character.[9] However, even this distinction is perhaps too simple, because several stalker films make minimal use of the killer's point of view, and others (especially some of the visually more sophisticated ones, such as *Halloween, Halloween II, Friday the 13th, Part 2,* and *The Slumber Party Massacre*) freely mix his point of view with those of other characters and/or complicate it through a series of visual ploys that are described at greater length below. Stalker films create tension not so much in terms of particular characters but, more generally, in terms of spectatorship and the act of seeing itself. They utilize strategies of point of view and restricted vision that intensify the basic attraction–repulsion dynamic of the horror genre and provide camera-centered equivalents of the labyrinth effect so central to the thriller (see Chapter 2).

The most celebrated use of such strategies is the elaborate opening shot of *Halloween,* which plunges us into the perspective of an unseen killer as he circles around a house prowling and peeking in windows, enters through the kitchen door, picks up a knife, goes upstairs, and puts on a mask, through whose eyeholes we watch him stab a semi-nude teenage girl and then descend to the front yard – where the film's first visible cut reveals him to be a six-year-old boy who has just murdered his sexually active sister. Such extended and intricate camera movements, which a few years earlier would have probably been too expensive and time-consuming to include in a low-budget horror film, were indebted to the development in the mid-1970s of the Steadicam, a special camera harness that facilitates smoother and less distracting "hand-held" (actually, torso-attached) camerawork. Though few stalker films were able to sustain *Halloween*'s sophisticated level of camera mobility, the use of Steadicam POV shots was incorporated into the cycle's general vocabulary of suspense-enhancing visual conventions.

Stalker films work to make the spectator unusually camera conscious, not because they are art films, but because the camera in them is explicitly narrativized, linked to the action of the story. They arouse a heightened awareness of framing, because the killer or a fresh corpse may pop out from anywhere in the offscreen space, and of camera movements, because these may at any moment indicate the hovering presence of the unseen killer. This presence is often signaled by additional cues, such as heavy breathing on the sound track, conspicuous jiggling of the camera, and visual distortion via wide-angle lenses and blurry focus. At other times, however, the presence of the killer may be uncertain or subliminal, suggested by a slight, nearly imperceptible unsteadiness of the camera. Sometimes the camera advances ominously toward a potential victim but turns out to represent the presence of a nonthreatening character – say, the heroine's boyfriend or a police-man or one of the numerous annoying pranksters who infest these films. Alternatively, the camera movement may turn out to indicate the presence of no one at all, merely creating a mood of generalized anxiety.

There is a teasing, gamelike quality to stalker films, filled with red herrings, practical jokes, false alarms, and false alarms that turn out to be real alarms. Stalker films presume an active spectator and encourage audience participation, which is often verbally exercised (in *Rocky Horror Picture Show* fashion) at movie marathons and video-screening get-togethers. It is surely no accident that the rise of the stalker-film cycle coincided with the beginning of the home-video boom.

The gamelike, participatory aspect of stalker films is reflected in the above-noted whodunit format of several of the films. More generally, stalker films tantalize the spectator with questions regarding not only the identity but also the nature of the killer. The central question becomes not so much whodunit as whatdunit – that is, what exactly is the he (or occasionally she) who is doing it: a flesh-and-blood person, a supernatural being, and/or an abstract, unkillable projection of the audience's own fears and desires?

Such questions were raised at the end of the first stalker film, *Black Christmas:* After the killer has apparently been identified and apprehended, a threatening, ineradicable presence still remains in the house. This theme was expanded in *Halloween,* which presents its monster, Michael Myers, as not only a cipher but also an enigma. Setting a pattern for future stalker-film villains, Michael has the power to appear anywhere almost instantaneously, despite his lumbering gait, and knives and bullets fail to kill or even weaken him. *Halloween* incorporates film clips from the science-fiction classics *The Thing from Another World* (1951) and *Forbidden Planet* (1956), implying that Michael Myers is best classified as an alien, akin to the bloodsucking vegetable creature in the former and the invisible Monster from the Id in the latter. Near the end, the shattered heroine (Jamie Lee Curtis) shakily surmises, "It was the Bogeyman," and the doom-saying doctor (Donald Pleasance) dourly assures her, "As a matter of fact, it was." After having been shot six times by a pistol at close range and toppling out of a second-story window, Michael disappears. His heavy breathing is heard over the final shots of the three homes where the main action occurred, suggesting that, in our security-obsessed neighborhoods, all houses are permanently haunted.

These issues become even more central in the last of the three major stalker-film series, initiated with Wes Craven's *A Nightmare on Elm Street* (1984) and continued through five sequels to date. The mainspring of the series is the ambiguous and fluid nature of its villain, Freddy Krueger (Robert Englund), a child-murderer who was lynched by enraged parents and has returned to prey upon their surviving offspring. Krueger is a real person who has become imaginary (he lives on as a bogeyman figure in the dreams of his victims), but he also has the power to penetrate the material world [Fig. 47]. The damage inflicted by Krueger in his victims' dreams is real, corporeal – their flesh is visibly scored with bloody gashes from the razor-fingered glove he wears – and he can also attain bodily form, making himself vulnerable to physical harm.

A Nightmare on Elm Street is perhaps the richest example of the stalker-film cycle, but it also deviates from the basic stalker format in several key respects: The voyeuristic use of point-of-view shots is almost entirely eliminated; the villain is more distinct; and there is a more intense, psychologically detailed focus on the teenage heroine (Heather Langenkamp). More typically, stalker films – with their limited scope, Us-versus-It clarity, rudimentary characterizations, and well-defined repertory of plot ingredients and visual tricks – aspire toward a stripped-down, almost mathematical purity, as efficiently machine-like as their relentless villains. However, that efficiency is achieved at considerable cost in depth, complexity, and subversiveness.

The limitations of the stalker-film format are illustrated by *The Funhouse* (1981), a horror movie made at the height of the stalker boom and containing many of the same basic elements. The story concerns four teenagers (including such generic stalker-film types as the obnoxious prankster, the short-lived promiscuous girl, and the indestructible virgin) who ill-advisedly decide to spend the night in a labyrinthine carnival fun house. There they are picked off by a lurking killer, who, in characteristic stalker fashion, wears a mask – in this case, a replica of Boris Karloff's monster from *Frankenstein.*

Although its basic situation resembles that of many stalker films and its first scene parodies the famous opening of *Halloween, The Funhouse* is not given a stalker-film treatment. The film's approach is too perverse and ambivalent to exist comfortably within the confines of the conventional stalker format; there is too much interest in exploring the Other Side, the side of the grotesque and the monstrous. The killer/stalker figure does not remain a faceless, opaque alien. He is soon

Figure 47. *A Nightmare on Elm Street:* Dream figure "Freddy Krueger" surfaces into the material world.

unmasked, revealed to be a hideously deformed freak, and invested with a certain *Phantom of the Opera* pathos. The carnival world is presented as an alternative reality, a crazy mirror reflecting the repressed, attractive–repulsive underside of the normal world, and not so different from that normal world as we might like to believe. Director Tobe Hooper's flair for depicting grotesque families, demonstrated previously in *The Texas Chain Saw Massacre,* is continued in this film, which develops the theme on two levels: the figurative family bond that unites the carnival people against the outside world, and the actual family bond that exists between the killer and his protective father, the seedy fun-house barker (Kevin Conway). These perverse family bonds are compared with the normal ones involving the heroine's middle-class family, not always to the latter's advantage.

The Funhouse is a disturbing film that, in the tradition of the great horror movies of the 1970s, challenges our complacency by undermining the distinction between the normal and the abnormal. The stalker-film cycle, on the other hand, seems a reactionary retreat from the adventurous subversiveness of the post-1970 horror-film boom. By distancing us from their monsters, by building an opaque and impenetrable wall between the normal and the monstrous, stalker films cut themselves off from much of the deep-diving ambivalence that is the special strength of the horror genre. Stalker films can be exciting, but they are rarely disturbing.

The stalker film, much like its resilient villains, has refused to die, despite the wishful predictions of many parents and film reviewers. After having apparently expired in the early 1980s, the *Halloween* and *Friday the 13th* series were revived for several more sequels. The unexpected commercial success of Wes Craven's *Scream* (1996), a complicated, self-referential compendium of previous stalker-film elements, gave an additional boost to this durable cycle. Meanwhile, leading figures of the horror renaissance of the 1970s, such as George A. Romero, Tobe Hooper, David Cronenberg, Brian De Palma, and Larry Cohen, have either floundered commercially or largely abandoned the horror genre.

Neo-Noir

In the early 1980s, it became apparent that a number of crime movies were being specifically patterned after film noir, the belatedly recognized, semisubmerged movement that had expressed the dark side of postwar America. By 1990, this still flourishing revival had acquired the label "neo-noir." Noir specialist Todd Erickson has pointed out a number of loose parallels between the historical context of classical film noir and the period that spawned neo-noir.[10] The problems of letdown and readjustment at the end of World War II were paralleled by the malaise that followed the Vietnam War. Anxiety over the status of women was intensified by the redomestication of working-force women after World War II and, correspondingly, by the rise of the modern feminist movement in the 1970s. The illicit sexuality and mercenary spirit that permeate classical noir found their equivalents, respectively, in the drugs-and-disco hedonism of the late seventies and in the morality-coated materialism of the go-go eighties.

Predecessors of the neo-noir movement (or, to put it another way, earlier successors of the classical noir movement) can be found in the French New Wave and in the revisionist detective films and conspiracy thrillers of the 1970s. Neo-noir first gained widespread recognition in 1981, with the release of two high-profile productions: *Body Heat,* which was identified by many reviewers as an overt recycling of classical noir elements (such as its sultry slat-shadowed atmosphere and its twisty James M. Cain–like plot of adultery, murder, and betrayal), and *The Postman Always Rings Twice,* a remake of the 1946 Cain-based film noir. Another significant neo-noir of 1981 was *Cutter's Way,* which, after initially bombing at the box office, gained a successful rerelease in response to extensive critical support.

These three films represent three different (and not mutually exclusive) possibilities for reviving film noir. The first, exemplified by *Body Heat,* encompasses homages or pastiches that attempt to recycle classical noir plot elements and to re-create the classical noir ambience, usually with the addition of more explicit sex and violence. Later efforts in this vein include *Blood Simple* (1984), which applies flashy noir-like stylistics to its bleakly ironic, grotesquely violent tale of illicit love and botched revenge in the Texas hinterlands; *Angel Heart* (1987), an example of detective noir, featuring an increasingly bewildered private eye (Mickey Rourke), a thickly atmospheric New Orleans setting, and a supernatural twist; and *Final Analysis* (1992), a cumbersomely plotted, at times visually extravagant tale of a cocky San Francisco psychiatrist (Richard Gere) who gets the smirk wiped off his face by a scheming woman (Kim Basinger).

A variant on the pastiche option involves the application of a murky noir-derived visual style (expanded into the realm of color photography, thanks to the development of faster film stocks) to movies that fall predominantly into other genres. In some cases, the recreated noir look seems little more than window dressing for innocuous subject matter, as in *Batman* (1989) and *Batman Returns* (1992); in others, it indicates a more substantial darkness at the heart of the film, as in the police–science-fiction hybrid *Blade Runner* (1982) [Fig. 48] and the grisly police thriller *Seven* (1995).

Conversely, there are noir pastiches whose plots evoke classical noir but whose styles are brighter, glossier, and more mainstream, with at most a patina of noirlike eccentricity. Examples include *Masquerade* (1988), a blend of film noir and Harlequin romance concerning a gullible young heiress (Meg Tilly) surrounded by double-crossers; *Shattered* (1991), a flashback-peppered account of an amnesia victim (Tom Berenger) who finds himself at the center of a bizarre swindle; and *Malice* (1993), featuring an inventive, convoluted screenplay about a college professor (Bill Pullman) suckered by his "Snow White" wife (Nicole Kidman).

Figure 48. *Blade Runner:* Noir look, different genre.

The second category consists of remakes of classical noirs. These neo-noir remakes are usually markedly different in approach from the originals. The 1946 *Postman* is sardonic, romantic, and balmy [Fig. 49]; the 1981 version is somber, carnal, and drizzly [Fig. 50]. *Against All Odds* (1984), a remake of 1947's *Out of the Past,* converts the most voluptuously fatalistic of classical noirs into a heroic redemption tale with a nonfatal femme and a fluffy white dog. *D.O.A.* (1988) similarly takes a more heart-warming approach in remaking the hard-edged, high-pressure 1950 film of a fatally poisoned man trying to solve his own murder.

The third neo-noir option could be called the "analogue." *Cutter's Way* tells of a tarnished California golden boy (Jeff Bridges) and his crippled, half-mad friend (John Heard) who get in way over their heads when they try to pin a brutal sex murder on a pillar of the community. Neither a pastiche nor a remake, *Cutter's Way* reconceives the noir impulse at a more fundamental level, linking its elusive sense of anxiety explicitly to contemporary sources: The secondary hero is an embit-

Figure 49. *The Postman Always Rings Twice* (1946): Balmy and romantic . . .

Figure 50. . . . and *The Postman Always Rings Twice* (1981): Somber and carnal.

tered Vietnam veteran, the main characters are sixties counterculture leftovers, and the suspected murderer seems precisely the type who would be a heavy contributor to the campaign chest of fellow Santa Barbara resident Ronald Reagan.

However, this third option of updating the social context has not been strongly pursued in the neo-noir movement. For the most part, neo-noir's relationship to contemporary social issues has been, like that of classical noir, indirect and abstract (though by no means nonexistent). More significant have been attempts to reconceive, rather than simply emulate, the eccentric stylistic vocabulary of film noir.

A leading figure in this respect is David Lynch, whose *Blue Velvet* (1986) is one of the most original products of the largely derivative neo-noir movement. The story of a clean-cut but very curious young man (Kyle MacLachlan) [Fig. 51] who takes a harrowing walk on the wild side of his seemingly wholesome hometown, *Blue Velvet* expands the semiexpressionist stylistics of classical noir with an array of surrealist, art-film, absurdist, avant-garde, pop-art, and postmodern devices. These flourishes include microscopic close-ups of bugs in rugged battle beneath a manicured lawn, banal absurdist dialogue ("Man, I like Heineken"; "It sure is a strange world"), unnaturalistic sound effects, enigmatic inserts of a guttering candle and a severed ear, and supersaturated all-American pop images of red roses, white picket fences, and blue skies. Lynch has pursued this eccentric and eclectic style to comparable, though not necessarily as effective, extremes in later noir-hued works, such as the feverish couple-on-the-run tale *Wild at Heart* (1990), the gaudy Gothic psychodrama *Twin Peaks: Fire Walk with Me* (1992), and the identity-dissolving mystery *Lost Highway* (1997).

Another major stylistic innovator in the field of neo-noir is Quentin Tarantino. His directorial debut, *Reservoir Dogs* (1992), is a blood-drenched, nihilistic heist film whose complex flashback structure evokes such classical noirs as *The Killers* (1946) and *The Locket* (1946). Tarantino's intricate structuring techniques were pushed several notches further in his breakthrough hit *Pulp Fiction* (1994), a panoramic crime movie that arranges three interlocked story lines in an overlapping 2-3-1 chronology. Although filled with noir references and motifs, *Pulp Fiction* also deviates from the grand tradition in crucial ways. It lacks a noir look; the expansive, brightly colored widescreen visuals seem derived from comedy directors like Frank Tashlin and Blake Edwards rather than from noir masters like Fritz Lang and Robert Siodmak. *Pulp Fiction* not only goes against the grain of film noir's charac-

Figure 51. *Blue Velvet:* Small-town kid (Kyle MacLachlan) discovers the dark side.

teristically dark, oppressive visual style (other neo-noirs, such as the sunny *The Grifters* [1990] and the traveloguish *Against All Odds,* had previously done this), but it also undermines noir's ominous, paranoid tone. Noirlike situations of dread and entrapment are constantly being set up (a dangerous date with a gangster's wife, a drug overdose, a boxer who refuses to take a fall, a messy accidental shooting in an automobile), only to receive comic or upbeat resolutions. Even the film's most doom-laden event, the death of charming hit man Vincent Vega (John Travolta), is offset by his "resurrection" in the final, out-of-sequence section of the film. Although many noirs, both classical and neo-, have dealt freely in black, sardonic humor, Tarantino in *Pulp Fiction* seems to have achieved a contradiction in terms: a *joyeux* film noir, a light-hearted dark film.

The small-town settings of such neo-noirs as *Blood Simple* and *Blue Velvet* indicate a general trend away from the predominantly urban orientation of classical noir. Whereas most classical noirs are set in whole or in part in the thriller trinity of New York, Los Angeles, and San Francisco, many neo-noirs have brought darkness to the heartland, with a special affinity for the situation of the drifter or fugitive who stumbles into a dead-end dump in the middle of nowhere. Examples include *The Hot Spot* (1990), in which an itinerant hustler (Don Johnson) encounters female trouble in a Texas backwater; *Red Rock West* (1993), in which a down-on-his-luck veteran (Nicolas Cage) limps into a Wyoming hamlet where he is immediately mistaken for a contract killer; *The Last Seduction* (1994), in which a ruthless Manhattan dame (Linda Fiorentino) is obliged to hide out in the upstate burg she calls "Mayberry"; *U-Turn* (1997), in which an unfortunate motorist (Sean Penn) is stranded in an arid Arizona death trap; and *Palmetto* (1998), in which a fresh-out-of-jail patsy (Woody Harrelson) gets sucked into a "foolproof" kidnapping scheme in a rain-soaked Florida fishing town. In neo-noir, the old-fashioned, often decaying small town has provided a more fruitful venue for the marginal lives, exposed vulnerability, and moody atmosphere that evoke the noir sensibility than have either the sprawling city (more suitable for the police thriller) or the tidy suburbs (more suitable for the stalker film). These isolated, anachronistic settings also indicate the hermetic quality of much neo-noir, located off the main highway of contemporary history.

The period ca. 1967–78 was marked by an unusually strong strain of antiheroism in the American cinema, extending into mainstream big-budget films and the action genres. Beginning in the late 1970s, Hollywood films became increasingly dominated by superheroism, whether in the family-oriented fantasy/adventure vein of the *Star Wars,* Indiana Jones, Superman, and Batman series, or in the more violent vehicles of Sylvester Stallone, Arnold Schwarzenegger, Bruce Willis, Steven Seagal, and other bulked-up action stars. Inheriting some of the transgressive function of 1970s horror films, the neo-noir movement has helped to keep alive a more vulnerable, morally ambiguous concept of the thriller hero.

In its more explicit treatment of such classical noir themes as sexual deceit and the femme fatale, neo-noir parallels and often blends into another recent category that could be called "sexual thrillers." These films share neo-noir's preoccupation with the gender anxieties generated by feminist political advances and the accompanying anti-feminist backlash. Some of them – such as *Fatal Attraction* (1987), *Basic Instinct* (1992), *Body of Evidence* (1993), *The Temp* (1993), and *Disclosure* (1994) – depict the threat posed by dangerously empowered women. Others emphasize the risks run by women who venture too far into the dangerous waters of sexual adventure: *Sliver* (1993), *Jade* (1995), and a multitude of straight-to-cable cheapies like *Secret Games* (1992), *Intimate Obsession* (1992), *Sexual Malice* (1994), and the unusually well-crafted neo-Gothic *Object of Obsession* (1994).

The key figure in the development of the sexual thriller has been high-priced screenwriter Joe Eszterhas, and the quintessential example of the form is the Eszterhas-written *Basic Instinct,* in which an unstable San Francisco policeman (Michael Douglas, the favorite target of recent femmes fatales) becomes entangled with a manipulative mystery writer (Sharon Stone) who may also be the ice-pick murderer he is hunting. Rather than simply embellish a thriller plot with explicit sexual interludes, *Basic Instinct* seeks to merge sex and suspense, as exemplified by the frenzied bedroom scenes in which Stone is riding astride the vulnerable Douglas and seems at any moment about to reach for the fatal ice pick that will provide the ultimate thrill.

PART THREE

Film Analyses

6

The Detective Thriller
The Kennel Murder Case (1933),
The Big Sleep (1946)

A s noted in Chapter 1, the thriller is an imprecise concept, widely applied and difficult to pin down. On the one hand, it spreads
itself over several acknowledged genres, such as spy, detective,
police, and horror. On the other hand, within an individual genre some
works may be considered thrillers and others not. In order to approach
this problem, therefore, it might be useful to seek a borderline in one
of those genres that contain both thrillers and nonthrillers.

Such an opportunity is provided by the detective story, one of the
earliest and most durable of thriller-related genres. The detective genre
has been subdivided into two primary categories by several critics and
authors, including acclaimed novelist Raymond Chandler. In his often-
quoted 1944 article "The Simple Art of Murder," Chandler draws a
strongly biased distinction between the "formal detective story," practiced by such authors as Agatha Christie and Dorothy L. Sayers, and
the "realistic style," pioneered by Dashiell Hammett (and carried on
by Chandler himself).[1] More recently, the same basic division has been
examined by John G. Cawelti, whose 1976 book *Adventure, Mystery,
and Romance* is discussed in Chapter 2, and Tzvetan Todorov, an important French theorist-critic whose extensive writings on literature,
language, and genre include the concise 1966 essay "The Typology of
Detective Fiction." Todorov labels the first type of detective story the
whodunit; Cawelti uses the term *classical detective story* to refer to the
same thing. The second type is called the *detective thriller* by Todorov
and *hard-boiled detective story* by Cawelti. Although both types feature
detective heroes and murder mysteries, the second (detective thriller
or hard-boiled detective story) is the one that is more pertinent to the
domain of the thriller.

As might be expected, the distinction between the detective whodunit and the detective thriller is not a clear and absolute one. A detective thriller usually contains some whodunit elements, and detective
whodunits are not totally devoid of thriller elements. Nevertheless, the

two forms are distinct enough that they can provide us with some important clues for tracking down the elusive concept of the thriller. This chapter examines two films: *The Kennel Murder Case* (1933), representing the classical/whodunit side of the detective genre, and *The Big Sleep* (1946), representing the hard-boiled/thriller side.

The classical/whodunit form, which characteristically centers on the solution of an exceptionally puzzling crime by a brilliant and eccentric sleuth, derives from the earliest stages of detective-literature history. The first detective story is widely considered to be Edgar Allan Poe's "The Murders in the Rue Morgue" (1841), in which the Parisian recluse C. Auguste Dupin employs his superior intellectual powers to unravel the bizarre solution to a pair of gory homicides. British author Wilkie Collins's *The Moonstone* (1868), centering on the baffling disappearance of an exotic diamond, features an investigator, Sergeant Cuff, with many of the qualities of later whodunit detectives, but he is only a secondary if striking character in a novel whose complex design far exceeds the scope of what would eventually become the classical detective story. The detective genre was further refined and greatly popularized by the debt-ridden British physician Arthur Conan Doyle, whose novella *A Study in Scarlet* (1887) introduced the most famous fictional sleuth: the London-based "consulting detective" Sherlock Holmes. Faithfully reported by his awed companion Dr. Watson and best suited to the short-story format, Holmes's adventures are more concentrated in scope (with a smaller roster of suspects) than the classical whodunit developed by Doyle's successors.

The form of the classical whodunit was crystallized during the so-called Golden Age of Detective Fiction, featuring a number of milder gentleman sleuths who followed in Holmes's footsteps. These descendants of Holmes (whose last case appeared in 1927) include E. C. Bentley's boyish aesthete Philip Trent (who first appeared in print in 1913), Agatha Christie's fastidious Belgian fusspot Hercule Poirot (1920), Dorothy L. Sayers's war-traumatized aristocrat Lord Peter Wimsey (1923), S. S. Van Dine's psychology-oriented connoisseur Philo Vance (1926), Frederic Dannay and Manfred Bennington Lee's pince-nez-sporting bibliophile (and their pseudonym) Ellery Queen (1929), Margery Allingham's blue-blooded twit Albert Campion (1929), Rex Stout's corpulent stay-at-home Nero Wolfe (1934), Nicholas Blake's tea-swilling wag Nigel Strangeways (1935), and many others.

Although a mainstay of popular literature, the whodunit type of detective story has been a minor force in commercial cinema. Because of its emphasis on wordy ratiocination over suspenseful action, it is not considered a strongly cinematic form. Hitchcock expressed his distaste for the whodunit, and he generally avoided the form (save for four or five partial instances) throughout his career.[2] There have been occasional major productions in the whodunit vein – for example, W. S. Van Dyke's breezily sophisticated *The Thin Man* (1934), René Clair's jocular Christie adaptation *And Then There Were None* (1940), Sidney Lumet's lavish production of Christie's *Murder on the Orient Express* (1974), and, in an offbeat variation, David Lynch's sensationalistic TV soap opera *Twin Peaks* (1990). However, the most active venue for the whodunit in movies was provided by the B-movie series of the 1930s and 1940s, each centered on a continuing detective hero, such as Ellery Queen, The Saint, Mr. Moto, and Sherlock Holmes. One of the earliest and longest-running detective-film series (1929–47) featured Philo Vance, the private-eye hero created by S. S. Van Dine (pseudonym of the American literary editor and art critic Willard Huntington Wright), a central figure of the Golden Age of Detective Fiction.

The Kennel Murder Case (1933) was the fifth entry in the Philo Vance film series, which, until its later years, enjoyed A rather than B production budgets. This film is an exemplary whodunit, containing virtually all the classic ingredients, down to the proverbial butler as a prime suspect. It is also an example of a specialized whodunit form known as the "locked-room mystery," featuring a corpse that is discovered in a sealed chamber with no apparent exit for the murderer. Literary examples of this tricky device include Poe's aforementioned "The Murders in the Rue Morgue" and one of the most famous Sherlock Holmes stories, "The Adventure of the Speckled Band" (1892).

The Kennel Murder Case was directed by Michael Curtiz, whose lengthy and prolific tenure at Warner Brothers established him as a studio workhorse of unsurpassed proficiency (besides *The Kennel Murder Case,* Curtiz made six other movies released in 1933). Among his best-known films are the wartime romance *Casablanca* (1942), the musical biography *Yankee Doodle Dandy* (1942), and the noirish melodrama *Mildred Pierce* (1945). The screenplay, credited to Hollywood veterans Robert N. Lee and Peter Milne, does a fine job of both fleshing out and streamlining Van Dine's prolix novel – adding several scenes that lead up to the first murder, expanding some characters and inventing a new one (Sir Thomas McDonald), while still managing to dispatch the story in a speedy 73 minutes. The debonair William Powell had played Philo Vance in three previous films and was soon to achieve greater fame as another sophisticated screen detective, Nick Charles of the *Thin Man* series, based on hard-boiled virtuoso Dashiell Hammett's softest-boiled novel.

The film opens at the Long Island Kennel Club's annual dog show, where noted canine-fancier Philo Vance is exhibiting his beloved Scottish terrier. Also competing is the eminently murderable Archer Coe, a wealthy and mean-spirited New Yorker with a long list of enemies. These include his niece and ward Hilda Lake, who resents his control over her money; Hilda's sweetheart Sir Thomas McDonald, whose prize pooch was possibly murdered by Archer; Brisbane Coe, who has long hated his brother Archer; Archer's personal secretary Raymond Wrede, whose infatuation with Hilda is adamantly opposed by his employer; Doris Delafield, Archer's neighbor and recently estranged mistress; Eduardo Grassi, Doris's current paramour, whom Archer has double-crossed in a deal to purchase his valuable Chinese antiquities collection; Liang, Archer's Chinese cook, who has a patriotic interest in preventing the sale of the collection; and the butler Gamble, a former con artist who has no discernible murder motive but looks extremely suspicious.

Archer Coe is soon discovered dead by apparent suicide, in a locked bedroom of his Manhattan mansion, with a gun in his hand and a bullet in his head. Upon hearing the news, Philo Vance cancels an imminent trip to Italy and assists the police investigation being led by District Attorney Markham and Sergeant Heath. Vance's skepticism of the suicide scenario is confirmed by the discovery that Archer Coe was both clubbed and stabbed before he was shot. His disgruntled brother Brisbane Coe, who had established a phony alibi with a feigned trip to Chicago, is the prime suspect, but Brisbane's corpse comes tumbling out of the hall closet. An injured Doberman, belonging to Doris Delafield, is discovered on the premises. Sir Thomas is stabbed in his apartment in the building next door, but the investigators suspect him of having faked the attack with a dagger – the murder weapon – that is found under his bed.

Using scale models of the pertinent buildings, Vance demonstrates that there were actually two different murderers whose paths accidentally crossed. The first clubbed and then fatally stabbed Archer Coe, in addition to braining the inquisitive Doberman when it wandered onto the scene. The second, Brisbane Coe, shot his already dead brother and then was himself killed by the initial murderer. Vance uses the injured Doberman to identify its attacker: the secretary Raymond, who impulsively killed Archer Coe in a dispute over Raymond's desire to marry Hilda.

For the purpose of distinguishing thriller from nonthriller, a crucial aspect of the classical/whodunit detective story is the *detachment* of the detective hero. His emotional and physical involvement in the events of the story is limited. The whodunit detective's involvement is primarily cerebral: figuring out the clues, with little risk, from the perspective of an observer on the sidelines. The ultimate extension of this trait is Rex Stout's massively sedentary Nero Wolfe, who declines even to step outside his Manhattan town house.

The Golden Age classical detective hero is often an aristocratic, upper-class figure, for whom detective work is merely an exotic hobby rather than a livelihood. A brilliant dilettante, he takes on cases because they capture his fancy, not because he needs the money. There is none of the "twenty-five bucks a day plus expenses" characteristic of the hard-boiled dicks of the detective thriller.

Philo Vance is a much more foppish figure in the Van Dine novels, wherein he wears silk kimonos, smokes gold-tipped cigarettes, and speaks in an affected dialect ("But really, y'know, I can't go in these togs. I'll hop into appropriate integuments").[3] Actor William Powell tones down Philo's foppishness in *The Kennel Murder Case,* but the swank associations are still strong: He has a very dapper appearance, wears light-colored gloves and a boutonniere [Fig. 52], and obviously does not have to work for a living. Philo is not hired for the case; he takes it on purely as a diversion. After canceling his vacation in order to investigate the murder, he muses nonchalantly, "This may prove far more interesting than a trip to Europe."

The classical sleuth does not get his hands dirty (Vance's ever-present gloves serve as a vivid image of this immaculateness). Though occasionally nicked by a bullet or bruised in a scuffle, he rarely suffers serious physical harm or succumbs to a femme fatale. Philo Vance does not even soil his hands (or gloves) with money. He is above all that.

A similarly dispassionate attitude characterizes the whodunit detective's personal relationship to both the murderer and the murder victim(s), who are usually strangers to him or, at best, slight acquaintances. The whodunit victim (like Archer Coe in *The Kennel Murder Case*) is almost always socially prominent – someone wealthy or powerful enough to give him stature and make his murder significant. However, as Cawelti notes in *Adventure, Mystery, and Romance,* the victim is not someone for whom either we or the detective feel a great deal of sympathy, because such feelings might upset the balance of the story, causing it to tilt toward pathos or tragedy.[4] It would then lose the serene composure typical of the classical detective story, which literary critic Joseph Wood Krutch called "one of the most detached and soothing of narratives."[5] Mystery writer Dorothy L. Sayers concurred, "It is better to err in the direction of too little feeling than too much."[6] An indicator of this detachment in *The Kennel Murder Case* is the fussy little doctor whose main concern over the victims is that their deaths and injuries are interfering with his meals, his sleep, or his World Series tickets. "Well, there are too many people in the world, anyway!" he grumbles, as he arrives to examine yet another bothersome corpse.

Similarly, the murderer in the detective whodunit is rarely an extraordinary figure. He (or she) is usually not a larger-than-life master criminal in the vein of Fritz Lang's Dr. Mabuse or the colorful supervillains of the James Bond and Batman films, nor is he a sociopath examined in great psychological depth like Dostoyevsky's Raskolnikov (*Crime and Punishment,* 1866) or Richard Wright's Bigger Thomas (*Native Son,* 1940). If he were, he might then become too fascinating in himself and draw attention away from the genius detective and his brilliant solution of the mystery, which are the primary concerns of the classical detective story.[7]

The classical detective story is commonly characterized by a very familiar, domestic, bourgeois context. One of the most striking aspects of *The Kennel Murder Case* is its heavy use of camera angles and compositions that give prominence to large domestic objects, such as lamps, tables, shelves, and, especially, the banisters and balustrades of the main staircase. However, the effect of such techniques here is not to create an oppressive and claustrophobic atmosphere (in contrast to detective-movie thrillers like *The Maltese Falcon* [1941] and *Murder, My Sweet* [1944]). Instead, their major function is to inflate the importance of the domestic setting, to give extra solidity and weight to the upper-middle-class world that is the main arena of the classical whodunit. The German cultural critic Walter Benjamin, in his journal *One-Way Street* (1928), maintains that the furniture is practically the main ingredient of the classical detective story: "The furniture style of the second half of the nineteenth century has received its only adequate description, and analysis, in a certain type of detective novel at

Figure 52. *The Kennel Murder Case:* The dapper classical detective (William Powell, right). (The Museum of Modern Art Film Stills Archive)

the dynamic center of which stands the horror of apartments." According to Benjamin, the very sturdiness and precise arrangement of the furniture seem to summon up an answering disruption of this too, too solid bourgeois world, "tremulously awaiting the nameless murderer like a lascivious old lady her gallant."[8]

The settings of the whodunit often have a quality of isolation, as exemplified by that favorite depository for murder victims, the country house. Cawelti notes that the action, even when set in the middle of the city, remains largely contained within a couple of circumscribed locales; there is little sense of the bustle and breadth of the city outside.[9] This pattern is generally reflected in *The Kennel Murder Case*. Although there are some diverse locations in the first half of the film (e.g., the Long Island dog show and Grand Central Station), the second half gravitates toward the Coe mansion and the apartment building next door.

The whodunit gives a clear sense of its spatial layout; the topography of the action is very anchored and readable. Many classical detective novels contain maps and diagrams to ensure that our orientation is clear; the book *The Kennel Murder Case* includes floor plans of the Coe mansion and Archer Coe's bedroom, plus a map of the two adjacent buildings involved in the murders. A remarkable image in the movie version shows Philo Vance towering over scale models of the two buildings [Fig. 53]. "I think I can fit the pieces of this jigsaw puzzle together," he announces confidently, as he lifts the roofs off the models to examine the floor plans beneath. This image is a wonderfully evocative expression of the classical detective's power and detachment, his control over the realm he investigates: He towers over the world of the case, godlike, looking down upon it from a position outside. The image also relates to the detective's moral function: He lifts the lids off the sanctuaries of the guilty and uncovers the dirty secrets hidden inside. Most important, it connotes the stability and controllability of the world of the classical whodunit, which is like a puzzle or miniaturized model with a clear layout and clearly defined rules. These associations are strengthened by the dissolve from Vance pointing out the location of Archer Coe's study in the scale model to a high-angle shot of the actual room, where the murder is seen taking place in flashback – as if the potentially disruptive force of the murder itself were contained within that miniature model world.

The recap of the suspects two-thirds of the way through the film of *The Kennel Murder Case,* in which each one is shown in close-up as he or she is fingerprinted, serves as another device for stabilizing the narrative and orienting the audience. It functions as a roll call, reminding us who all the suspects are and enabling us to get our bearings. Such devices provide a vivid contrast to *The Big Sleep,* whose plot is so confusing that, legendarily, even the director, the screenwriters, and author Raymond Chandler himself could not figure out who was killing whom at a certain point in the story.

The detective thriller derives from a later direction in the history of detective fiction: the "hard-boiled" movement, whose sordid and violent worldview was a reaction against the more forthright artificiality of the classical whodunit and the effeteness of its gentleman-detective heroes. (As comic poet Ogden Nash succinctly suggested, "Philo Vance / Needs a kick in the pance.")[10] In contrast to the British-dominated, upscale matrix of the classical whodunit, the hard-boiled school was based in the United States and directed at a more lowbrow audience.

Figure 53. *The Kennel Murder Case:* Godlike detachment of the classical detective (William Powell). (The Museum of Modern Art Film Stills Archive)

Its breeding ground was the pulp magazines (named after their cheap, rough-textured paper) that rose in popularity in the 1910s and 1920s. The most famous and influential of the pulps was *Black Mask,* which was founded in 1920 but didn't hit its stride until the mid-1920s.[11]

Black Mask produced the first acknowledged practitioner of the hard-boiled style, Carroll John Daly, and the first hard-boiled writer to receive widespread critical acclaim, Dashiell Hammett. A former employee of Pinkerton's National Detective Agency, Hammett in 1923 began writing stories that featured a ruthless and somewhat indistinct private eye known only as the Continental Op (i.e., an operative working for the Continental Detective Agency). Hammett's first full-length novel, *Red Harvest* (serialized in *Black Mask* in 1927–8 and published in 1929), is a corpse-glutted tale in which the Op pitilessly plays a corrupt city's rival factions against each other in an orgy of escalating violence. His best-known novel, *The Maltese Falcon* (serialized in 1929 and published in 1930), dropped the customary first-person narration of hard-boiled mysteries in order to provide a clearer, more critical portrait of its detective-hero, the predatory charmer Sam Spade. Hammett's most admired successor in the hard-boiled detective school was Raymond Chandler, author of the moody Philip Marlowe series (1939–58), and his most popular successor was Mickey Spillane, author of the lowly regarded but highly profitable Mike Hammer series (1947–present). The hard-boiled style was given more widespread appeal by Ross Macdonald, creator of the compassionate Lew Archer series (1949–76); this broadening of the tradition has been carried on by such multifaceted detective protagonists as Joseph Hansen's morose (and gay) Dave Brandstetter (1970–present), Sara Paretsky's pugnacious (and female) V. I. Warshawski (1982–present), and Walter Mosley's wary (and black) Easy Rawlins (1990–present).

Cawelti observes that the hard-boiled detective story (or detective thriller, in Todorov's aforementioned terminology) has proven to be a much more significant form in the cinema than has the whodunit.[12] As noted earlier in this chapter, the film whodunit has occupied a minor niche, largely restricted to B pictures; important directors, such as Hitchcock and Lang, have shied away from it. On the other hand, the detective thriller, in either its pure form or closely related offshoots, has been the occasion for a number of major films by major filmmakers, including *The Maltese Falcon, The Big Sleep, Out of the Past* (1947), *Kiss Me Deadly* (1955), *Vertigo* (1958), *The Long Goodbye* (1973), and *Chinatown* (1974).

The Big Sleep is based on Raymond Chandler's first novel, published in 1939. The novel introduced Chandler's private-eye hero Philip Marlowe, who, beneath his tough surface, is more world-weary and softhearted than are Hammett's sharkish sleuths, the Continental Op and Sam Spade. The director of the film, Howard Hawks, is widely regarded as one of the masters of classical Hollywood filmmaking. Noted for their clean, precise style and their sensitivity to the interplay between actors, Hawks's films characteristically depict characters attempting to live by a code of professionalism in a world precariously poised between self-control and chaos. Although Hawks specialized in male-oriented action genres, such as the western and the war movie, his films are notable for their strong female characters; moreover, they often contain uncommonly mature romantic relationships, with a feeling of genuine partnership between man and woman. *The Big Sleep* is a fine example of these qualities.

Hawks's films also feature exceptionally good screenwriting. The screenplay for *The Big Sleep* is credited to three distinguished writers: William Faulkner, the eminent novelist, who during his less eminent period toiled as a screenwriter; Leigh Brackett, a noted author of science-fiction and fantasy literature; and Jules Furthman, a prolific master of Hollywood genre writing. Additional scenes and rewrites were contributed without credit by Philip G. Epstein, a veteran Warner Brothers collaborator who specialized in mixtures of wit and romance.[13] Much of the sharp dialogue in *The Big Sleep* was taken almost verbatim from Chandler's novel. However, the screenplay made several major alterations in order to accommodate censorship restrictions (especially in regard to the book's depictions of homosexuality, a pornography ring, and the lewd behavior of lascivious little sister Carmen Sternwood) and to incorporate the stronger romantic dimension of the film.

Humphrey Bogart, who had given a definitive private-eye performance as Hammett's aggressive Sam Spade in *The Maltese Falcon* (1941) [see Fig. 20], brought a warmer and more relaxed tone to his portrayal of Philip Marlowe. Lauren Bacall, who plays Vivian Rutledge, had made her film debut opposite Bogart in Hawks's 1944 classic of wartime intrigue, *To Have and Have Not*. The onscreen romantic chemistry of Bogart and Bacall (who also fell in love offscreen) created a sensation. *The Big Sleep*, which had been completed in early 1945, was held back from release and altered. When the film was finally released in August 1946, material amplifying the Bogart–Bacall relationship had been added, and material dealing more specifically with the investigation had been deleted. (The original version of *The Big Sleep* has recently been exhumed from the Warner Brothers vaults and exhibited at museums and revival houses. The following discussion of the film is based solely on the 1946 version with which audiences and critics have been familiar for the past fifty years.)

The film's complicated plot commences with Marlowe being summoned to the Sternwood mansion, where he is immediately sized up by the infantile and oversexed Carmen, younger of the family's two daughters. In the mansion's orchid-filled hothouse, the perspiring detective meets General Sternwood, a burnt-out invalid. He hires Marlowe to investigate a man named Arthur Geiger, who is attempting to blackmail the general for some of Carmen's misadventures. Sternwood is additionally upset over the recent disappearance of Shawn Regan, a surrogate son whom Marlowe had also known and admired. Before leaving, Marlowe encounters Carmen's hostile but alluring older sister, the divorcée Vivian Rutledge.

Marlowe begins his investigation by visiting Geiger's rare-book store, whose pretentious facade masks a blackmail ring and other unspecified, unsavory activities. After sparring with Geiger's unfriendly sales clerk Agnes and dallying at a nearby book store with a much friendlier female clerk, Marlowe follows Geiger and his handsome male "shadow" Carol Lundgren to Geiger's bungalow. Gunshots ring out in the night, and Marlowe finds Carmen stoned silly in front of a hidden camera, with Geiger's bullet-riddled corpse at her feet.

Friendly cop Bernie Ohls summons Marlowe to mist-shrouded Lido Pier, where a limousine containing the Sternwoods' dead chauffeur is fished out of the ocean. A compromising photo of Carmen comes into the possession of petty con man Joe Brody, who reveals that the chauffeur, infatuated with Carmen, had killed her nemesis Geiger. Then Brody himself is shot dead by Carol Lundgren, in mistaken revenge for his employer Geiger's murder.

With Carmen's blackmailers dead and the compromising evidence recovered, the case is apparently finished. However, Marlowe is personally very much interested in Vivian and puzzled by her relationship to gambling czar Eddie Mars, who seems to have a mysterious hold upon her. Marlowe is also still curious about the missing Shawn Regan, who is rumored to have run off with Eddie Mars's wife Mona. After being beaten up by Mars's thugs as a warning to drop the case, Marlowe is approached by Jonesy, an odd little hoodlum with a unexpected sense of integrity. Jonesy, in love with the slippery Agnes, is acting as her go-between to sell Marlowe information regarding the whereabouts of the missing Mona Mars. Going to meet Jonesy in the deserted, dimly lit Fulwider office building, Marlowe finds him being questioned by Mars's ruthless enforcer, Canino [see Fig. 7]. As Marlowe watches unseen from an adjoining office, Jonesy bravely shields Agnes and then is poisoned by Canino.

Information obtained from the coldhearted Agnes sends Marlowe on a foggy nighttime drive to a rural hot-car garage, where he is knocked cold by Canino. Marlowe awakens to find himself tied up and in the presence of both Vivian and Mona Mars, who has been hiding out to deflect suspicion from her husband in the Shawn Regan disappearance. Throwing her support to Marlowe, Vivian helps him to escape and to gun down Canino. Marlowe then lures Eddie Mars into a trap at the Geiger bungalow. There it is revealed that Mars has been blackmailing

Vivian by convincing her that Carmen had killed Regan – a murder possibly committed by Mars himself. The infuriated Marlowe causes Mars to be killed by his own gunmen, who have been lying in ambush outside. Marlowe and Vivian, still menaced by the gunmen but secure in their love for each other, wait for the police to arrive.

In his essay "The Typology of Detective Fiction," Tzvetan Todorov provides a useful method for conceptualizing the distinction between the whodunit and the detective thriller. Todorov says that a work of detective fiction consists of two stories, two paths that are followed: (1) the story of the crime, and (2) the story of the investigation. The first story concerns a crime (usually a murder) that has been committed but that the audience has not seen, because it occurred either in the past or offstage. Then the detective arrives on the scene and commences the second story, in which he investigates the crime and discovers its solution.[14]

According to Todorov, the whodunit throws most of its weight onto the first story, the story of the original crime. The second story, the investigation, has little importance in itself. Its main purpose is to recuperate the first story, to bring it to light, to provide the solution to its mystery. This imbalance produces the very peculiar dynamics of the whodunit: The crucial first story is inactive, already accomplished, whereas the second, which is present and active, is a story in which nothing happens. As Todorov says, the characters of the second story do not act, they learn.[15]

The detective thriller reverses the priorities of the whodunit: It suppresses the first story and vitalizes the second. The story of the past crime under investigation becomes less important, while that of the investigation itself is given more weight. As a result, suspense is more prominent in the detective thriller; what is going to happen next gains ascendance over what has happened in the past.[16]

It should be noted, however, that *The Big Sleep* is not really a prime example of intense, sweaty-palmed, edge-of-the-seat suspense. Though there are some effective suspenseful sequences, such as the murder of Jonesy and the showdown with Canino, overall these are neither very numerous nor very lengthy. The film's status as a thriller rests more crucially on other factors besides suspense, such as its general mood, labyrinthine structure, and presentation of the hero.

Not only what happens next but also to *whom* it happens are substantially more important in the detective thriller. One of the primary ways in which the second story, the story of the investigation, be-comes vitalized is that the detective hero is more personally involved. In contrast to the characteristic detachment of whodunit detectives like Philo Vance, the thriller detective becomes acutely vulnerable on a number of levels:

1. Physical. The thriller detective is constantly exposed to violence. He is often wounded, beaten up, tortured, drugged, or thrown into jail. In *The Big Sleep,* Marlowe is beaten up twice and threatened with fire-arms several times. At one point late in the film, he complains, "I'm tired. My jaw hurts, and my ribs ache. I killed a man back there, and I had to stand by while a harmless little guy was killed." It is difficult to imagine Philo Vance or Hercule Poirot making such a speech. *Murder, My Sweet* (1944), in which Marlowe (played this time by Dick Powell) is repeatedly beaten and drugged into unconsciousness [see Fig. 19], and *Chinatown* (1974), in which Jake Gittes (Jack Nicholson) is kayoed with a wooden crutch and slashed through the nostril with a switch-blade [see Fig. 39], are just two among many possible examples of the tremendous punishment routinely endured by thriller detectives, in contrast to the occasional scuffles of the whodunit detective.

2. Emotional. More so than the whodunit, the detective thriller pre-sents the murder victim as a sympathetic character whose loss is keen-ly felt and about whom the detective cares deeply. Examples in *The Big Sleep* are Marlowe's admired if absent friend Shawn Regan and espe-cially Jonesy (Elisha Cook Jr.), the ill-fated little hoodlum whom Mar-lowe encounters late in the film. The Jonesy episode adds a crucial ele-ment of guilt to Marlowe's emotional involvement in the case. Because he does not intervene quickly enough to prevent Jonesy's death, Mar-lowe continues to be haunted by it – "I stood around like a sap," he re-calls bitterly. The murder shakes Marlowe deeply and contributes to his nearly hysterical vindictiveness when he finally turns against the criminal kingpin Eddie Mars.

Even more important, the thriller detective can become romantical-ly or sexually involved with one or more of the women he encounters in the course of the investigation.[17] The whodunit detective, with oc-casional exceptions, tends to be something of a neuter – it is hard to imagine Philo Vance making a pass at, say, Hilda Lake (Mary Astor) in *The Kennel Murder Case.* Vance's creator S. S. Van Dine, in a magazine article outlining the rules for detective-story writing, stated flatly, "There must be no love interest."[18] Van Dine's mystery-writing col-league Dorothy L. Sayers agreed, "The less love in a detective-story, the

Figure 54. *The Big Sleep:* Hard-boiled dick (Humphrey Bogart) softens up sultry bookstore clerk (Dorothy Malone).

better."[19] (Classical detective authors did not always follow their own rules; both Van Dine's Philo Vance and Sayers's Peter Wimsey eventually succumbed to the little god's arrows.)

In *The Big Sleep,* not only does Marlowe fall head over heels in love with Vivian Rutledge, but the entire world of the film is highly sexualized, erotically charged. Within the first fifteen minutes, Marlowe encounters four women who seem sexually promising: the lubricous Carmen ("You're cute!"); the more abrasive Vivian ("You're a mess, aren't you?"); the prim, pretty librarian ("You don't look like a man who'd be interested in first editions"); and the sultry bookstore clerk ("You begin to interest me – vaguely") [Fig. 54]. Later, this list is augmented by the female cabdriver who eagerly responds to Marlowe's request for a "tail job," the short-skirted hostess who sidles up to him at Eddie Mars's casino, and the waitress who obligingly lights Marlowe's cigarette at the café. *The Big Sleep* depicts a world filled with sexual possibilities for the detective – in contrast to the world of the classical whodunit, where sexuality seems largely irrelevant, except perhaps as a murder motive contributing to the solution of the mystery.

However, *The Big Sleep* is atypical of hard-boiled detective thrillers in one important respect: the very central and positive nature of its love story [Fig. 55]. The film version of *The Big Sleep* at times seems as much a love story as a detective story (unlike Chandler's novel, wherein Marlowe keeps his distance from Vivian). The growth of the relationship between Marlowe and Vivian from friction to attraction to trust to active partnership is a main concern of the film. It competes with the mystery/detective elements, at times overshadows them, and eventually dovetails with them, when the split-second teamwork displayed by the couple in defeating the killer Canino both crystallizes their romantic bond and resolves an important part of the mystery-plot action.

This romantic dimension is a special feature of *The Big Sleep,* distinguishing it (but not necessarily separating it) from most other examples of the genre. In more typical detective thrillers, the detective may fall in love, but the relationship ends unhappily, either by being unfulfilled (the detective's love interest dies or otherwise departs at the end of the story) or by involving a femme fatale – a deceitful woman who betrays him. Another common occurrence is the hard-boiled detective's participation in casual sexual encounters, involving flirtation and physical pleasure rather than deep romantic commitment. Mickey Spillane's best-selling Mike Hammer novels provide many instances of this; Marlowe's rainy-afternoon encounter with the bookstore clerk (Dorothy Malone) in *The Big Sleep* also fits the category.

3. Moral. This type of involvement can take two basic forms for the thriller detective. The first is temptation. The detective may be offered bribes or sexual favors. He may be compromised by emotional ties, such as friendship, as in the 1953 Chandler novel (and 1973 Robert Altman film) *The Long Goodbye.* By these means, the detective may be enticed to look the other way rather than pursue the case and expose the guilty. Although not a major factor in *The Big Sleep,* this theme surfaces in Vivian's unsuccessful attempts to divert Marlowe ("Who told you to sugar me off this case?") from delving too deeply into the Shawn Regan situation.

The second form of moral involvement concerns judgment and enforcement. The thriller detective frequently not only solves the case but also becomes an active agent of justice and retribution. Rather than merely turning the guilty party over to police, the detective may

Figure 55. *The Big Sleep:* As much a love story as a detective story.

be moved to execute the culprit – either directly, as when Marlowe guns down Canino in *The Big Sleep,* or indirectly, as when the furious Marlowe forces Eddie Mars to step into a hail of bullets (the indirect option is also occasionally employed by classical detectives such as Peter Wimsey and Philo Vance). The thriller detective's function as a moral avenger, acting righteously if unofficially in the name of society, links him to the hero of the police thriller, discussed in Chapters 4 (see "The Flawed-Cop Cycle"), 5 (see "Supercops"), and 9.

Marlowe delivers moral judgments throughout *The Big Sleep.* After the little man's death, Marlowe eulogizes, "You did all right, Jonesy." When the faithless Agnes complains, "I got a raw deal," Marlowe retorts without sympathy, "Yeah, your kind always does." Fueled by the murder of Jonesy, Marlowe's moral indignation reaches a peak in his diatribe against Eddie Mars: "He's a blackmailer, a hot-car broker, a killer by remote control! He's anything that looks good to him, anything with money pinned to it, anything rotten!" After goading Mars's loyal wife Mona with this outburst, Marlowe grins, "She's okay – I like her," and wonders if Vivian could measure up to the same standard. A few minutes later, her nervy proficiency provides him with the answer: "You looked good, awful good. I didn't know they made 'em like that anymore." Like many other thriller detectives, Marlowe becomes deeply involved in the moral aspects of the case, whereas whodunit detectives (as Cawelti notes) seem motivated more by scientific curiosity or gamelike diversion.[20]

The distinction between the whodunit and the detective thriller involves elements not only of story but also of form and structure. The whodunit has a *centripetal* structure: concentrated, tightly interconnected, tending toward the center. As in *The Kennel Murder Case,* the crimes (including motives, suspects, and victims) often fall mostly within a family circle.[21] The purest form of this tendency is the "manor-house mystery," set at a country estate; literary examples include Agatha Christie's first Hercule Poirot mystery *The Mysterious Affair at Styles* (1920) and A. A. Milne's popular *The Red House Mystery* (1922), the latter singled out for scorn in Chandler's aforementioned essay "The Simple Art of Murder."[22] The detective thriller, on the other hand, has a *centrifugal* structure – loose, diffuse, tending away from the center. The detective thriller is a more epic form than the whodunit; it takes in more territory, spreads its focus more widely. *The Big Sleep* creates a more complex, amorphous space than does *The Kennel Murder Case* – a space that is essentially expanding and unbounded, where it is harder for us to get our bearings. It would be difficult to map out this space or reduce it to a scale model, as is done literally in *The Kennel Murder Case.*

This centrifugal quality also extends to the scope of the detective's case. Cawelti points out that, in the detective thriller, the shape of the private eye's mission shifts and expands.[23] The case seems relatively simple and straightforward at first, but then the plot thickens, grows more devious and widespread. Evil and disorder become generalized and ingrained rather than isolated and detachable. Sometimes the detective's entire society, or at least its power structure, is revealed to be substantially corrupt. The original crime that is being investigated is just a thread that leads into a much larger and more complex web of conspiracy and deception, and the detective and audience become more and more entangled in that web. This process relates to the idea of being captured and enthralled that is so central to the thriller (see Chapter 1). In *The Big Sleep,* Marlowe is originally hired to investigate the blackmailer Geiger, but this original mission becomes nearly buried under the mass of subplots and shady dealings into which it leads. Similarly, in *Murder, My Sweet,* Marlowe's initial mandate to find a thug's long-lost sweetheart eventually exposes a nest of fraud, larceny, blackmail, and murder among the rich and phony; and in *Chinatown,* what starts out looking like a simple "bedroom case" gets vaster in its implications the more Jake Gittes sticks his bandaged nose into it, until he has uncovered a conspiracy that encompasses the future of all Los Angeles.

As discussed in Chapter 2, the thriller favors labyrinthine, mazelike plot structures, filled with twists and tangles. *The Big Sleep,* in fact, has become legendary for its especially complex, convoluted story line. A famous anecdote (alluded to earlier) recounts how Hawks, while shooting the film, was unable to figure out who had killed the Sternwoods' chauffeur, Owen Taylor. He checked with the screenwriters, who didn't know, and finally with Raymond Chandler, who also didn't seem to know.[24] Hawks at that point let the matter drop. A curious footnote to this often-repeated tale is that the novel does, indeed, explain (or, at least, strongly suggest) who killed Taylor: Taylor himself, in a suicidal plunge off the pier.[25]

Nevertheless, the fact remains that, in contrast to the exhaustive explanations of the typical whodunit, Hawks elected to leave this mystery, as well as many other mysteries in the story, unclear. For instance, is Carmen initially being blackmailed for gambling debts or something more sinister? What exactly is going on in the back room of Geiger's bookstore? What is contained in Geiger's cipher-coded notebook? Did Carmen or Eddie Mars kill Shawn Regan? On several points (such as Owen Taylor's death), the film is less clear than the novel is, withholding or muddying explanations that Chandler had provided. Some of these equivocations serve the purpose of sidestepping censorship restrictions; others seem less clearly motivated. As Hawks recalled, "The writers passed the script on to me and said, 'There are a lot of things that don't make sense.' I said, 'Good. Let's try and see whether the audience likes that.'"[26]

The Kennel Murder Case also features a plot that could be described as complex and labyrinthine. In addition, there are mazelike qualities in the spatial layout of the action (e.g., the basement passageway between the two buildings). However, this labyrinthine potential is not strongly realized in the film because, crucially, the hero, Philo Vance, is *outside* the labyrinth. He does not have "partial vision" (to use Pascal Bonitzer's phrase); he has total vision. Vance has a godlike vantage point from which he can survey the whole layout. He is detached, emotionally and physically, from the events; he is not trapped within them. Vance has too much control to be a true thriller hero; as mentioned in Chapter 1, the thriller involves a certain loss of control for both hero and spectator.

Let us imagine, however, that we were to take the same basic story of *The Kennel Murder Case,* and, instead of Philo Vance, another character, such as Raymond Wrede (the guilty man) or Sir Thomas McDonald (the wrong man), were made the protagonist. Imagine the film concentrating on Sir Thomas: He is being framed for the murders, the police are grilling him, this snide amateur detective is badgering him with questions. On top of all this, somebody jumps out of the dark and stabs him, but nobody will believe it – everyone assumes that Sir Thomas stabbed himself in order to provide an alibi. . . . In this case, we would have more of a thriller (a film noir, perhaps), because the film would now be taking the perspective of the person who is inside the labyrinth, who is all tangled up in it and cannot see clearly, and we, the viewers, would be inside the labyrinth with him. In comparison with *The Kennel Murder Case, The Big Sleep* places us deeper inside the labyrinth. Although not entrapped to the extent of a film-noir protagonist, Marlowe is significantly less in control than Philo Vance is; his vision is more restricted; he is more a part of the mysterious, treacherous world he investigates than he is its detached observer and interpreter.

The Big Sleep has the loose, episodic, digressive structure characteristic of many thrillers, in contrast to the whodunit, where everything is more relentlessly geared toward the central mystery and its final solution. The style of *The Kennel Murder Case* is snappy, tight, to the point. Cuts, *wipes* (i.e., optical effects in which a shot appears to push the preceding one off the screen), and *zip* (or *swish*) *pans* (i.e., the camera panning so quickly that the image blurs) are frequently used to create an emphatic link between something shown or mentioned at the end of one scene and something shown or mentioned at the beginning of the next. This produces a sense of focused, forward propulsion toward a fixed point. For example, Sergeant Heath's shouted query, "Any report on that wire?" is followed by a cut to a speeding train, a wipe to a train conductor beginning to dictate a reply to the telegram in question, and another wipe to the text of the reply ("BRISBANE COE NOT

ABOARD THIS TRAIN") as it is read in New York by District Attorney Markham. A few minutes later, a similar series of transitions shows the police tracking down Brisbane Coe's luggage at Grand Central Station.

The style of *The Big Sleep,* on the other hand, is sprawling, voluptuous, lingering. The film dawdles; it dwells on atmosphere, wallows in it, wraps it around us. *The Big Sleep* devotes time to developing these elements rather than to clarifying the plot, so that the viewer becomes enmeshed, suspended in a thick mood of intrigue and mystery. The seductive atmosphere is sustained by such evocative details as the junglelike foliage of General Sternwood's hothouse; the afternoon rainstorm looming and bursting outside the window of the Acme Book Shop; the exotic bust, beaded curtain, and assorted Orientalia at Geiger's bungalow [see Fig. 4]; the shiny coupes glistening with rain and gliding through fog; the lights coming on as Marlowe broods at the café counter in the gathering dusk; the translucent windows of the office where Jonesy is killed. It is a measure of Hawks's directorial skill that these details are so fluidly incorporated into the film's action, registering strongly despite rarely being singled out in close shots or emphasized in dramatically angled foregrounds (in contrast to Curtiz's heavier touch with details in *The Kennel Murder Case*). They become an integral part of the general ambience that surrounds the characters, coexisting and interacting with them.

Such atmospheric details are sometimes considered a distraction in the plot-dominated whodunit. In addition to his proscription against romance, S. S. Van Dine declared, "A detective story should contain no long descriptive passages, no literary dallying with side-issues, no subtly worked-out character analyses, no 'atmospheric' preoccupations."[27] Less dogmatically, G. K. Chesterton (in his essay "A Defence of Detective Stories," discussed in Chapter 2) eloquently described how the detective story could enhance the mystique of the modern city. Chesterton's observation, based on the then-developing style of the classical detective story, seems even more pertinent to the later detective thriller. The elements identified by Chesterton tend to be implicit and marginal in the classical whodunit, which concentrates its attention on the solution of the puzzle. They are more explicit and central in the detective thriller, which has greater freedom to digress, to linger on description and atmosphere and a sense of place. The whodunit is all of a piece, whereas the thriller tends to break up into a series of pieces. *The Big Sleep* often wanders off the main path of the narrative to encompass digressions and set-piece scenes that contribute little or nothing to the solution of the mystery: the interlude with the seductive clerk in the bookstore, the prank phone call to the police station, the suggestive horse-race repartee between Marlowe and Vivian, the song Vivian sings at the casino.

In the whodunit, the destination is more important than the route, whereas in the detective thriller there is more emphasis on a journey through a world. Both of these concepts are central to the thriller: a *journey* – movement – through a *world*, or, more precisely, a certain kind of world.

Thrillers emphasize movement. Some (such as *The 39 Steps,* 1935; *North by Northwest,* 1959; *The Fugitive,* 1993; *Speed,* 1994) are virtually extended, nonstop chases from beginning to end. Even in less extreme forms, thrillers tend to cover a lot of ground. Cawelti observes that the hard-boiled detective is typically on the move throughout the story.[28] This applies well to Marlowe in *The Big Sleep,* especially during the film's last twenty minutes, which take him from the Fulwider office building where Jonesy is killed to the curbside rendezvous with Agnes, then to the remote countryside garage ("Ten miles east of Realito"), and finally back to the city for the final showdown at Geiger's bungalow. In contrast, *The Kennel Murder Case* is more sedentary, particularly toward the end, when it settles down mainly in the two adjacent buildings that are involved in the murders.

The world of the whodunit, as demonstrated by *The Kennel Murder Case,* is solid, weighty, bourgeois. *The Big Sleep* has a softer, more sensuous, more exotic quality, articulated by fog, rain, night, crickets, sirens wailing in the distance. In *The Big Sleep,* the Sternwood mansion seems grander and more ornate than the Coe mansion in *The Kennel Murder Case,* yet it also seems airier, more weightless, not as heavy and solid. *The Big Sleep,* like many other thrillers, creates a double world that is familiar but also exotic, marvelous, and hovering, halfway into a dream. Over the course of *The Kennel Murder Case,* the world shrinks (literally, in the case of the scale models) and becomes ever more tangible. In *The Big Sleep,* the world expands and becomes more tenuous: Fog and night close in, and everything grows less distinct. This is a world where we lose our bearings, where we get lost and tangled, where we become enthralled and surrender ourselves to the exotic, exhilarating sensations it offers us. This is the world of the thriller, as represented by one of its primary forms, the detective thriller. Other forms, reflecting the same general tendencies in their particular ways, are covered in the ensuing chapters.

7

The Psychological Crime Thriller
Strangers on a Train (1951)

In his history of crime fiction, *Bloody Murder* (1985), the British novelist and critic Julian Symons draws a fundamental distinction between the "detective story" (by which he means essentially the same thing as the whodunit or classical detective story, discussed in Chapter 6) and the "crime story."[1] Because the term "crime story" might be misleadingly overgeneralized, the more specific alternative "psychological crime thriller" will be used from this point on.

As the name indicates, a *psychological crime thriller* is dominated by the psychological motivations and emotional relationships of characters affected by a crime. The question of "whodunit" – central to the classical detective story and less central but still important to the detective thriller – is deemphasized or completely eliminated. There is less concern with concealment and more with characterization.

Raymond Chandler complained that the puzzle-solving aspect of detective stories is inherently obstructive to characterization. In order to conceal the murderer's identity, the writer is obliged to "fake character" – in other words, crucial aspects of the murderer's personality (and also of other prime suspects' personalities) have to be withheld or falsified.[2] In a similar vein, G. K. Chesterton called the detective story "a drama of masks and not of faces" and compared it to a masquerade ball in which no one becomes personally interesting until the clock strikes twelve.[3]

In the psychological crime thriller, the identity of the criminal is usually revealed right away or, at least, very early on. This enables a more open and detailed treatment of the emotional pressures experienced by the criminal, by those characters threatened by the criminal, and by those characters close to the criminal or victim. In the detective story, Symons says, the characterizations of everyone except the detective are perfunctory, superficial, and subordinate to the figuring out of the mystery plot. Too much psychological complexity or subtle characterization might get in the way of the puzzle. In the psychological crime thriller, on the other hand, the characters and the effects of the events upon them are the most important elements.[4]

In the classical whodunit, the method of murder is often bizarre, complicated, or misleading.[5] Some rare poison, exotic animal, or unusual weapon may have been used, as in the famous Sherlock Holmes story "The Adventure of the Speckled Band" (1892), in which a deadly Indian swamp adder is the murder weapon, or Rex Stout's first Nero Wolfe mystery, *Fer-de-Lance* (1934), wherein the murderer employs a specially constructed golf club that, upon impact, ejects a needle smeared with the venom of a South American viper. In addition, the victim may appear to have been killed in one way but was actually killed in another – as in *The Kennel Murder Case* (1933; see Chapter 6), in which Archer Coe appears to have died from a gunshot but was actually stabbed to death with a rare Chinese dagger.

In the psychological crime thriller, the method of murder is usually neither fancy nor misleading. It is straightforward (e.g., plain, old-fashioned shooting or strangling) and does not assume importance in itself. In *Strangers on a Train,* the killer's modus operandi is efficiently blunt: Bruno Anthony simply walks up to his victim, strangles her, and calmly walks off.

The psychological crime thriller is, as Symons says, "constructed forwards."[6] In contrast to the classical whodunit, there is less concern with what happened in the past than with what is going to happen next – to the killer, the suspect, the potential victim. Is the killer (such as Bruno Anthony) going to be caught? Is the false suspect (such as Guy Haines) going to be able to clear himself? Is the intended victim (such as Guy's wife or Bruno's father) going to realize the danger she or he is in?

A variation of the form has the primary psychological burden falling on someone who is emotionally close to a murderer or suspected murderer. In this case, the character's internal dilemma might be something along the lines of, Am I married to a murderer? Should I trust him? Should I betray him? Am I the next victim? Examples include *Gaslight* (1944), in which a woman (Ingrid Bergman) is being driven insane by her outwardly concerned husband (Charles Boyer); *Le Boucher* (a.k.a. *The Butcher,* 1969), wherein a French schoolmistress (Stephane Audran) falls in love with a likeable butcher (Jean Yanne) who may also be butchering local women; and *Jagged Edge* (1985), in which a lawyer (Glenn Close) has similar misgivings regarding her client-turned-lover (Jeff Bridges). This type of plot falls somewhere between the whodunit and the purer forms of psychological crime thriller: The identity of the killer may be concealed, but there are usually only one or two suspects and no central detective figure. If *Strangers on a Train* had concentrated on the point of view of Guy Haines's perplexed fiancée, Ann Morton, the film might have fallen into this subcategory of the psychological crime thriller.

The psychological crime thriller has much in common with the detective thriller as described by Tzvetan Todorov (see Chapter 6); however, as noted just above, it goes much further in minimizing or eliminating the concealment factor. In addition, the detective figure, rather than being the center of the action, is usually peripheral or completely absent in the psychological crime thriller. Symons writes: "Most often the central character is just somebody to whom things happen."[7] The protagonist's inexperience with the world of crime increases the sense of vulnerability that is so important to the thriller. *Strangers on a Train*'s Guy Haines, a clean-cut tennis player who suddenly finds himself embroiled in a madman's scheme, is an excellent example of this principle.

The psychological crime thriller was pioneered by Edgar Allan Poe in such stories as "The Tell-Tale Heart" (1843) and "The Black Cat" (1843), each related from the demented perspective of a guilt-racked murderer. It was further developed by R. Austin Freeman (*The Singing Bone,* 1912), Francis Iles (*Malice Aforethought,* 1931), and Freeman Wills Crofts (*The 12:30 from Croydon,* 1934), all classical detective writers whose variations in this vein became known as "inverted detective stories," because of their strategy of revealing the guilty party at the beginning rather than the end. After World War II, this type of crime story became more prevalent, as the classical whodunit and even the hard-boiled detective story began to exhaust their novelty.

The author whom Symons nominates as the leading practitioner of the psychological crime thriller is Patricia Highsmith, an American-born writer who enjoyed her greatest success in Europe. Highsmith's first novel, *Strangers on a Train* (1950), was the source for the Alfred Hitchcock film discussed in this chapter. As Symons notes, Highsmith's novels often feature male "couples" (such as Guy and Bruno in *Strangers on a Train*) whom a crime yokes together in a twisted, obsessive relationship.[8] Highsmith's other novels include *The Blunderer* (1954), in which a bungling copycat ruins a murderer's perfect crime; *The Talented Mr. Ripley* (1955), centered on the amoral opportunist Tom Ripley (featured in four later novels); and *Those Who Walk Away* (1967), in which the protagonist (whose wife recently committed suicide) is irresistibly drawn to the man (her unforgiving father) who wants to kill him.

Other psychological crime novels cited by Symons include Ira Levin's trickily structured *A Kiss before Dying* (1953; film versions, 1956 and 1991), in which an ambitious young psychopath murders his pregnant girlfriend and then insinuates himself into her wealthy family, and the French team Pierre Boileau and Thomas Narcejac's *D'entre les morts* (1956), the source for Hitchcock's *Vertigo* (1958). Among the prominent authors that could be added to Symons's list are the posthumously acclaimed pulp innovator Jim Thompson, whose lurid excursions into sexual and criminal deviance (*The Killer Inside Me*, 1952; *A Swell-Looking Babe*, 1954; *The Grifters*, 1963) have been a major influence on the neo-noir film movement, and the respected British novelist Ruth Rendell, whose fatalistic tales (*A Judgement in Stone*, 1977; *Live Flesh*, 1986; *A Fatal Inversion*, 1987) frequently explore the deadly symbiosis between criminal and victim.

The psychological crime thriller was a form that particularly attracted Hitchcock and provided the basis for some of his most important and popular movies. It maximizes suspense and highlights the subjective aspects that Hitchcock favors in his films (see Chapter 4), as opposed to whodunit puzzles or action spectacles (elements like car chases and shootouts have a very minor place in Hitchcock's work). Hitchcock did, of course, work in other categories of thriller, such as spy (including *Sabotage*, 1936; *Notorious*, 1946; *Torn Curtain*, 1966), detective (*Vertigo*), Gothic (*Rebecca*, 1940; *Under Capricorn*, 1949), and horror (*Psycho*, 1960; *The Birds*, 1963). However, even in those instances, the films often include strong traces of the elements Symons identifies with the psychological crime thriller: for example, *Sabotage*, which focuses on a woman (Sylvia Sidney) who comes to realize that her husband (Oscar Homolka) is a terrorist; *Notorious*, in which a traitor's daughter (Ingrid Bergman) is caught in a lethal triangle between the American agent (Cary Grant) who recruits her and the neo-Nazi conspirator (Claude Rains) who marries her; and *Vertigo*, which starts out like a detective thriller but becomes more of a psychological crime thriller as it goes on.

Hitchcock thrillers that fit primarily into the psychological-crime mode include *Blackmail* (1929), in which a policeman (John Longden) and his girlfriend (Anny Ondra) cover up her involvement in a homicide that he is investigating; *Suspicion* (1941), in which an insecure young bride (Joan Fontaine) suspects that her ne'er-do-well husband (Cary Grant) is trying to kill her; *Shadow of a Doubt* (1943), wherein a teenage girl (Teresa Wright) realizes that her beloved Uncle Charlie (Joseph Cotten) is the notorious "Merry Widow Murderer"; *Rope* (1948), in which two young men (John Dall, Farley Granger) murder a friend and then brazenly entertain guests with the corpse on the premises; *I Confess* (1953), whose priest (Montgomery Clift) becomes the prime suspect in a murder that has been sacramentally confessed to him; *Dial M for Murder* (1954), in which a straying wife (Grace Kelly) is railroaded to the gallows by her conniving spouse (Ray Milland); and *Frenzy* (1972), in which a violent man (Jon Finch) is framed for a series of sex murders committed by his friend (Barry Forster).

An early and enthusiastic reader of Highsmith's *Strangers on a Train,* Hitchcock quickly purchased the movie rights to the novel. His first choice to write the screenplay was Dashiell Hammett, and, when that fell through, he turned to another hard-boiled master, Raymond Chandler.[9] The detective novelist's collaboration with Hitchcock was stormy and unproductive; after two unsatisfactory drafts, Chandler was replaced by Czenzi Ormonde, a little-known protegée of the screenwriter-playwright Ben Hecht. The final screenplay changed Guy Haines's occupation from architect to tennis player, eliminated an important private-detective character, and added the Washington, D.C., setting. Most important, the movie converts Guy into a more conventional hero, stronger and less flawed than in the book, which (somewhat like a film noir) concentrates on his complicity and eventual disintegration.

Robert Walker, whose performance as Bruno Anthony dominates the film, was an inspired casting choice by Hitchcock. Walker, who previously specialized in playing sincere, awkward young men, had never taken a such a sinister role before; moreover, the actor's career was at a low ebb when Hitchcock summoned him. This casting coup was counterbalanced by Hitchcock's lack of enthusiasm for Farley Granger and Ruth Roman as the romantic leads.[10] A success with critics and public, *Strangers on a Train* ended a slump for Hitchcock and ushered in a period of high creativity that lasted into the mid-1960s. (As with *The Big Sleep* [see Chapter 6], an element of potential confusion has been introduced by the existence of different versions of the film. In recent years, some video outlets have offered a slightly different, British-release version of *Strangers on a Train*. That version contains additional dialogue during the early scene in which Bruno presents the "criss cross" plan to Guy, and it omits the brief epilogue in which a chastened Guy and Ann shy away from a friendly priest on the train. The following analysis is based on the familiar American-release version.)

The film begins with the apparent chance meeting of two young men on a Washington-to-New-York train: Guy Haines, an amiable tennis star, and Bruno Anthony, a brash eccentric, replete with mother complex. For a stranger, Bruno knows a lot about Guy: his political ambitions; his plans to marry a Senator's daughter, Ann Morton; his anticipated divorce from his promiscuous wife Miriam. Bruno, after complaining about his father, regales Guy with crackpot theories, including a "criss cross" plan for a perfect crime: Two strangers, such as they, could swap murders, Bruno eliminating Guy's onerous wife, Guy dispatching Bruno's odious father, each murder lacking an apparent motive to lead the police to the killer. Guy nervously departs, leaving behind an engraved cigarette lighter that had been given to him by Ann.

Guy stops off at his hometown of Metcalf to finalize the divorce plans with Miriam. She reneges, and Guy makes a violent scene in front of several wide-eyed witnesses. Taking Guy's compliance for granted, Bruno travels to Metcalf, follows Miriam to an island at an amusement park, and strangles her. Later that night, Bruno accosts Guy outside the latter's Washington apartment with news of the deed, and he threateningly reminds Guy of his obligation in the murderous bargain. Ann's suspicions are aroused by Guy's nervous behavior in front of herself, her stuffy father, Senator Morton, and her frisky younger sister, Barbara. The police are also suspicious, and they begin tailing Guy.

Bruno, impatient for Guy to carry out the remaining murder, insinuates himself into Guy's elite Washington circle. At a society party, Bruno is so struck by the resemblance between the murdered Miriam and the similarly bespectacled Barbara that he goes into a trance and nearly strangles a simpering matron. A horrified Ann confronts Guy, who admits all and wins back her trust. Guy goes to the Anthony mansion, apparently to murder Mr. Anthony but actually to warn him. Bruno, suspecting a trick, is waiting there and vows revenge on Guy. Ann and Guy realize that Bruno intends to return to the Metcalf murder scene and, under the cover of darkness, plant Guy's cigarette lighter as incriminating evidence. Guy, engaged in a Forest Hills tennis tournament, determines to win his match quickly so that he can intercept Bruno before nightfall.

After getting off to a fast start, Guy's tennis match bogs down into a lengthy duel. Arriving in Metcalf, Bruno drops the fatal lighter down a storm drain but eventually recovers it. Guy finally wins his match and hurries onto a Metcalf-bound train, while Bruno waits at the amusement park for the sun to set. Closely followed by the police, Guy reaches the amusement park and chases Bruno onto a merry-go-round, which goes out of control when a policeman accidentally shoots its operator. Guy and Bruno grapple on the careering carousel, until a sudden stop causes to it disintegrate [see Fig. 1]. Bruno is crushed to death in the spectacular crack-up; the lighter clutched in the dead man's hand corroborates Guy's story and leads to his exoneration.

Strangers on a Train exemplifies some general thriller properties discussed previously in this book. One is the thriller's expansive, centrifugal quality, its tendency to spread out rather than converge inward (see Chapter 6). Even though the structure of Strangers on a Train is considerably tighter and more concentrated than that of The Big Sleep, it still contains a great deal of shuttling back and forth between different locales (Washington, Metcalf, Forest Hills) as well as between different areas within those locales (the downtown area and the outlying amusement park in Metcalf; the various residences in Washington and Bruno's mansion in the suburb of Arlington). Much like the roving detective Marlowe in The Big Sleep, the hunted hunter Thorndike in Man Hunt (see Chapter 8), and the scrambling cops Doyle and Russo in The French Connection (see Chapter 9), the main characters of Strangers on a Train are constantly on the move.

Another way in which Strangers on a Train relates to this thriller-esque emphasis on motion is through its prominent use of trains. Hitchcock made other movies in which significant portions of the action are set on trains: The 39 Steps (1935), Secret Agent (1936), The Lady Vanishes (1938), North by Northwest (1959). Cultural historian Morris Dickstein has noted that trains were popular settings in the studio-bound thrillers of the 1930s and that they have always been very appropriate vehicles for the thriller spirit: They throw people together in situations fraught with intrigue, and they signify the movement from a secure world to an insecure world that typifies the thriller plot.[11] The compartments, passageways, and doorways in a train have a built-in suspense potential: A train is like a mobile labyrinth, filled with blind spots and hiding places. A train also conveys a palpable sense of imminence, involving constant motion that one can both see and hear, as it follows a track toward an unavoidable and perhaps fateful destination.

In these respects, the train both connects with and differs from another element in Strangers on a Train that has special relevance to the thriller: the amusement park. This setting evokes the sense of disorientation one finds in a thriller, as well as the sense of moving into a heightened, transformed environment. With its whirling rides and speed and dizziness, the amusement park also relates to the visceral side of thriller – the side that goes straight to the gut and provides us with intense sensations (see Chapter 1). Although both the amusement-park setting and the train setting in *Strangers on a Train* connote motion and a passage away from the ordinary, safe world, the amusement park is associated primarily with chaotic, purposeless, directionless movement. The train, on the other hand, moves down the track toward a specific destination – an association emphasized in the opening sequence of two separate paths, Bruno's and Guy's, that relentlessly converge into a single railroad track. The amusement park in *Strangers on a Train* entails circular motifs: the merry-go-round, Ferris wheel, tilt-a-whirl, and various other rides that go round and round without going anywhere. Even more than the train, the amusement park is an especially labyrinthine place – a place where movement does not lead anywhere, where one gets lost, enthralled, entangled.

The central thriller theme of the double world – at once ordinary and extraordinary, mundane and adventurous – is given an explicitly psychological dimension in *Strangers on a Train*. Bruno represents a submerged, id-dominated night world that destabilizes Guy's placid daylight world and charges it with menace and excitement. At times this concept is expressed heavy-handedly – for example, when the camera angle is precipitously tilted to show Guy's world turned literally askew as he mounts the stairs outside his apartment and hears Bruno's voice call out of the shadows, summoning him to the dark region on the other side of the fence.

A more finely nuanced expression of this theme occurs during the scene of Bruno and Guy's first meeting on the train. In Chapter 3, it was noted that the style of German expressionist cinema, based on the external expression of internal feelings through setting, lighting, decor, and other visual elements, had been especially influential on the mainstream thriller movie. As a young assistant director and director, Hitchcock had worked in Germany during the heyday of the expressionist film movement and was, by his own account, greatly affected by it.[12]

An example of this expressionist influence is provided by the backgrounds and compositions of Guy and Bruno's first conversation, in which Hitchcock cuts back and forth between over-the-shoulder shots of the two men. The shots facing Bruno are deep, cluttered, and fragmented, presenting a riot of clashing shapes and lines, with uneven slat shadows streaking across his face and body, a striation of venetian blinds on the lower left, a pattern of squiggly lines on a rectangular glass partition on the upper left, three long bright stripes radiating across the ceiling behind his head, and various plant leaves and small circular lights peppering the deeper background. (Similarly complex, dissonant compositions frame Bruno in the scene with his mother and the scene at the National Gallery.) The reverse shot facing Guy is (much like Guy himself) shallow and sedate, stabilized by the large dark block of Guy's coat and vest. From the start, the two worlds of the film are played off each other. However, there are already hints of an overlap between them, in the squiggly lines and jittery leaves behind Guy on the left, suggesting a latent, unstable side that links him to Bruno and will soon cause him to lash out at Miriam ("I could strangle her!"). The opening train scenes strongly establish Guy on the left side of the frame and Bruno on the right; but, at the end of the sequence – when Bruno says, "Your wife, my father: criss cross!" – the two men stand up and switch positions. Guy crosses over to the right side of the frame and Bruno to the left, announcing the intermixture – criss cross! – of the film's two worlds.

This process of crossing over is carried further in the scene in which Bruno informs the horrified Guy of Miriam's demise. The scene is staged around the gateway of a massive iron fence, mostly with Bruno in the shadowy area behind the fence bars on the left and Guy in a brighter, more open area on the right [Fig. 56]. Early in the scene, a series of over-the-shoulder shots shows Bruno's shoulder in the darkened left foreground and Guy in the brighter center of the frame, but with the shadows of the fence bars across his face and a complicated pattern of metalwork behind him. The effect is of Bruno's dark, crazy world relentlessly closing in upon Guy's bright, rational one. Near the end of the scene, a shot from Bruno's point of view looks out through the ornate bars of the fence as a police car pulls up to Guy's residence. Guy ducks behind the bars with Bruno, and the next through-a-fence-darkly shot now represents their combined points of view. Guy's world is merging with Bruno's – "You've got *me* acting like I'm a criminal!" the murder's beneficiary complains.

The dark, submerged aspect of Bruno's world is strikingly expressed in the tour-de-force shot of Miriam's murder reflected in the lens of her eyeglasses. As Hitchcock scholar Gene D. Phillips has noted, the fluid, distorted shapes evoke a fun-house crazy mirror; they also suggest watery depths, with Bruno's grotesquely elongated hands recalling the lobster claws that emblazoned his necktie (designed by Hitchcock himself) in the opening scene.[13] The flashy, chaotic side of Bruno's world finds its supreme expression in the amusement park, with its dazzling lights and whirling rides. In contrast are the two primary environments of Guy's world: (1) the tennis court, characterized by decorum, regularity, straight lines, sunshine, and openness, and (2) Washington, D.C., with its gleaming neoclassical monuments and temples of law and government. The train, combining elements of both instability and regularity, serves as a medium of contact and passage between the two worlds – a relationship brought out most strongly in the crosscutting that links tennis court, train, and amusement park in the extended suspense climax of the film.

Suspense is a minor factor in the whodunit *The Kennel Murder Case* and even in the detective thriller *The Big Sleep,* as discussed in Chapter 6. In *Strangers on a Train,* this prime thriller ingredient comes to the fore, reflecting both the particular talents of Alfred Hitchcock ("The Master of Suspense") and the particular strengths of the psychological crime thriller, whose emphases on internal pressures and forward construction make it especially receptive to suspense.

Some general principles of suspense have been discussed in Chapter 2. The remainder of the present chapter concentrates on specific issues, techniques, and applications of suspense, as exemplified primarily by sequences from *Strangers on a Train.*

1. Tense. In Chapter 2, suspense was conceived (following Noël Carroll's essay "Toward a Theory of Film Suspense") in terms of an "interrogatory" or question–answer model, in which the narrative poses questions and then withholds the full disclosure of the answers. One way of distinguishing a suspense thriller from other types of stories based on concealment and interrogation is that those other types (such as the whodunit) often emphasize questions posed in the past tense. *The Kennel Murder Case* places its primary weight on such questions as: Who kill*ed* Archer Coe? What *was* the weapon used? How *did* the killer bolt the door from the outside? In a thriller like *Strangers on a Train,* on the other hand, the primary questions are posed in the future tense, which is inherently more suspenseful: *Will* Guy carry out his part of the bargain and murder Mr. Anthony? *Will* Guy win the tennis match in time? *Will* Bruno retrieve the incriminating lighter?

Figure 56. *Strangers on a Train:* Bruno's dark, crazy world closing in upon Guy's bright, rational one.

A problem raised by this model is, How do questions posed in the *present* tense relate to the concept of suspense? These present-tense questions often concern judgmental issues relating to identity and states of being. In *Strangers on a Train,* is Bruno Anthony just a harmless eccentric, or *is* he dangerously insane? In *The Big Sleep,* what *is* Vivian Rutledge's relationship to Eddie Mars? *Is* she trustworthy? In *Man Hunt, is* Alan Thorndike as civilized as he thinks he is? In *The French Connection, is* Sal Boca just a small-time crook, or *is* he the key to a big-time drug deal? The psychological crime thriller is especially well suited to explore these present-tense questions, which can then feed into the future-tense questions that are the meat of suspense. For example, the question, Is Bruno dangerously insane? is perhaps not suspenseful in itself, but it contributes to such suspense-laden questions as, Is he so insane that he will murder Guy's wife? That he will destroy Guy?

Noël Carroll describes different ways in which the interrogatory model can be complicated beyond a simple question–answer structure. For example, a scene may introduce or answer more than one question, may sustain and intensify rather than answer a question, may provide an incomplete answer to a question, or may, by answering one question, immediately open up another one.[14] An example of the last case occurs in *Strangers on a Train* when Guy goes to the Anthony mansion to warn Bruno's father. At the end of that scene, the betrayed Bruno aims a gun at Guy as the latter nervously walks toward the exit. After several tense seconds, the question, Will Bruno shoot Guy? is answered when Bruno announces that, to avoid waking Mother, he will postpone his revenge – "I'll think of something better than that," he vows. This immediately opens up the new questions of, What new scheme will Bruno hatch? and Will it succeed? The subsequent scene of Ann's visit to the Anthony mansion answers the first question (she perceives that Bruno's scheme involves planting the cigarette lighter), but this only sustains and intensifies the second question: Will the scheme succeed?

One might add to Carroll's list the possibility of one suspenseful question serving strategically to divert our scrutiny from another. François Truffaut, in his book-length interview with Hitchcock, points out an example that occurs when Guy sneaks into the Anthony mansion and is confronted by a fearsome-looking dog on the stairs. According to Truffaut, this "small suspenseful diversion" functions to distract our attention and prevent us from figuring out too quickly that Guy does not intend to murder Mr. Anthony, and that Bruno rather than his father is waiting upstairs.[15]

Carroll also observes that a suspenseful narrative involves an interplay between *macroquestions* (i.e., central, overriding questions that structure all or most of the plot) and *microquestions* (i.e., smaller, more quickly resolved questions that often contribute to the former).[16] For example, in *Strangers on a Train,* the microquestions, Will Guy finish his tennis match in time? and Will Bruno fish the lighter out of the storm drain? contribute to the overriding macroquestion, Will Bruno succeed in his scheme to frame Guy for murder?

2. Time. Suspense, in which anticipation and protraction are key factors, centrally involves control over time. This makes it especially germane to cinema, which has the ability to manipulate time in exceptionally diverse and precise ways. In the interview, Truffaut remarks, "Your particular style and the very nature of suspense require a constant play with the flux of time, either by compressing it or, more often, by distending it." Hitchcock replies, "The ability to shorten or lengthen time is a primary requirement in filmmaking. As you know, there's no relation between real time and filmic time."[17]

As a prime example of this property, Truffaut cites the tennis-game/train-trip climax of *Strangers on a Train,* noting how the action is freely compressed (e.g., during the tennis match) and extended (e.g., when Bruno sits at the amusement park, waiting for the sun to set). Truffaut notes that the compression of time at certain points expresses Guy's "frantic haste" to win the match and Bruno's panic at losing the lighter.[18] Although I am not sure that Truffaut's specific interpretations here are entirely accurate (relative to the adjacent scenes, time during the lighter-retrieving scene seems more agonizingly extended than tightly compressed), his general point is illuminating: The manipulations of time in *Strangers on a Train* often express psychological and emotional content while also building suspense.

The beginning of the tennis match is presented in extended detail. We see the first game in its entirety, the steady pace here reflecting Guy's control and determination as he applies himself to his task. The pace is then stepped up as Guy rolls through the first two sets of the match. However, the most pronounced condensation occurs when the tide turns and Guy's opponent wins game after game in rapid succession. The accelerated tempo here expresses Guy's frustration and loss of control, a nightmarish sensation of being overwhelmed by a sudden avalanche of misfortune. Time is extended again for the parallel actions of Bruno fishing for the lighter and Guy struggling through the deuce-filled final game of the tennis match, each man displaying reserves of inner strength as he perseveres through a grueling challenge. The pace is picked up for Guy's dash to the train station and Bruno's arrival at the amusement park, but then it slows down dramatically for Bruno's vigil as he waits for sundown so that he can complete his mission: planting Guy's lighter on the island where Miriam was murdered.

It is noteworthy that Bruno displays little agitation during this extended segment. Instead he exudes an eerie sense of stasis, sitting by the tree and staring fixedly, in contrast to Guy's greater nervousness as he sits on the train, squirming in his seat, glancing at his watch, and looking back over his shoulder at the setting sun. There are moments throughout the film when Bruno is characterized by an unnerving stillness: when he stands by the amusement-park entrance and catches Miriam's eye, when he appears threateningly on the steps of the Jefferson Memorial, and, most famously, when his head remains immobile amid a gallery of swiveling tennis spectators. Bruno's chaotic interior occasionally breaks through during momentary losses of self-control, but his more common attitude is one of smooth composure.

The extension of time in the sunset sequence evokes the disturbingly quiet side of Bruno's unquiet personality. It also recalls the nightmarish stases of Gothic horror stories, their overwhelming sense of entrancement and enthrallment, of being drawn into the inescapable heart of the labyrinth. Perched amid tree branches and the spokes of a whirling ride, Bruno is like a spider in the center of his web, alert and poised, waiting for the opportunity to pounce [Fig. 57]. The first part of the film's climax is dominated by Guy at the tennis match, with Bruno (except for the dropped-lighter segment) seen only in brief glimpses. The second part is correspondingly dominated by the less active Bruno, as the film shifts its primary locale from the tennis court, which is Guy's domain, to the amusement park, which is Bruno's domain. These factors contribute to a pervasive sense of Bruno's power and control at this point in the film, increasing the apparent odds against Guy and thereby (in accordance with Carroll's theory) intensifying the suspense as the final showdown approaches.

3. Probability. As noted in Chapter 2, Noël Carroll emphasizes the importance of probability in creating suspense – i.e., suspense will be more intense the more unlikely a desired outcome appears to be. Carroll adds that this probability principle is very active and fluid in an effective suspense sequence. Editing structures call attention to probability factors (e.g., cutaways to a clock ticking down or to a rescuer being delayed by a flat tire), repeatedly remind us of them, and readjust them in light of changing conditions. This produces a continual reemphasis and recalibration of the probability factors in a suspense sequence. Carroll also notes that a certain balance needs to be maintained. If the desired outcome seems too easily attainable, audience disinterest may result. On the other hand, if the desired outcome appears too wildly improbable, with massive obstacles piled on outrageously, the successful result may become unconvincing and even laughable.[19]

Once again we turn to the extended climax of *Strangers on a Train,* this time as an example of fluctuating probability factors in a suspense sequence. The sequence starts with Guy's chances looking pretty good as he gets off to a fast start in the tennis match. They worsen when Guy's opponent stages a comeback, but they improve dramatically

Figure 57. *Strangers on a Train:* Spider (Robert Walker) poised in web. (The Museum of Modern Art Film Stills Archive)

when Bruno drops the lighter down the storm drain and get even better ("Advantage, Mr. Haines!") when Bruno clumsily knocks the lighter to a lower level. The negative factor of Bruno recovering the lighter is quickly offset by the positive factor of Guy finally winning the match. Guy's unsuccessful effort to shake off the police appears to hurt his chances, but their decision to postpone an arrest helps those chances. The setting sun: advantage, Mr. Anthony. Guy's train arriving in Metcalf: advantage, Mr. Haines. The sight of Bruno advancing toward the pier darkens Guy's prospects, but the long line of people waiting for the boats and the boat man's recognition of Bruno brighten those prospects. Guy's arrival at the amusement park and his spotting of Bruno continue his advantage, but this evaporates during their fight on the berserk merry-go-round (Bruno's almost superhuman strength has been previously established). Guy's chances hit an all-time (and ex-

ceedingly suspenseful) low as he hangs precariously from the edge of
the whirling carousel with Bruno stomping on his fingers. The tide then
quickly turns with the collapse of the carousel, Bruno's fatal injury, and
the boat man's information to the police. Bruno's dying-gasp attempt
to incriminate Guy produces a final oscillation of the odds, but the appearance of the lighter clinches game, set, and match for Mr. Haines.

4. *Knowledge.* Suspense is a more complicated proposition than
simply "What's going to happen next?" It also involves the audience's
position in relation to what's going to happen next. One very important factor in suspense is the position of knowledge that is created at
a particular point in the film. The knowledge factor has two basic poles:
the position of a character inside the film, and the position of the spectator outside the film. These two positions may or may not coincide.
We may know more or less than the character who is the primary subject of suspense, or we may be in the same position of knowledge.

A film can put us in shifting positions of knowledge: We can be less
ignorant, more ignorant, or equally ignorant in relation to the characters from one scene to the next, or even from one moment to the next.
An example is Guy's nocturnal visit to the Anthony mansion. At first,
we know less than Guy does (we do not know if he really intends to
murder Bruno's father). Then we possibly know more than he does (we
might realize before Guy does that the figure in the bed is not Bruno's
father). Finally, as Guy nervously exits the house with Bruno's gun
pointed at his back, we are in an equal position of knowledge – neither
Guy nor we know whether Bruno really intends to shoot him.

The importance of knowledge in creating suspense is presented in
another way in a famous Hitchcock interview passage that distinguishes between "suspense" and "surprise." The example he uses is
that two people are sitting in a room and talking, and suddenly a bomb
goes off without warning: surprise. Alternatively, the audience is informed well in advance that the bomb is under the table and that it is
set to go off at one o'clock, while in the background a clock is seen
inching toward the fatal hour: suspense. Hitchcock explains:

In these conditions the same innocuous conversation becomes fascinating
because the public is participating in the scene. The audience is longing
to warn the characters on the screen: "You shouldn't be talking about such
trivial matters. There's a bomb beneath you and it's about to explode!" In
the first case we have given the public fifteen seconds of *surprise* at the moment of the explosion. In the second case we have provided them with fifteen minutes of *suspense.* The conclusion is that whenever possible the
public must be informed.[20]

It should be noted that Hitchcock sometimes departs from his own precepts and chooses to exploit surprise rather than suspense. For example, in a stunning scene from *North by Northwest,* the murder of the official Townsend at the United Nations is played primarily for surprise. The fugitive hero Thornhill (Cary Grant) is trying to explain his predicament to Townsend, when suddenly the latter gasps and topples forward with a knife in his back. If he had chosen, Hitchcock could have easily played that scene for suspense by boosting the audience's knowledge. The assassin could have been shown pulling out the knife and aiming it while Thornhill obliviously continues talking. In that case, the audience, in a position of knowledge superior to the hero's, would likely be in a state of edge-of-the-seat suspense, wanting to say, "Watch out! There's the killer! Do something!" Instead, Hitchcock shows the assassin retreating behind a doorway and then concentrates our attention on the conversation between Thornhill and Townsend. Hitchcock goes for surprise here, and the results are very effective, though not particularly suspenseful.

5. Identification. Identification is another important factor affecting the audience's position toward suspenseful events, It contributes to and complicates – but is not the same as – what Carroll calls the "moral" or "desirability" factor (see Chapter 2). Identification, as noted by Carroll (who avoids using the concept at all), is a term fraught with psychological implications that go beyond its common and often imprecise application to movie watching.[21] With that disclaimer in place, I shall proceed to use the term *identification* in the loose sense of anything that enables us to feel an affinity (not necessarily complete or exclusive or unquestioning) with a particular element in the film. The most familiar form of identification is identification with the characters, which can be based on a number of nonexclusive and often overlapping factors:

Emotional factors: The character's feelings are evoked strongly and convincingly and sympathetically enough that we can, to some extent, share them.

Moral considerations: We feel strongly that the character is in the right and therefore share her or his moral perspective.

Physical point of view: We share a character's field of vision. An extreme case occurs frequently in stalker films (see Chapter 5) that compel us to see through the eyes of the killer, even though other major bases for identification (such as emotional and moral) may be strongly contradicted.

Commonality: We recognize a character's thoughts, feelings, or actions as familiar to our own experience and therefore find it easy to participate vicariously in them.

Admiration: We find aspects of the character compellingly attractive and therefore worthy of emulation, mainly on an idealized fantasy level (hence the importance of movie stars as identification figures).

Shared curiosity: We are equally in the dark; we want to discover the truth as much as the character does. This is one reason why detectives (official or unofficial) make such good identification figures – they become our representatives within the story and find out the things we want to know.

In relation to this curiosity factor, there can even be cases in which our primary identification is not with any character in the story but with the story itself – that is, the telling of the story, its movement to unwind itself and reach a resolution. This type of identification is based on our desire for completion, relief, an end to the suspense. In some cases, our sympathy or moral allegiance with a character may be weak, but considerable suspense can still be generated, simply because we want to see things come to a head, resolve themselves. A frequently cited example of this possibility occurs in *Strangers on a Train* when Bruno is desperately reaching for the lighter that has fallen through the grate [see Fig. 8]. Even though the audience should be rooting against Bruno, because he is the villain and is trying to frame the hero, the scene evokes a strong desire to see Bruno pick up that !@#$%&* lighter – just to get it over with, to resolve the suspense.

The above-mentioned commonality factor, in which we identify with feelings or situations because they are familiar to us, is another element that contributes to our complicit allegiance with Bruno in the lighter scene. (Who among us hasn't suffered similar exasperation with a misplaced object?) Such situations illustrate the potential benefits in suspenseful ambivalence that can accrue from creating fallible and humanized antagonists as opposed to awesome and otherly supervillains like Dr. Mabuse and Dr. No (see Chapters 3 and 5, respectively).

In some situations, however, the commonality factor can operate independently of any particular character. A suspenseful situation can evoke a feeling that inspires universal, almost primal apprehension, even though the characters in the scene may be unsympathetic and even though they may not be experiencing that feeling themselves. In their interview, Truffaut raises the extreme example of a hypothetical film about the 1944 bomb plot to assassinate Hitler, and Hitchcock responds:

Even in that case I don't think the public would say, "Oh, good, they're all going to be blown to bits," but rather, they'll be thinking, "Watch out. There's a bomb!" What it means is that the apprehension of the bomb is more powerful than the feelings of sympathy or dislike for the characters involved.[22]

In a sense, we identify with suspense itself, with a desire both to be caught up in suspenseful anxiety and to be released from that anxiety, no matter who or what is involved. We can become carried away by the sheer momentum of the narrative and its suspense mechanisms, and this sometimes makes it easier for us to override the possible qualms involved in an ambiguous allegiance with a morally questionable character.

The complexity of suspense is enhanced when these different factors shift from one position to another or fall into ambivalent positions between. Our identification may switch from one character to another (as in *Psycho;* see below), or it may be consistently divided between opposed characters (as in Michael Mann's *Heat,* as discussed in the Carroll section in Chapter 2, and, more covertly, in *Strangers on a Train,* as will be discussed shortly), or we may identify with one character in some ways and another character in other ways (as in stalker films, which evoke identification, in different ways, for both the killer and the heroine). We may know more than the character knows one moment, less the next moment. The outcome may be desired or dreaded or both. An example of the last case occurs near the end of Hitchcock's *Psycho,* when inquisitive Lila Crane (Vera Miles) hesitates at the door to the Bates fruit cellar, drawing an exultantly divided audience response along the lines of (1) No, don't go down in the cellar, because something awful may be there, and (2) Yes, do go down there, because we're dying to find out what it is! All of these cases relate to the ambivalence that is so important to the thriller, that pulls us in different directions at once (see Chapter 1).

As might be expected from the acknowledged Master of Suspense, Hitchcock orchestrates these different suspense factors into especially rich patterns, a veritable symphony of suspense. Some of these patterns have been described above; in addition, *Strangers on a Train* creates shifting patterns of identification. There are three major focal points of identification in the film (Guy, Bruno, and Ann), in addition to several minor ones (such as Barbara, the policeman Hennessy, and the mother whose son is imperiled on the merry-go-round).

The two most forceful of these are Guy and Bruno. (It is difficult to ascertain to what extent this dual emphasis is a function of the film's design, and to what extent it is a function of the weak characterization of Ann.) Throughout *Strangers on a Train,* heavy use is made of cross-cutting (see "Attraction Films and Chase Films" in Chapter 3), partly for purposes of suspense and partly for the thematic purpose of drawing extensive parallels between Guy and Bruno, who are presented as doubles or alter egos. Just a couple of the many instances of this theme are the dissolve from Guy shouting, "I said I could strangle her!" to Bruno flexing his manicured hands, and the cut from Bruno looking at his watch after the murder to Guy looking at his watch on the Washington-bound train. The film has a divided, mirrorlike structure. Several critics have commented on its extensive system of parallels and doubles; Hitchcock himself boasted, "Isn't it a fascinating design? One could study it forever."[23]

The split in our identification between the two men reaches its greatest intensity when Guy is struggling to win the tennis match while Bruno is struggling to reach the lighter. Before this sequence, there have been other elements to entice our complicit allegiance with Bruno: his genuinely trying parental situation, his puncturing of the obnoxious little boy's balloon (shades of W. C. Fields), his puncturing of the respectable facades of such characters as Judge Cunningham and Guy himself ("Marrying the boss's daughter: that makes a nice shortcut to a career, doesn't it?") – a trait that links Bruno with the comparably outspoken and more obviously sympathetic Barbara. A distinctive feature of *Strangers on a Train* is that Bruno is constantly threatening to take over Guy's position as the protagonist – to take over the film, so to speak, just as he is taking over Guy's life by exchanging roles with him in the "criss cross" scheme.

It is as if the film were constantly threatening to turn over, go wrong side up, and become Bruno's film rather than Guy's. Something roughly similar to that does in fact occur in a later Hitchcock film, *Psycho,* which starts out as the fugitive Marion Crane's film, and then, midway through, flips over, as the putative villain Norman Bates (like Bruno, a psychotic killer obsessed with his mother) takes over the film and becomes its main (though not exclusive) protagonist.

Figure 58. *Strangers on a Train:* Bruno (Robert Walker) wears out his welcome at a society party.

Psycho is an extreme case, but Hitchcock frequently employs complex patterns of viewer identification, in which we are split between different characters, or constantly shifting between them, or placed in situations that compel us to question our previous allegiance with a character (see the final section of Chapter 4). The party scene of *Strangers on a Train,* in which Bruno almost strangles Mrs. Cunningham [Fig. 58], is an especially intricate example of shifting among multiple viewpoints. In this scene, the film gives us reason to identify with Bruno (as we participate in his mental process of connecting Barbara with the dead Miriam), with Barbara (as she looks on in horror and realizes that, in his mind, it is herself Bruno is strangling), with Ann (as she puts two and two together and begins to suspect that Bruno murdered Miriam), and with Guy (as he is forced into an increasingly compromising position by Bruno's crazy antics). Of the competing points of view in this scene, the one that registers least strongly is probably Guy's, reflecting his growing displacement by Bruno. The proliferation of points of view here can also be seen as an expression of Bruno's chaotic intrusion upon Guy's once orderly world.

Figure 59. *Strangers on a Train:* Stolid Guy Haines (Farley Granger, left) comes perilously alive on a runaway merry-go-round.

In his films, Hitchcock seizes upon the capacity of suspense to suspend us, to leave us up in the air. He then builds upon that capacity by shifting us around and placing us in ambiguous and morally confusing positions, in order to increase our sense of vulnerability and undermine our sense of complacency. Although the suspense is always resolved at the end of a Hitchcock film (with one notable exception), that deeper sense of suspension is never quite erased. His happy endings often contain an element of underlying unease or forced jocularity (*Strangers on a Train* has both), and, in one daring and revealing instance, he declined to provide even the pretense of resolution, ending *The Birds* in a state of vast and explicit suspension.

One of Hitchcock's central and most frequently remarked themes is the precariousness of our moral and social order. Adapting the double world of the thriller in a manner that reflects his Victorian and Catholic roots, he dramatizes the ways in which our ordinary, seemingly orderly existence teeters over a seductive, suppressed night world that we ignore at our peril and confront at a possibly even greater peril. Hitchcock's films jolt his heroes out of their artificial security and drag them through a gauntlet of danger and chaos, as terrifying and exhilarating as a ride on a runaway merry-go-round. The characters do not necessarily emerge from this ordeal with great gains in enlightenment and strength; if not devastated, they often end up warily withdrawing back into their shells (as in the epilogue of *Strangers on a Train*) or judiciously "forgetting" much of what they have learned. During that harrowing interlude, however, Hitchcock's somewhat frozen protagonists come perilously alive [Fig. 59]; even the stolid Guy Haines becomes a reckless gambler – in the words of the tennis announcer, "a complete reversal of his usual watch-and-wait strategy." These themes connect Hitchcock's central concerns very strongly to the domain of the thriller, similarly involving a leap from a secure, unadventurous world into an insecure, adventurous realm where we are complicitly and even pleasurably plunged into darkness and pain, in order to emerge at last into a light of day that, after such compelling night, might seem more than a little unreal.

8

The Spy Thriller
Man Hunt (1941)

T he subject of this chapter is the spy genre, which encompasses the general areas of espionage, international intrigue, and the clandestine side of global conflict – the shadow war that is fought off the battlefield, often in the very midst of everyday life. There has been an especially close link between the spy story and the concept of what is popularly if loosely considered to be a thriller. The few writers who have attempted general overviews of the literary thriller, such as Ralph Harper, Jerry Palmer, and (more implicitly) Michael Denning, concentrate mainly on the spy genre and seem to consider it *the* archetypal thriller form. One reason for this preeminence of the spy thriller is the breadth of its scope – conspiracy on a global scale, an entire world in the balance, potential enemy agents lurking in every city, street, and building – against which the individual heroism and vulnerability of the protagonist can be more sharply defined. Harper writes, "In the thriller there is always a war on or a war about to go on. . . . This is the reason why secret agent stories are the touchstones of thriller literature; they represent evil unlimited."[1]

Like the detective story, the spy story is a genre with a significant literary pedigree. As John G. Cawelti and Bruce A. Rosenberg note in their genre overview *The Spy Story* (1987), one can trace precedents for the spy story all the way back to Greek mythology. The wily Odysseus is involved in spylike activities in both the *Iliad* and *Odyssey;* the Trojan Horse can be seen as an early example of a clandestine operation.[2] James Fenimore Cooper's Revolutionary War–set *The Spy* (1821), which includes an American undercover agent as one of its main characters, is considered the first important fictional treatment of spying. A few Sherlock Holmes stories, such as "The Naval Treaty" (1893) and "The Bruce-Partington Plans" (1908), treat of espionage within a detective-story context, and Rudyard Kipling's *Kim* (1901) deals with the subject within an adventure-tale context. Around the turn of the century, a number of popular British books by such authors as George

Chesney, E. Phillips Oppenheim, and especially William Le Queux dealt with imagined invasions of Britain. This paranoid scenario was incorporated into a touristic/adventurous framework (see the first Hitchcock section in Chapter 4) in Erskine Childers's embryonic spy thriller *The Riddle of the Sands* (1903), about two British chums on a sailing holiday that leads to the discovery of a secret German plan to invade England. Joseph Conrad wrote two major psychological novels connected with espionage, *The Secret Agent* (1907; filmed as Hitchcock's 1936 *Sabotage*) and *Under Western Eyes* (1911), each using subversive political activity as a springboard for dramas of guilt and betrayal.

However, the spy thriller did not begin to crystallize as a genre until around the time of the First World War. In other words, the spy thriller is strongly connected to the historical arrival of modern warfare. In this respect, the spy thriller functions in relation to modern warfare much like such critics as Chesterton and Cawelti propose the detective story functions in relation to the modern metropolis (see Chapter 2). As they suggest, the detective story keeps a sense of exotic mystery and romantic adventure alive in the context of the modern-day, technologized, mass-minded urban environment. In a similar manner, the spy thriller maintains a sense of mystery, adventure, and individual heroism in the context of modern, technologized, mass warfare. The spy story provides a variation on the general concept (introduced in the Chesterton section of Chapter 2) that the thriller is a response to modern life, which is perceived under normal circumstances (or even not so normal, as in the case of a world war) to be inhospitable to the adventurous in the traditional sense.

Rather than being an indistinguishable cog in a vast impersonal war machine, the fictional spy (or the civilian caught up in the world of espionage), although he (or she) might belong to a large organization, is usually working alone or as part of a small team. Even though not a general or a political leader, this lone, often obscure individual has the power to make a crucial difference in large-scale events. Possession of one vital secret (the Ultra secret, the Enigma code, the plans for D-Day) can change the course of the entire war. Dr. No or Goldfinger or Blofeld will spread chaos on a global scale – unless this one man, James Bond, can stop him. These cases provide a possibility for significant individual action that might be otherwise lacking in the context of mass warfare, where it is more a matter of one soldier, one battle, one political maneuver among many. As Michael Denning observes in his analysis of the British spy novel, "The secret *agent* returns human *agency* to a world which seems less and less the product of human action."[3] Fritz Lang's 1941 *Man Hunt* contains an extreme case of the idea that a single individual, working alone and undercover, can make a crucial difference in the global struggle: The hero, a British big-game hunter, stalks the leader of Nazi Germany, Adolf Hitler.

During the period from around 1915 to 1945 (i.e., the pre-cold-war era), the spy genre was dominated by a type of hero who is in some ways the equivalent of classical detective heroes such as Lord Peter Wimsey and Philo Vance. The classical spy hero is usually an amateur or dilettante as far as espionage is concerned. He is not a professional or career spy. He is often an aristocrat or gentleman, though usually of the hardy sportsman type rather than the foppish Philo Vance type. He is frequently an innocent bystander who gets caught up in a spy conspiracy through an accident or a case of mistaken identity. The hero of *Man Hunt,* Captain Alan Thorndike, is a nonprofessional and a gentleman, caught up in the world of espionage, although, as we eventually learn, his initial involvement is not as accidental or innocent as that of more typical amateur heroes.

The key pioneer in the development of the classical spy story was the Scots-born political eminence John Buchan, whose spy novels consciously incorporated the romance/adventure tradition of Sir Walter Scott and Robert Louis Stevenson into the context of modern-day political conflict.[4] His influential *The Thirty-Nine Steps* (1915) relates the adventures of Richard Hannay, an entrepreneur/adventurer who stumbles upon a German plot to steal British naval secrets. Buchan's novel popularized an important thriller device that often goes hand in hand with the accidental spy hero: the double chase. In *The Thirty-Nine Steps,* an American journalist claiming knowledge of an assassination plot is killed in Hannay's London apartment, and Hannay finds himself wanted for the murder. On the run from the authorities, he both pursues and is pursued by the real culprits, mostly through the rugged Scottish countryside. The hero in this configuration becomes a man between – caught between two opposing forces and threatened by both of them. Such situations relate to the thriller's characteristic strategies of enhancing vulnerability, doubling, and overloading – the hero is getting it from all sides.

The Thirty-Nine Steps became the basis for Alfred Hitchcock's acclaimed 1935 film *The 39 Steps.* Hitchcock and his screenwriter Charles Bennett retained little of Buchan's novel save for the general idea of the double chase, which was later recycled by the director in such films as *Young and Innocent* (1937), *Saboteur* (1942), *Spellbound* (1945), *Strangers on a Train* (1951), *North by Northwest* (1959), and *Frenzy* (1972). Other thriller movies that make extensive use of the double-chase structure include *This Gun for Hire* (1942; based on Graham Greene's 1936 novel), in which a hunted assassin (Alan Ladd) hunts the employers who have double-crossed him; *No Way Out* (1987), in which a Pentagon investigator (Kevin Costner) races to find the truth before he is framed for murder and espionage; and *The Fugitive* (1993; based on the 1963–7 TV series), in which a falsely convicted man (Harrison Ford) escapes to search for the real killers. The germ of a double-chase structure can be found in *Man Hunt*. In addition to being pursued by Nazi agents, Thorndike is sought by the British authorities – first for extradition to Germany and later for the murder of the Nazi killed in the subway. However, the police side of the double threat is not strongly developed by the film, in which law officers rarely appear.

The Buchan tradition of the two-fisted gentleman spy was carried on in the 1920s by such authors as Sidney Horler, Valentine Williams, Dornford Yates, and "Sapper" (pseudonym of H. C. McNeile), whose heroes (most popularly, Sapper's Bulldog Drummond) battled Bolsheviks, mad scientists, master criminals, and other troublemakers. The spy novel was brought to a new level of sophistication by two of the genre's most important authors, Eric Ambler and Graham Greene, both left-leaning Britons who began their careers in the 1930s. As Cawelti and Rosenberg point out, early spy novels in the Buchan tradition had concentrated on the threat to traditional British values posed by outsiders such as anarchists and German agents, but both Ambler and Greene placed more emphasis on the enemy within, often in the form of respectable homegrown fascists and rapacious big-business interests.[5] Ambler and Greene frequently used the amateur-spy formula, but their protagonists are ordinary, even shabby, in comparison with the elitist heroes of Buchan and his contemporaries.

Ambler's early works in this vein include *Background to Danger* (1937), in which a British journalist gets mixed up in spy maneuvers in Eastern Europe; *Epitaph for a Spy* (1938), in which a vacationing schoolteacher is bullied by the French authorities into helping them catch a spy; and the exceptionally suspenseful *Journey into Fear* (1940), in which a British armaments-company emissary to Turkey finds himself stalked by an assassin. Graham Greene, the most distinguished writer to work extensively in the spy genre, employed the amateur-spy formula in *The Confidential Agent* (1939), in which an overmatched Spanish envoy to Britain is hounded by fascist agents; *The Ministry of Fear* (1943), in which a guilt-ridden recluse stumbles upon a Nazi spy ring; *Our Man in Havana* (1958), in which a fake spy finds his masquerade becoming real; and Greene's original screenplay for Carol Reed's *The Third Man* (1949), in which a visiting American writer (Joseph Cotten) reluctantly serves as an undercover police agent in postwar Vienna. (Films centering on undercover police work – such as *The Friends of Eddie Coyle* [1973], *Rush* [1991], *Point Break* [1991], and *Donnie Brasco* [1997] – often fall closer to the spy genre than they do to the mainstream police thriller.)

During the pre-1945 period, there was one particularly noteworthy exception to the prevailing trend of the amateur-spy story. This was *Ashenden; or, The British Agent* (1928), an episodic, semiautobiographical novel by the eminent British author W. Somerset Maugham. Set mainly in Switzerland during World War I, *Ashenden* features a professional (though not career) spy rather than an amateur or accidental spy, and it portrays espionage as a grim, dirty business rather than a lark or temporary form of escapism. Some of Ashenden's adventures provided the basis for Hitchcock's 1936 film *Secret Agent.*

Since World War II, professional spies, employed by large government agencies, have been the predominant (though by no means exclusive) focus of spy fiction. These include Ian Fleming's glamorous James Bond (first appearing in 1953), William Haggard's cool-headed administrator Charles Russell (1958), John le Carré's modest but shrewd George Smiley (1961), Len Deighton's impertinent man-with-no-name, dubbed Harry Palmer in the movie versions (1962), John Gardner's squeamish charlatan Boysie Oakes (1964), Adam Hall's analytical iron man Quiller (1965), Brian Freemantle's disgruntled slob Charlie Muffin (1977), and Tom Clancy's squeaky-clean Company man Jack Ryan (1985).

As discussed in the opening section of Chapter 4, the spy film rose to prominence during the mid-1930s, in response to the growing international tensions of the time. Previously, the most active phases of the genre had been a flurry of propagandistic espionage movies in the World War I era and a later, smaller vogue (ca. 1927–32) of seductress-spy dramas in the Mata Hari vein. The most distinguished spy movie of the silent era was Fritz Lang's *Spies* (*Spione,* 1928; see the Lang section in Chapter 3), about professional German agents battling an independent supervillain (a plot situation similar to those of several James Bond tales). The leading figure in the post-1930 spy-film renaissance was Alfred Hitchcock, who directed seven spy movies between 1934 and 1942. Much like the classical spy novels of the post-1914 era, spy movies of the late thirties and early forties made frequent use of such devices as the amateur/accidental hero, the touristic setting, and (even before the war) a fervent call to arms addressed to an overly complacent citizenry.

The last element is especially prominent in *Man Hunt,* which was released in June 1941 (that is, nearly two years after the outbreak of the war in Europe, and less than six months before America's entry into it). Various factors had inhibited prewar Hollywood films from criticizing the fascist aggression of Germany, Italy, and Spain. These restraints included the fear of losing important foreign-market revenues, the waning but still vocal isolationist bloc in Congress, and the strictures of Hollywood's Production Code Administration, which refused to approve scripts it considered propagandistic. The first film to challenge these barriers significantly was 1939's *Confessions of a Nazi Spy* (see the spy-film section of Chapter 4), which painted an alarming picture of Nazi-sponsored subversive activities in the United States.

Even after the outbreak of war in Europe and the crushing early losses suffered by the Allies, Hollywood films had to tread carefully. A general fairness doctrine was enforced by the PCA (e.g., portrayals of bad Germans had to be counterbalanced by portrayals of good Germans), and overt appeals to intervene in the war were strongly discouraged. *Man Hunt* went farther into this disapproved territory than had any previous Hollywood feature (with the possible exception of Charles Chaplin's controversial 1940 satire *The Great Dictator*). Though the PCA ordered the removal of some of the film's depictions of German brutality, its portrayal of Nazi Germany is overwhelmingly negative, and its call for intervention unmistakably partisan.[6] Portions of *Man Hunt* perhaps seem strident and didactic today, but they might appear less so when one takes into account the urgency of the international situation in early 1941 and the desire of antifascist filmmakers to make up for lost time in sounding the alarm.

Man Hunt begins in mid-1939 with a lone hunter stalking through a heavily guarded forest to the edge of a cliff, from which he aims his rifle at a house below. In his gun sight is Adolf Hitler. Before the hunter can fire, he is spotted by a guard and captured. He is interrogated by a refined Gestapo officer (George Sanders) who recognizes his captive as Alan Thorndike (Walter Pidgeon), the world-famous British hunter.

Thorndike insists that he had no intention of assassinating Hitler; his goal was merely a bloodless "sporting stalk," undertaken for the sheer challenge. Though skeptical, the Gestapo officer offers to release Thorndike if he signs a confession stating that he undertook the assassination with the approval of the British government. When Thorndike refuses, he is tortured and then pushed off the cliff to make his death appear accidental.

Thorndike does not die. Though badly injured, he eludes a search party and makes his way to a London-bound ship, on which a plucky British cabin boy helps him to hide. The voyage is joined at the last moment by a gaunt German agent posing as Thorndike. Disembarking on a foggy London night, Thorndike immediately finds himself surrounded by a pack of Nazi spies. He ducks into an apartment house, where he encounters Jerry (Joan Bennett), an uninhibited young woman of apparent ill repute. Smitten by Thorndike's genteel manner, she hides him in her flat. Jerry indignantly refuses all his offers of payment, except for an arrow-shaped pin for her cap.

Thorndike calls upon his brother Lord Risborough, an obtuse British diplomat, and makes plans to flee the country. The Gestapo officer arrives in London, posing as an English gentleman, Quive-Smith. He and his minions trap Thorndike in an Underground (subway) station. The gaunt German chases Thorndike into a train tunnel and is electrocuted in the struggle. The dead man is identified as Thorndike, and Thorndike himself, described by witnesses, is sought by the police for murder.

Thorndike flees to the Dorset countryside and lies low in a small cave. Quive-Smith captures Jerry and, after killing her, finds information that leads him to Thorndike's lair. The Nazi seals up Thorndike in the cave and pressures him to sign the confession. To break Thorndike down, he confronts him with evidence of Jerry's death: the cap with the arrow-shaped pin. The shock strips away the last vestiges of Thorndike's civilized self-deception, and he realizes that he had indeed unconsciously intended to shoot Hitler. He hastily improvises a bow and arrow from the materials at hand, using Jerry's pin as the arrowhead, and kills Quive-Smith with it. With his last breath, the Nazi shoots Thorndike. As war rages in Europe, Thorndike recovers from his wound. After joining the RAF, he makes an unauthorized parachute jump into Germany, armed with a precision rifle and resolved now to finish the job of destroying Hitler.

Man Hunt is based on *Rogue Male* (1939), the best-known novel by British author Geoffrey Household, who wrote several spy stories strongly influenced by John Buchan but featuring a greater concern with psychological issues. Household's tense novel is narrated in the first person by its unnamed hero and interweaves the external action of his flight with the internal workings of his mind as he grapples with his true motives for stalking the tyrant. The final confrontation between Quive-Smith and the hero of the novel is closely reproduced in the movie version. However, much else has been changed. The London section, which constitutes nearly half the movie, is very brief in the book, consisting mainly of the chase in the Underground station. Most of the book's action comprises Buchan-like chases through the countryside; Lang's film is more concerned with the transformation of the city into a duplicitous thriller environment. Nearly all of the movie's characters are greatly expanded from the novel or completely invented. Jerry, the young woman who shelters Thorndike, exists only in the movie version; in the novel, her basic narrative function is served by a stray cat whom the hero befriends.

The movie also makes the novel's political background more specific and its antifascist message more explicit. The Nazis' use of dirty tricks and forced confessions is compared to their political manipulation of the 1933 Reichstag fire as a tool to discredit their opponents. The film ends, as the novel could not, with the actual outbreak of the war and Thorndike's participation in it. Most important, the film adds the character of Thorndike's brother, a British diplomat who has recently represented his government on a "mission of appeasement." This phrase is clearly a reference to the misguided appeasement policies of Prime Minister Neville Chamberlain, culminating in the infamous Munich Pact of September 1938, which granted extraordinary concessions to Hitler and paved the way for the war to come. The Chamberlain reference strengthens the allegorical dimension of the hero's actions: Just as Great Britain (and the other democratic powers) had failed to pull the trigger on Hitler in several political showdowns of the late 1930s, so Thorndike fails to dispatch the Führer when he has him in his sights on the cliff above Berchtesgaden.

The screenplay for *Man Hunt* was written by former newsman Dudley Nichols, one of the most prestigious screenwriters of the era. Nichols's screenplays, such as *The Informer* (1935), *Stagecoach* (1939), and *This Land Is Mine* (1943), are characterized by their seriousness of theme, prominent use of symbolism, strong emphasis on issues of conscience, and tendency toward didacticism. These concerns generally coincided with those of director Fritz Lang, although Nichols, unlike Lang, was not especially drawn to thrilleresque subjects. He and Lang were to collaborate once again, on *Scarlet Street* (1945), a chilling yet lively film noir that represents an artistic high point in both their careers. (20th Century–Fox's first choice to direct *Man Hunt* had been John Ford, for whom Nichols had often written successfully.)

Fritz Lang, the illustrious director of *Man Hunt,* was highlighted in Chapter 3 as one of the key figures in the evolution of the movie thriller. As noted, Lang was associated with the influential German expressionist cinema movement, whose attributes include a reshaping of the visible world to express abstract forces and inner states of feeling. Such techniques were adapted to mainstream filmmaking in modulated form, and expressionism's suitability for expressing such feelings as anxiety and dread made it eminently relevant to the thriller. Lang was particularly instrumental in articulating the thriller environment, a multileveled labyrinthine world saturated with a mood of paranoia and conspiracy.

These qualities are strongly in evidence in *Man Hunt.* Especially impressive is the economy and force with which London is established as a dread-filled thriller metropolis. "Stop worrying, my boy," Thorndike smugly tells the anxious cabin boy after the ship arrives in London. "This is England. I'm home again." Yet, within moments of his setting foot on shore, the city has been transformed from an expected refuge into a perilous labyrinth overrun with disconcerting mixtures of the familiar and the sinister. Everywhere he turns, Thorndike finds the foggy streets blocked by stealthy figures who have the appearance of stylized stage Cockneys but upon closer inspection are revealed as German-speaking thugs. He dashes to a passing taxicab only to find the gaunt German agent (identified in the film's credits as "Mr. Jones") sitting in the back seat and trying to pull him inside [Fig. 60].

The confident Thorndike we saw disembark from the ship, along with the familiar, stable London he expected to find, are soon eroded. Midway through the film, Thorndike and Jerry visit a shop to buy the promised pin for her cap. The proprietor greets them in German: "Guten Morgen, mein Herr. Guten Morgen, Fräulein. . . ." Startled, Thorndike does a double take and looks back toward the window, as if to reassure himself that he is still in London and not some new nightmare suburb of Berlin. The proprietor is apparently only a harmless immigrant, but

Figure 60. *Man Hunt:* British fugitive (Walter Pidgeon) nearly nabbed by spectral Nazi agent (John Carradine). (The Museum of Modern Art Film Stills Archive)

Thorndike's wildest fears are coming to seem less and less far-fetched. Jumping onto a departing subway train, he again finds the gaunt Mr. Jones waiting for him. This specter seems to have the uncanny ability to pop up anywhere, now in the form of a prosperous businessman ensconced behind a copy of the *London Times*. In a final, especially cruel revelation, Jerry runs from the Nazis into the reassuring arms of the local bobby. The policeman begins speaking harshly in German and hands her back to his *Kameraden*. We are not too far here from the endlessly duplicitous world of Feuillade's Vampires and Lang's Dr. Mabuse, in which the solidity of the modern city is continually undermined by reversals, disguises, and diabolical sleight of hand.

Another legacy of Lang's expressionist heritage is the abstract quality of his films; they are not particularly realistic in terms of such common-

ly applied standards as the authenticity of the locations, the psychological particularity of the characters, and the sense of a continuum extending beyond the boundaries of the frame. Lang's films (especially
those made before 1950) are more concerned with being expressive;
they have something of the quality of myth or Greek drama. They employ stylized sets and lighting to create a self-enclosed, claustrophobic world. The characters often have an allegorical quality; they seem
as much symbols or archetypes as flesh-and-blood persons. Thorndike
in *Man Hunt* stands for British vacillation on the eve of World War II.
The Gestapo officer even says to him, "You're symbolic of the English
race," and Thorndike replies, "I'm beginning to think you're symbolic
of yours." One of Lang's earliest films, *Destiny* (*Der müde Tod,* 1921),
features Death himself, in black hood and robe, as one of the main characters. The spectral, black-clad Nazi agent played by John Carradine
in *Man Hunt* could as easily be called Mr. Death as Mr. Jones; the cabin boy refers to him as "that walking corpse."

As discussed in Chapter 3, Lang during his German period developed a method for conveying a sense of vast conspiratorial and fatalistic forces through the structure of his films (especially *Spies; M*
[1931]; and *The Testament of Dr. Mabuse* [1933]), in which seemingly
disparate pieces come together to form an intricate, interlocking pattern. After moving to Hollywood, Lang lacked the absolute control over
script development and production conditions necessary to impose
such a rigorous shot-to-shot design upon his films. In his American
films, Lang relies more heavily on the creation of a general mood of
cold menace and on an organizing system of symbols, motifs, and parallels to link different parts of the film together. This observation about
Lang's style is not meant to imply that other directors' films do not also
employ interlinked patterns of imagery but simply that this dimension
tends to be closer to the surface in Lang's work. It is more overt, and
it combines with the intricate plot twists and the starkly geometrical
compositions (dominated by straight lines, sharp angles, and broad
shapes) to infuse Lang's films with a strong sense of an overriding pattern that encages the characters.

The most prominent of these symbolic chains in *Man Hunt* concerns
arrows, centering on the pin in Jerry's cap and on Jerry herself (as
Thorndike tells her, "You're like that little arrow on your hat: straight
and shining"). During the scene at the pawnshop [Fig. 61], the German-
accented proprietor jokingly points the arrow first at Thorndike ("You
should have that and put it in the gentleman's heart") and then, more

Figure 61. Arrows: In *Man Hunt,* Thorndike (Walter Pidgeon) presents a lethal gift to Jerry (Joan Bennett) . . . (The Museum of Modern Art Film Stills Archive)

ominously, at Jerry ("You will have it still when you die"). The arrow is eventually turned in the other direction, toward the enemy, first as the weapon that Thorndike uses to kill Quive-Smith and finally as the arrow emblem (positioned at precisely the same angle as the arrow on Jerry's cap) on the airplane that aims Thorndike into the heart of Hitler's Germany. The first instance of the arrow motif occurs when Thorndike is captured by the Nazis, and a small statue of Saint Sebastian – pierced by the arrows of martyrdom – is prominently included in the background of several shots [Fig. 62]. This association suggests one interpretation of the arrow motif: The weapon wielded by Thorndike ("a precision rifle") is initially misdirected and harms himself, but by the end it is directed at its proper target, Hitler.

Another relevant aspect of the Saint Sebastian image is that Sebastian survived his martyrdom: Left for dead by the Emperor's archers, he was nursed back to health by a pious woman and lived to be martyred on another day (less picturesquely this time, by cudgeling). This association links the arrow imagery to another of the film's central patterns, concerning resurrection. In the final scenes, Thorndike dies (he appears to have been fatally shot by Quive-Smith) and is reborn as a symbol of Britain's and the free world's awakened resolve to destroy Hitler.

This final symbolic transformation has been prepared throughout the film, which puts Thorndyke through a series of preliminary deaths, burials, and rebirths, culminating in his final destruction and resurrection. The first in this series occurs when the Nazis attempt to execute Thorndike by pushing him off a cliff, but he miraculously survives. Another takes place when Thorndike kills the Nazi agent Mr. Jones in the subway tunnel. That death serves as a surrogate death for Thorndike – Mr. Jones, now unrecognizably mangled, was carrying Thorndike's passport, so the world assumes Thorndike to be dead. In the film's climax, Thorndike is shot by Quive-Smith and apparently killed, after having been shut up in a cave that is like a tomb – as Quive-Smith says, "You're sealed up, as in a grave." An earlier gravelike image occurs when Thorndike evades the Nazi search party on the ship by concealing himself under a hatch in the floor of the captain's cabin.

Thorndike's surrogate deaths all involve a physical descent, a movement downward in some way: down from the cliff, down into the hold of the ship, down into the Underground, down into the ravine for the final confrontation with Quive-Smith. The idea of descent here is metaphorical as well as physical – specifically, it represents a movement downward along the evolutionary scale, to a more savage or primitive state.

The coexistence of the civilized and the primitive, with a partial regression to the primitive, is one of the major themes of *Man Hunt* (and also of several classical spy novels by such authors as Buchan, Horler, and Ambler), providing a variation on the characteristic thriller device of infusing the archaic and adventurous into the modern and mundane. The film opens with an image of a primeval forest, wrapped in mist. Thorndike starts out using a high-powered precision rifle but eventually reverts to a more primitive weapon, the bow and arrow. The Gestapo headquarters is filled with emblems of high culture, such as the chessboard, the statues, and the musically decorated lamp shade, but it is also a site of torture and barbarism. The Gestapo commandant, who takes pride in the Nazis' return to the "primitive virtues," stares thoughtfully at the chessboard while the sounds of Thorndike's savage

Figure 62. . . . and a Gestapo officer (George Sanders, left) interrogates Thorndike in front of Saint Sebastian, in *Man Hunt.* (The Museum of Modern Art Film Stills Archive)

beating recede offscreen. A single, startling close shot transforms the avuncular, pipe-puffing German doctor into a murderous beast, his eyes glittering with maniacal glee as he suddenly lunges forward to shove Thorndike over the cliff to his presumed death. When Jerry serves them fish-and-chips, Thorndike has to eat it with his fingers, and he remarks with bemused amazement, "I forgot that fingers came before forks!" [Fig. 63]. Later, he uses not only his fingers but his teeth, like an animal, to tear up the confession Quive-Smith has coerced him to sign.

The three major "deaths" or descents experienced by Thorndike all involve images that evoke the cave, humankind's first primitive home. The grave and the cave are two central images in *Man Hunt,* and they are closely linked. Most obvious, there is the tomblike cave in which

Figure 63. *Man Hunt:* "I forgot that fingers came before forks!" (The Museum of Modern Art Film Stills Archive)

Thorndike hides at the end [Fig. 64]. Earlier, when he escapes after being pushed off the cliff, there is a lengthy shot that shows him framed through a cavelike tunnel formed by tree branches. This image is precisely echoed in the composition of one of the most striking shots in the film: a cross-sectional view looking straight down the tubular Underground tunnel where Thorndike hides from the gaunt Nazi agent. In addition to its visual impact, this shot powerfully embodies the film's thrilleresque creation of a double world, at once civilized and savage. We are in the bowels of the modern metropolis, amid one of its technological marvels; but, at the same time, it is as if we were back in the caves and forests of prehistoric times, with men hunting each other like wild beasts.

Morris Dickstein has written of the thriller hero, "Only by passing through adventure and danger, by descending into suppressed elements of his own civilized identity, can the individual restore himself to the apparent safety and security of society."[7] *Man Hunt* gives this

Figure 64. *Man Hunt:* The cave and the grave. (The Museum of Modern Art Film Stills Archive)

common thriller theme a special inflection and urgency, in terms of the film's treatment of the civilized–primitive theme and its relationship to the oncoming war. *Man Hunt* suggests that in order to fight the savagery of the Nazis, one also must revert to savagery. One has to descend or die symbolically, as Thorndike does, in order to rise again (the image of the circle is linked to the idea of escape, as well as to the cave/grave). The film begins with its hero at a great height, on top of the cliff from which he is aiming a rifle at Hitler. Then Thorndike is brought low, again and again, in ways that strip away his civilized veneer, before finally being raised up in the airplane . . . from which he will now descend once more, rifle in hand, to hunt the biggest game of all.

9

The Police Thriller
The French Connection (1971)

The police thriller is self-evidently distinguished from other subcategories of crime film in that it is a story in which the police
and police work take the center stage. This contrasts with the
other crime-film varieties, such as the detective film, psychological
crime film, and gangster film, in which the police are usually present
but more peripheral to the action.

The police film has a less pertinent literary background than do other major branches of the movie thriller, such as the detective film, horror film, and spy film. There has been no shortage of crime/mystery
stories featuring policemen, beginning with Émile Gaboriau's Monsieur
Lecoq in the 1860s, but the fictional police story has experienced diffi-
culties in developing a distinct identity apart from the detective story.
Some police protagonists, such as Josephine Tey's Alan Grant (first
appearance, 1929) and Ngaio Marsh's Roderick Alleyn (1934), derive
from Golden Age gentleman detectives like Philo Vance and Lord Peter
Wimsey; others, such as Earl Derr Biggers's Charlie Chan (1925) and
Georges Simenon's Jules Maigret (1932), are intuitive and philosophical in the manner of G. K. Chesterton's Father Brown; still others, such
as Freeman Wills Crofts's Inspector French (1924) and Basil Thomson's
Constable Richardson (1933), are more methodical in technique and
conventional in personality. However, in all of these cases, the basic
formula deviates little from that of the detective story (whether whodunit or hard-boiled), with an individualistic sleuth solving the puzzle
of an eccentric and complicated crime.

The first significant departures from this pattern occurred ca. 1950.
They were provided by the form of story known as the *police procedural,* which is strongly grounded in the everyday routine of a police unit.
Lawrence Treat's *V as in Victim* (1945), concerning a New York City
unit, is sometimes cited as the first, still embryonic example of the
form. The key figure in defining the procedural form is widely considered to be Ed McBain, who inaugurated his well-known 87th Precinct

series with *Cop Hater* in 1956. Other notable examples of the police-procedural novel include the London-set George Gideon series (1955) by J. J. Marric, the Stockholm-set Martin Beck series (1965) by the wife–husband team of Maj Sjöwall and Per Wahlöö, and the New York-set Norah Mulcahaney series (1972) by Lillian O'Donnell.

The basic form of the literary police procedural was strongly influenced by extraliterary sources, including the popular radio show *Dragnet* (1949–50) and its even more popular television version (1951–9); later television series such as *The Lineup* (1954–60) and *M Squad* (1957–60); and semidocumentary crime films such as *The Naked City* (1948) and *He Walked by Night* (1949). Like the semidocumentary crime film (see Chapter 4), the police procedural carries over a wartime spirit into postwar life; literary scholar Stephen Knight has pointed out the procedural's foregrounding (and often simultaneous undermining) of such war-enhanced values as bureaucracy, technology, and collectivism.[1]

The police procedural represents a partial repudiation of the elitism and artifice inherent in the detective story. In a police procedural, there can be several separate cases investigated in the course of the narrative, and more than one police detective centrally involved in the investigations. Even when the story is dominated by a central character, there is more emphasis on teamwork – the contributions of other investigators, technicians, informants – than is commonly found in the detective story. Rather than the dazzling deductions of a brilliant sleuth, there is a greater reliance on methodical procedures such as legwork, lab work, forensics, research, surveillance, and interrogation. As in the psychological crime thriller, the identity of the criminal may be quickly revealed, and a parallel structure, moving back and forth between the pursued criminals and the pursuing police, is sometimes employed. The crimes investigated tend to be (relatively) mundane rather than tricky or esoteric, and the police protagonists are (relatively) more ordinary and less set apart than the lone-wolf private detective. They are often married, and there is more attention given to their domestic and off-duty life.

In general, the police procedural places a greater emphasis on the milieu that its protagonists inhabit. As procedural novelist Hillary Waugh has written, "These are stories, not just about policemen, but about the world of the policeman."[2] There is much attention given to the camaraderie and bickering of the police station, the interrelated activities of different branches of the police department, the criminal demimonde that the police detective constantly rubs up against, and the day-to-day pressures of police work, whether they come from disapproving superiors, neglected family members, the misinformed public, or internal demons. In the popular police novels of Joseph Wambaugh (such as *The New Centurions* [1970] and *The Choirboys* [1975]), such pressures, rather than the solving of crimes or the capture of criminals, are often the primary focus of the book.

Police protagonists are both more powerful and less powerful than private detectives. They are more powerful because they have the official authority of the Law behind them, as well as the manpower, technology, and other tangible resources of the police department. They are less powerful because they are organization men and women – in contrast to private detectives, who are usually independent operators, working out of their own offices. The very name "private eye" connotes that detective's independence. The police detective is more of a "public eye," being a public servant and therefore subject to the constraint of regulations, the inertia of bureaucracy, and the scrutiny of press and public.

Because of its emphasis on time-consuming routine and its deemphasis of star-friendly individualism, the police procedural has had only limited impact in the cinema. It has proven more amenable to the television-series format, as attested by such popular and highly regarded shows as *Hill Street Blues* (1981–7), *Homicide: Life on the Street* (1993–present), and *NYPD Blue* (1993–present). *The French Connection* represents an unusually close and successful movie equivalent of the police procedural, making use of many though not all of the elements mentioned above.

The police subcategory of the crime movie was fairly slow to come to prominence in film history. The first major group of movies to center on policemen was the "G-Man" cycle of the late 1930s, constituting a reaction to the gangster film and glorifying crime-busting lawmen such as FBI agent James Cagney in the pattern-setting *G-Men* (1935) and New York undercover cop Edward G. Robinson in *Bullets or Ballots* (1936), both directed by William Keighley. As discussed in Chapter 4, police protagonists figure prominently in such postwar film cycles as the semidocumentary crime film, the flawed-cop film, and the syndicate-gangster film. The police-centered crime film entered its most active and commercially successful period with the advent of the modern police thriller, which was spearheaded by such major hits as *Bullitt* (1968), *The French Connection* (1971), and *Dirty Harry* (1971).

In addition to its box-office success, *The French Connection* achieved a prestige equaled by neither *Bullitt* nor *Dirty Harry* nor any other police thriller until *The Silence of the Lambs* (1991). *The French Connection* received critical accolades and numerous honors, including Academy Awards for best picture, actor, director, screenplay, and editing.

The film is loosely based on Robin Moore's 1969 nonfiction book, which details a major drug bust made in early 1962 by two New York police detectives, Eddie Egan and Sonny Grosso (renamed Jimmy Doyle and Buddy Russo in the movie). Many factual details were greatly altered in the transition from page to screen. Although given short shrift by director William Friedkin, Moore's book (whose form is similar to that of a fictional police procedural) is quite exciting in a different, more low-key way.[3]

The producer of the film, Philip D'Antoni, had previously produced *Bullitt,* and he continued to specialize in police dramas in both film and television. After several unsuccessful attempts to come up with a workable screenplay, D'Antoni hired Ernest Tidyman, a novice screenwriter and former crime reporter who had recently written the black-detective novel *Shaft* (1970). The notoriously combative Friedkin subsequently claimed that most of the script had been made up by himself and the main actors, based on their interaction with real-life police detectives, including Egan and Grosso. The matter was brought to arbitration and resolved in Tidyman's favor.[4]

Friedkin had yet to make his mark as a filmmaker. *The French Connection* was his fifth feature film, but his most significant previous efforts had been two television documentaries: *The People vs. Paul Crump* (1962), a plea on behalf of a death-row prisoner, and *The Thin Blue Line* (1966), a sympathetic overview of the pressures of police work.

As a film director, Friedkin has displayed a distinctive though not always successful mixture of action-film directness and art-film ambiguity. He prefers to imbed the film's ideas in its action, avoiding explication and editorialization, and employing fragmented, impressionistic structures that encourage the audience, as Friedkin has said, "to draw their own conclusions, whatever they may be."[5] This approach has often resulted in a lack of narrative clarity that is unusual for mainstream Hollywood cinema. *The French Connection* represents Friedkin's most successful stylistic fusion, with the famous chase scene epitomizing the action-film side, the ambiguous final gunshot (patterned after the enigmatic monoliths in *2001: A Space Odyssey* [1968]) epitomizing the art-film side, and the film's antidrug message implicitly but powerfully expressed through its settings and structure.[6]

Friedkin used similar methods to more uneven effect in his next movie, *The Exorcist* (1973), an enormous box-office success in spite of a plot that was largely incomprehensible to anyone who had not read William Peter Blatty's source novel. Since *The Exorcist*, Friedkin's career has precipitously declined, its most interesting work being *Sorcerer* (1977), an ambience-heavy, dialogue-light remake of *The Wages of Fear* (1953; see "European Influences, . . ." in Chapter 5) that surpasses the original in spectacle but falls far short in characterization; *To Live and Die in L.A.* (1985), a West Coast companion piece to *The French Connection,* rendered in L.A. glitz rather than New York grit; and the harrowing *Twilight Zone* television episode "Nightcrawlers" (1985), yet another Friedkin journey through hell, set at a roadside café where the nightmare of the Vietnam War literally comes to life.

The French Connection raised little-known character actor Roy Scheider to prominence and prominent character actor Gene Hackman to leading-role stardom. The film makes effective use of the contrasting styles of its main actors, with Hackman's rough-edged flamboyance as Doyle counterpointed by Scheider's ordinary-guy understatement as Russo, and both of them counterpointed by the Continental suavity of Fernando Rey (Charnier), a Spanish actor best known for his work with the great international filmmaker Luis Buñuel. Egan and Grosso, the real-life models for Doyle and Russo, have supporting roles as, respectively, the fretful supervisor Simonson and the Federal agent Klein.

The French Connection begins in the mild Mediterranean winter of Marseilles. An undercover policeman is tailing an affluent businessman named Alain Charnier. Charnier's right-hand man, Pierre Nicoli, kills the cop with a bullet in the face.

Winter is harsher in Brooklyn, where two narcotics policemen, the colorful "Popeye" Doyle and his quietly loyal partner "Cloudy" Russo, chase a drug dealer into a desolate, trash-strewn lot. That evening, at a noisy nightclub, Doyle's suspicions are aroused by the sight of a small-time hood, Sal Boca, acting like a big-time spender. Doyle and Russo begin staking out Boca's candy store; they connect him to Joel Weinstock, a wealthy Manhattanite who has been involved in previous drug deals. While bullying the pathetic clientele of a junkies' bar, Doyle learns from an undercover agent that a large heroin shipment is expected to reach the city soon. Also assigned to the case are two Federal Bureau of Narcotics agents, Klein and Mulderig, the latter a sorehead with a low opinion of Doyle.

Charnier and his associates arrive in Manhattan. The heroin purchase is headed by Weinstock, who cautiously decides to delay payment. Doyle tails Charnier through midtown Manhattan but loses him in a subway station. Charnier flies to a meeting in Washington, D.C., where he is stalled by a nervous Boca. On the flight back to New York with Nicoli, Charnier confides that he is worried about the persistent Doyle; Nicoli offers to handle it.

As Doyle is returning to his apartment building, Nicoli attempts to shoot him from a nearby rooftop. Doyle chases him to an elevated subway station, where the gunman escapes on a departing train. While Doyle careens through the busy streets in a commandeered automobile, the desperate Nicoli hijacks the train, which finally crashes to a halt. Nicoli shakily descends from the platform and finds an exhausted Doyle waiting for him at the foot of the stairs. When the unarmed man turns to flee, Doyle shoots him in the back.

The police covertly seize Charnier's car and tear it apart. The hidden heroin is discovered inside; then the car is reassembled and returned. Charnier drives to the rendezvous in a decrepit area of Ward's Island. Right after the drug sale to Weinstock and his partners is completed, the police move in [Fig. 65]. Sal Boca is killed in the shootout; the others surrender. Charnier slips away to an abandoned building, followed by Doyle. In the shadows, Doyle mistakenly kills the Federal agent Mulderig. Unfazed, Doyle runs off in pursuit of Charnier; a single gunshot echoes through the ruins.

One of the most striking aspects of *The French Connection* is its vigorous editing style, which sustains a sense of both off-balance disorientation and headlong forward propulsion. Although these qualities are most apparent in the big chase scene, they are also operative throughout the film. Transitions are handled in a jagged manner; scenes often begin and end abruptly, sometimes in midconversation and even midsentence. There is only a limited attempt made to orient the spectator to new situations and locations, whether through preliminary script exposition or establishing long shots. Instead, we are plunged into one new situation after another, with the action already in progress, often by means of a jarring close shot that makes it initially difficult to get our bearings.

In several cases, explanatory and bridging material was scripted and even filmed but later eliminated by Friedkin; smooth orientation of the spectator is usually sacrificed in favor of maintaining the film's precipitate pace and its general mood of edgy confusion. For example, a scene was shot that showed Doyle intimidating, then charming a pretty bicyclist who ends up in bed with him. In the final version of the film, all we see are a few brief shots of Doyle's car coming up behind the young woman, then some traces of her presence in the following scene of Russo visiting Doyle's apartment. A preceding scene established Doyle's friendship with the owner of a cheap bar; all that remains is a shot of Doyle rising from a drunken stupor and heading out of the bar into the chilly dawn.[7]

Sound-track transitions are handled as jaggedly as the visual ones. Throughout the film, sound and image are slapped together in a free and easy manner, with offscreen voice-over dialogue often having a loose or unclear relation to the images over which it is heard, as in the sequence in which Doyle and Russo first stake out Sal & Angie's candy store. The most striking instance of the film's rough-edged sound style occurs at the nightclub where Doyle first spots the free-spending Sal Boca. In this scene, different elements of the sound track are selectively manipulated, so that some sounds are amplified while others are unnaturalistically muted or eliminated. When Doyle and Russo first enter the nightclub, the song performed by the singing trio is heard to the exclusion of all other sounds in the scene; we see Doyle and the other characters talking but cannot hear what they say. As Doyle's attention is drawn to Sal Boca's table, a high-pitched drone note is heard, after which the lopsided balance of the sound track is reversed: The sound of the singing trio (although they continue to sing) drops out completely, while Doyle and Russo's conversation dominates the scene (other conversations continue to be seen but not heard). Then, after Doyle concludes, "That table is definitely wrong," the voices of the singing trio, along with other ambient sounds (such as the voices at Boca's table), join the two cops' conversation, and the scene ends with a more conventionally realistic sound mix.

This sequence exemplifies the modified subjective dimension of the film's style: We experience events in a way analogous – but not necessarily identical – to that of the main characters. As the sound-track manipulations in the nightclub scene illustrate, we slip in and out of Doyle and Russo's perspective, scrambling to keep up with them, much as they scramble to keep up with the slippery Charnier and his associ-

Figure 65. *The French Connection:* Marseilles drug lord (Fernando Rey, center) fleeing from police on decrepit Ward's Island. (The Museum of Modern Art Film Stills Archive)

ates. Using a different kind of style, *The French Connection* achieves an overall effect similar to that of *The Big Sleep* (and, to a lesser extent, *Strangers on a Train* and *Man Hunt*): We are immersed in an ever-expanding labyrinth where it is difficult to get our bearings, where we are entangled, enthralled, and exhilarated.

One of the benefits of the film's editing style is that it enables *The French Connection* to emulate the form of the police procedural, appropriating its connotations of authenticity while mostly avoiding the weight of methodical exposition that has made the genre difficult to adapt to the commercial cinema. There are many scenes depicting routine police activities (tailing Sal Boca's car, watching the luncheonette, listening to the wiretap [Fig. 66], standing in the cold outside Weinstock's apartment building), in which little happens to advance the plot, but the jagged, truncated editing patterns maintain a feeling of pace and energy.

The culmination of the film's editing techniques is the celebrated chase in which Doyle's car hurtles down a busy avenue in a frantic attempt to catch up with an elevated train bearing his would-be assassin Nicoli. One reason for the effectiveness of the chase scene is that it functions as an intensification of the consistently kinetic, off-balance style employed throughout *The French Connection.* (An instructive contrast is provided by Friedkin's 1995 mystery thriller *Jade,* in which a frenetic car chase through San Francisco comes off as an isolated and overblown set piece in relation to the glossy, ornate style of the film as a whole.)

The chase in *The French Connection* has been frequently compared to the equivalent scene in *Bullitt,* which had previously set the standard for cop-film car chases (see "Supercops" in Chapter 5). However, the differences between the two scenes are more striking than their similarities. The predominant tone of the chase in *Bullitt* is transcendent mastery, whereas that of the chase in *The French Connection* is claustrophobic desperation.

The most evident contrast concerns the environments in which the two chases occur. Traffic in the *Bullitt* scene is light; there are few visible pedestrians; the streets of San Francisco have the nearly deserted appearance of a Sunday morning. After beginning in the city and making effective use of its sharp turns and hilly terrain, the chase moves into the less populated outskirts and finally onto a country highway. The last part of the chase, after Bullitt (Steve McQueen) pulls up alongside the two hoods he is pursuing, is entirely devoid of traffic. In contrast, the avenue down which Doyle speeds in *The French Connection* is constantly cluttered with obstacles in the form of vehicles, pedestrians, and stationary hazards such as the forest of pillars beneath the elevated track.

This contrast is underscored by the respective visual styles of the two scenes. The camera is tighter, closer to the action in *The French Connection;* the shots are generally briefer, the editing more fragmented. *Bullitt* cuts to wide and high-angled vistas to give an overall sense of the spatial layout at certain points in the chase. There are no equivalents of such shots in the *French Connection* chase: The few long shots are brief and moving extremely rapidly, with a clutter of obstructions whizzing through the foreground. Near the beginning of the chase, we briefly see the train and Doyle's car in high angle; from then on, the pre-

Figure 66. *The French Connection:* Doyle (Gene Hackman) and Russo (Roy Scheider) carry out routine police procedures. (The Museum of Modern Art Film Stills Archive)

dominant perspective is low, immersed – notably in over-the-shoulder shots of Doyle peering up at the tracks above and in traveling shots mounted at the level of the car's front bumper as it ploughs through heavy traffic.

In general, the chase scene in *Bullitt* is more spacious and stable, whereas that in *The French Connection* places us more in the midst of things and makes it more difficult to obtain a sense of orientation. The high points of the chase in *Bullitt* (such as a lurching descent down an undulating San Francisco hill and a hair-raising squeeze between a truck and a highway guardrail) are more spread out, interspersed with relatively lengthy shots of the two cars cruising along. In *The French Connection,* the equivalent high points (such as the near-miss of the woman with the baby carriage and the near-collision with the moving van) are more closely packed together, with little sense of letup, less time to catch one's breath.

Finally, there is a marked difference in the emotional temper of the two scenes. The characters in *Bullitt* barely break a sweat; the emphasis is on the cool, tight-lipped professionalism maintained by both hero and villains. The chase in *The French Connection* is physically and emotionally much more grueling for both Doyle (seen sweating, screaming, pounding on the steering wheel) and Nicoli (seen cornered, frantic, losing his head [Fig. 67]), with the two men in a state of battered exhaustion by the time of their final confrontation.

The chase scene in *The French Connection* is in some respects similar to the climax of *Strangers on a Train* (see Chapter 7). It splits the emotional focus between hero and villain, thereby adding an element of destabilizing ambivalence to the scene. Even though Nicoli is clearly the villain of the piece, presented with far less appeal than is Bruno Anthony in *Strangers on a Train,* his desperation and sense of entrapment are conveyed so vividly that he commands a certain amount of sympathy and identification.

There are also similarities between the chase in *The French Connection* and that in one of the earliest films described in this book: D. W. Griffith's 1912 short *The Girl and Her Trust* (see Chapter 3), which climaxes with a locomotive in pursuit of a railroad handcar bearing two thieves and the kidnapped heroine. Although the chase in *The French Connection* is more elaborate, the basic strategies employed in the two scenes have much in common. Both films cut back and forth between two moving vehicles, while a third viewpoint (taken from a speeding camera truck) races alongside the other two, blurring the objects in the foreground and conveying a sheer intoxication with speed. The main element that *The French Connection* adds to this equation is subjectivity: reaction close shots and point-of-view shots that plunge us into the perspectives of pursuer and pursued, each deep inside the labyrinth.

A central concern of the police thriller is indicated by the origin of the word "police" itself – from the Greek *polis,* meaning "city," as in "metropolis" ("mother-city"). "Police" and "city" are, etymologically speaking, the same word.

As previously noted, the city, in its modern labyrinthine form, is the primary thriller environment. Nowhere is this truer than in the police thriller, which is often as much about the city as it is about the police. *The French Connection* is as much about New York City as it is about cops and drug dealers. *Dirty Harry* is as much about San Francisco as

Figure 67. *The French Connection:* Hit man Pierre Nicoli (Marcel Bozzuffi) cornered, frantic, losing his head. (The Museum of Modern Art Film Stills Archive)

it is about Harry Callahan and the psycho he is trying to catch. *Seven* (1995) is as much about its rainy, rotten, unnamed city as it is about the manhunt for a murderous religious maniac. *L.A. Confidential* (1997) is as much about movie-haunted Los Angeles in the transitional 1950s as it is about its heroes' battle against high-level corruption.

The police thriller is centrally concerned with descriptions and interpretations of the modern urban environment. There are a few notable police thrillers that are set mostly in the country, including *On Dangerous Ground* (1952; see "The Flawed-Cop Cycle" in Chapter 4), *Witness* (1985), *One False Move* (1992), and *Fargo* (1996). However, in the majority of those examples, the action begins in a vicious, violent urban environment, which the displaced police or criminals carry with them like a virus, disrupting the rural world they enter.

As noted in Chapter 2 (see "Pascal Bonitzer: Partial Vision"), the city is a quintessential labyrinth. The very form of the city, filled with corners and compartments and passageways, makes it a place of limited vision and fragmentary impressions that is difficult to grasp as a whole. Also, as suggested before, the thriller tends to transpose associations of the woods or wilderness onto the modern city, turning it into a glass-and-concrete version of the enchanted or primeval forest.

However, the city differs from the wilderness in the obvious but crucial sense that it is a man-made environment, not a natural one. Accordingly, there is another set of polarities central to the concept of the city. This involves the two extremes of utopia and dystopia, or, to put it another way, heaven and hell. Most of the early literary utopias (or ideal societies) prominently feature cities as the epitome of humanity's highest aspirations – as in Thomas More's *Utopia* (1516), Fra Tomaso Campanella's *City of the Sun* (1602), Johann Andreae's *Christianopolis* (1619), Francis Bacon's *The New Atlantis* (1627), Edward Bulwer-Lytton's *The Coming Race* (1871), and Edward Bellamy's *Looking Backward* (1887). There are also traditional religious associations of the city with heaven: the City on the Hill, the Holy City, Jerusalem.

The heavenly or utopian city has become a less tenable image in recent times. The tendency has been instead to portray the city in terms of its negative associations, as Babylon or Sodom, a place of corruption and sin – and as a potential dystopia (or "bad place"). This image is frequently found in science fiction (e.g., *Metropolis* [1926], *Alphaville* [1965], *THX 1138* [1971], *Blade Runner* [1982]): the city as a place of absolute soullessness, alienation, and enslavement of the mind and body. The ultimate form of dystopia is hell.

Director Fritz Lang created in his 1926 classic *Metropolis* the most famous film dystopia – a city that, like the London of Lang's *Man Hunt* (see Chapter 8), conceals a primitive underside, honeycombed with subterranean passages beneath its civilized facade. A digression midway through *Metropolis* recounts the story of the Tower of Babel – an idealistic, well-planned attempt to build a utopian community, a city that literally reaches to the heavens – but this glorious project collapses into the dystopia of the modern metropolis. A vision of radiant unity gives way to dark images of disharmony, violence, oppression, terror, confusion, and cavernous labyrinths. This vision is not too distant from the city depicted in *The French Connection,* with its splintered, polyglot crazy quilt of ethnic and class enclaves.

The police thriller, more than any other thriller-related genre (even the horror film), plays on the image of the city as hell. In most other forms of thriller, the central opposition is between the city as an ordinary, oppressive, 9-to-5 place and the city as a magical, adventurous, thrillingly dangerous place. The police thriller does not neglect that opposition, but it also emphasizes another one: It concentrates more on moralizing the urban environment, so that the opposition ordinary–adventurous is equaled or surpassed by the opposition heaven–hell. The issue of the city as a good or evil place becomes even more important than that of the city as an adventurous or unadventurous place.

In the modern police thriller, there is precious little heaven around, and everything is pretty much hell – or, at best, poised precariously between the bottom edge of purgatory and the beckoning pit of inferno. As film scholar William Park writes in "The Police State" (1978), an article on post-1967 police movies, these films take place in "a completely fallen world . . . this worldly hell." He draws a link between their vogue and the closely following rise of horror films (e.g., *Rosemary's Baby,* 1968; *The Exorcist,* 1973; and *The Omen,* 1976) dealing explicitly with demons and satanism.[8]

Other thriller heroes encountered in this book, such as the detective, the spy, and the film-noir patsy, move through urban environments that, although they may be menacing and oppressive, are substantially romanticized, glamorized, filled with voluptuous atmosphere. Such elements are not necessarily absent in the police thriller – for instance, *Dirty Harry* employs some very colorful locations – but there is a strong pull toward a deromanticized, deglamorized world. This side is especially pronounced in *The French Connection,* which presents the city as relentlessly drab, sordid, ugly – a virtual wasteland.

However, a significant feature of *The French Connection* is that it presents us with more than one urban environment. There are several, which contrast with each other and also overlap and shade into each other in various ways. *The French Connection* opens not in New York but in Marseilles. The Marseilles scenes do not seem essential for developing the story, but they do serve other important functions: They relate to the sense of breadth, of covering a lot of ground, that is central to many thrillers (see the end of Chapter 6). They also relate to the theme of the exotic (see the section on John G. Cawelti in Chapter 2). As in *The Maltese Falcon* (1941), *Man Hunt, The Lady from Shanghai* (1948), *Invasion of the Body Snatchers* (1956), *The Exorcist, Black Sunday* (1977), *Die Hard* (1988), and many other thrillers, the destructive agency comes from abroad, as a foreign element.

The main function of the Marseilles scenes is to set up a contrast with the New York scenes. The film begins, ironically, with the heavenly image of a church (Marseilles's famous Notre-Dame-de-la-Garde) atop a hill. Unlike New York, Marseilles is presented as spacious, clean, quiet, uncongested, affluent, gracious. However, we soon discover that this heavenly place (much like the refined Charnier himself) is not what it seems. The film's first murder, featuring a visceral close shot of a blood-drenched face, reveals that Marseilles is also a place of corruption and murder beneath its civilized, gracious veneer. The scene then shifts to New York City, depicted, in contrast to Marseilles, as cramped, dirty, noisy, crowded, squalid, nasty. The action very quickly moves to the barren lots where Doyle and Russo chase down the drug dealer: a hellish wasteland littered with garbage, graffiti, rust, debris, and smoldering, sulfurous fires.

The film continues to emphasize the contrast between the two cities by alternating scenes set in New York and Marseilles – until that point when Marseilles, in the form of the drug dealer Charnier and his associates, comes to New York. At this point, the film splits up New York and develops a contrast between two of its boroughs, Manhattan and Brooklyn. In this configuration, Manhattan and Marseilles slide together. Manhattan, like Marseilles, is identified primarily with the wealthy and powerful – with Charnier and Weinstock, elegant apartments and hotels, high-priced shops and restaurants. Brooklyn, where Popeye Doyle works and lives, is depicted as a much seedier, lower-class environment, populated by small-timers and losers, such as Sal Boca and the drug dealer who gets slapped around in the first New York scene. The lower echelons of the criminal world hang out in Brooklyn, while the uppercrust of the underworld operate in midtown Manhattan. The film gives much emphasis to shots of the characters crossing bridges in and out of Manhattan; these shots reinforce the sense of passing between two different worlds. Doyle seems to lose power in Manhattan, where he is constantly struggling to keep up with Charnier, who finally gives him the slip in the midtown subway station. This debacle represents a low point for Doyle, his futility emphasized by the shot of him receding down the long tunnel as the train pulls out. Outside of Manhattan, however, Popeye is stronger: He intimidates everyone in the junkies' bar, he chases down Nicoli on the hijacked train.

Perhaps the most puzzling episode in *The French Connection* is the single scene set in Washington, D.C., where Sal Boca meets with Charnier in front of the U.S. Capitol. This location-shot scene (which has no equivalent in the book) is not necessary for developing the plot; the essential information could have easily been shifted to another locale or conveyed through dialogue after the fact. The depiction of Washington itself is curious. The city is almost completely deserted – we see perhaps two pedestrians walk by in the distant background. The way the location is filmed emphasizes a sense of emptiness, stillness, stagnancy. Washington here is an empty shell, a dead place. This White City, the official center of power, ultimately seems irrelevant to what is going on in the mean streets, in the combat zone, where obscure figures like the elusive Charnier and his nemesis Doyle are fighting the real war to decide the fate of America's embattled cities.

In addition, the film develops a series of deep, cavernlike locations, photographed so that they appear similar to each other: the nightclub, the junkies' bar, the basement where Doyle and Russo wiretap Boca, the dank underground passageway where Doyle briefly loses Charnier, the subway station where Doyle recedes into near-nothingness, the underground parking garage where Russo tails Boca. These cavernous locations prefigure the film's ultimate space: the abandoned building where Doyle loses Charnier – a dripping, decaying, completely disgusting locale.

The final scene of *The French Connection* can be seen as an apocalyptic vision of the future of the modern city. This vision conveys, more powerfully than any amount of message-laden dialogue could have done, why stopping Charnier's drug shipment is so important. "Shit" (the street-slang term for heroin) is turning the city into shit. A similarly understated connection is made earlier in the film, at the end of the scene in which Charnier, on the New York-bound airplane, tacitly authorizes Nicoli to kill Doyle. Charnier's unspoken behest is immediately followed by a cut to a rainy auto-accident scene, strewn with bloody corpses. In an almost thrown-away bit of dialogue, the Federal agent Klein tells the policeman Simonson, "We found a set of works on the kid driving the sports car over there." The implicit parallel here fixes responsibility on Charnier (and others like him) for both actions: the attempted murder of a policeman and the vehicular homicides caused by a drug-addled kid. High in the sky, the immaculate Charnier never gets his hands dirty, never actually orders the death of Doyle [Fig. 68], much less those of the more circumstantial victims of a heroin shipment, but he and his fellow drug lords nonetheless bring down a plague of blood and filth on the blighted cities far below.

Illuminated, like much of *The French Connection,* by low, shadow-stretching rays of the winter sun, the abandoned building in the final scene becomes like a tomb or a ruin left behind by a lost civilization.

Figure 68. Death from on high: Doyle (Gene Hackman) dodging a sniper's bullet in *The French Connection.* (The Museum of Modern Art Film Stills Archive)

The film's conclusion is a vision of total desolation, entropy, futility. It is a horrifying vision, and it ultimately consumes the hero. In the final shot, it is as if Doyle disappears through the gate of hell. He is swallowed up by the labyrinth, but, unlike Guy Haines in *Strangers on a Train* and Alan Thorndike in *Man Hunt,* Popeye Doyle does not reemerge into the light of day.

10

Conclusion

Having wound our way through the far-flung and mysterious maze of the movie thriller, it might be useful to get our bearings with some general observations. It might also be worthwhile to take note of a few unexplored passageways before we head for the exit and emerge into the light of day.

As noted from the start of this book, the thriller is a familiar but imprecise concept: a genre that isn't a genre, or, at least, a genre that cannot be subjected to the same definitional precision as other, more delimited genres. The thriller is a vast, ill-defined region whose horizons are the marvelous realms of romance and adventure in one direction (traditionally, the East) and the mundane, low-mimetic domains of comedy and melodrama in the other direction.

In the preceding chapters, I have tried to steer a middle course between two approaches that have characterized the few previous attempts to deal generally with the thriller. On the one hand, there are those writers (such as Brian Davis, Lawrence Hammond, and John McCarty) who pragmatically accept the imprecise nature of the thriller and the subjective criteria underlying common applications of the label, but who offer few tangible guidelines outside of the vague and seemingly arbitrary preferences of the author. On the other hand, there are those (such as Jerry Palmer and Charles Derry) who boldly define the subject in a way that indeed illuminates some of its outstanding examples and central concerns but also excludes too many key works that have been widely perceived as thrillers.

Throughout this book, I have worked backward, inductively: If a particular film or type of film has seemed, by its particular properties and/or general reception, to qualify as a thriller, I have tried to keep my approach elastic enough to include it. I have also proposed some specific concepts and parameters for defining the subject, but not so rigidly that the exclusion or inclusion of any one of them would necessarily determine a film's status as a thriller. For example, suspense is probably the most universally agreed-upon component of a thriller, yet (as discussed in Chapter 6) the shortage of this element in *The Big Sleep* (1946) need not disqualify the film as a thriller.

Nevertheless, certain key aspects of this elusive subject have inevitably slipped from my grasp. Rather than sum up with confident conclusions, I prefer to point out four of the problem areas that have been insufficiently addressed in my attempt to pin down this exceptionally problematic genre: categorization, hybridization, emotionalization, and contextualization.

Categorization

The problems raised by the imprecision of the term *thriller* point to more general questions regarding the identification of genres. *Genre* is a French equivalent of the Latin term *genus* (kind, race). That term was used by the eighteenth-century Swedish scientist Carolus Linnaeus in his influential system of botanical/zoological classification to indicate a level of similarity located between the more generalized level of "order" and the more specific level of "species." (For human beings, the order is Primates, the genus is *Homo,* and the species is *sapiens.*) The term *genre* was first used to categorize literary compositions in the early nineteenth century. It was then retrospectively applied to earlier systems of literary classification, most famously the classic distinction among tragedy, comedy, and epic outlined in the Greek philosopher Aristotle's fountainhead of genre criticism, *Poetics* (ca. 330 B.C.). The concept of genre has since evolved to encompass somewhat disparate and not entirely equivalent entities. Although it has become common practice to draw a distinction between the broad classification "genre" (e.g., horror film) and the more narrow "subgenre" (e.g., vampire film), the current usage of genre might call for wider and more flexible distinctions.

The thriller seems to constitute a large category within the spectrum of genres, more accurately described by such terms as "metagenre" (as I suggest in Chapter 1) or "umbrella genre" (as Charles Derry suggests in his book *The Suspense Thriller*).[1] Similarly large generic categories include "comedy" (encompassing satire, farce, parody, slapstick, screwball, sitcom, and many others) and "wonder-tales" (a.k.a. "the fantastic" – encompassing fantasy, horror, and science fiction). These metagenres occupy a level roughly analogous to that of "order" (or the even more generalized category, "class" – e.g., mammals) in Linnaean classification. They often need to be broken down into smaller units before they can be subjected to the critical methods (such as the identification of iconography and narrative patterns) that are commonly used to identify and analyze more circumscribed genres such as the western and the musical.

Going even further in the direction of generality, film scholar Alan Williams has suggested that narrative, experimental, and documentary are the primary film genres, and all other "genres" merely subgenres of those three basic aesthetic modes.[2] Moving in the other direction, toward greater specificity, one can draw a distinction between the more stabilized, historically broad genres or subgenres (such as satire, horror, detective) and historically specific movements or cycles (such as Restoration comedy, Gothic horror, Golden Age detective). In addition, the concept of genre is often applied in a generalized, adjectival sense, detached from the original generic category or historical cycle. For example, the picaresque novel, characteristically relating the episodic adventures of a wandering rogue, flourished from the sixteenth through the eighteenth centuries; among the best-known examples are *Lazarillo de Tormes* (1554), *Gil Blas* (1715–35), and *Moll Flanders* (1722). As an abiding genre, it expired over two hundred years ago, but the descriptive term *picaresque* can still be meaningfully applied to recent works that are somewhat similar to the original picaresque in content, form, and spirit – for example, Gus Van Sant's chronicle of male hustlers *My Own Private Idaho* (1991) or Oliver Stone's serial-killers saga *Natural Born Killers* (1994). "Gothic (horror)" and "screwball (comedy)" are other examples of terms that have outlived their original generic contexts and are now used mainly in an adjectival sense.

The concept of genre has lumped together a number of related but nonequivalent entities, including basic aesthetic modes (such as narrative film), metagenres (such as wonder-tales), stabilized genres (such as horror), subgenres (such as the vampire story), historically specific cycles (such as the lesbian vampire cycle of ca. 1970), adjectival descriptions derived from genres or generic cycles (such as Gothic), and undoubtedly others. I am reluctant, however, to arrange these categories into a taxonomic table in the manner of Linnaeus, because they are fluid and provisional, subject to the shifting perspectives of artistic ambiguity, historical evolution, and critical approach. For example, the term *film noir*, once specific to a historical cycle of the crime film, has exceeded its original context to become a widely applied adjectival term and possibly even a full-fledged, stabilized genre (as Todd Erickson suggests in his essay "Kill Me Again: Movement Becomes Genre" – see the section on neo-noir in Chapter 5).[3] Similarly, depending on the angle of approach chosen by the analyst, horror might be conceptualized as a metagenre, a stabilized genre, a subgenre of the wonder-tale, a subgenre of the thriller, or a hybridized component of the 1950s "monster movie" cycle. For the moment, I shall venture only that genre is a messy and amorphous concept – an obvious but often underacknowledged truth that has been forcefully borne upon me by this extended excursion through the thriller, one of genredom's messiest and most amorphous divisions.

Hybridization

Another factor undermining the precision of genre classification is *hybridization,* the mixture of forms, which is a significant dimension of all major genres. Film historian Janet Staiger points out that widespread genre mixing is not an especially recent phenomenon, born of increased decadence and/or sophistication, but has always been a predominant factor in the commercial cinema. "Hollywood films have never been 'pure,'" Staiger asserts.[4] The issue of hybridization is especially germane to those genres (or metagenres) that are flexible and ill defined on a semantic level – that is, open to a wide range of iconographic and thematic variations (see Chapter 1). One important area of hybridization involves the extensive and fluid border regions between genres that have a particularly close kinship – such as horror and science fiction, or comedy and melodrama. In the case of the thriller, the most significant border genre is the adventure tale (as discussed in the section on Chesterton in Chapter 2), and several examples of thriller–adventure hybrids have been previously cited (e.g., *The Perils of Pauline* [1914], *The Wages of Fear* [1953], *Jaws* [1975]).

There are also, of course, numerous opportunities for hybridization among the constituent genres that are gathered under the wide umbrella of the thriller. Examples of these have been occasionally noted in the preceding chapters – for instance, the semidocumentary–film noir hybrid *He Walked by Night* (1949), the horror–science fiction hybrid *Alien* (1979), the police–heist hybrid *Heat* (1995). For the sake of organizational clarity, however, the emphasis has been on discrete categories, such as spy thriller, detective thriller, and horror thriller. Insufficient attention has been paid to those films in which hybridization rather

Figure 69. *The Crow:* Ghost–vigilante hybrid.

than categorization is emphasized – that is, where a mixture of genres is foregrounded, even flaunted, and functions as an essential part of the film's system of meaning. A notable example is *Blade Runner* (1982), which resonantly combines elements of science fiction, police thriller, hard-boiled detective film, and film noir. These different generic components function as part of the film's dense mélange of anachronistic and futuristic elements, contributing to the perceptual confusion that underlies its central theme of the tenuous boundary between human and nonhuman. Recent thriller-related examples of ostentatious and expressive hybridization include the ghost–vigilante movie *The Crow* (1994) [Fig. 69], the police–disaster film *Speed* (1994), the heist–horror hybrid *From Dusk till Dawn* (1996), the western–gangster film *Last Man Standing* (1996), and the western–horror hybrid *John Carpenter's Vampires* (1998).

Emotionalization

Perception of the thriller is further clouded by the fact that it is defined in part by its evocation of a particular emotional response or visceral stimulus. This quality reflects the thriller's evolution from such sensation-oriented forms as the Victorian sensation novel, amusement-park thrill rides, and the early "cinema of attractions" (see Chapter 3). It distinguishes the thriller from emotionally more neutral genres, such as the western and science fiction, in which films may be serious or comic, action-packed or static, intense or relaxed, without jeopardizing their status within their respective genres.

Like comedy, melodrama, and, perhaps most drastically, erotica, the thriller addresses an implied emotional/visceral mandate. In comedies that mandate is "Make me laugh," in melodramas (or tear-jerkers) it is "Make me cry," in erotica it is "Make me aroused." In thrillers the mandate is "Make me squirm." Or, to put it another way: Pierce me with intense, even agonizing sensations that will transform my ordinary world and charge it with the spirit of adventure.

This generic property raises the possibility of the thriller that is not thrilling, akin to the comedy that is not funny or the erotic film that is not a turn-on. Although the intention can still be discerned, and more objective criteria can be applied to identify a film as a thriller, there exists an area of subjective emotional response that is an important component of the genre. This component is difficult to measure and falls outside the realm of normal academic discourse, but it seems presumptuous to deny that it exists and that it affects how we identify and evaluate thrillers.

While I was writing this book, a friend asked me to name my favorite thriller movie. I faltered over the answer, because I realized that there were two different ways of interpreting the question:

1. Which film do I consider to be the loftiest masterpiece that also happens to fall within the wide zone of the thriller?
2. Which is the thriller that *thrilled* me the most – that is, the one that had the greatest visceral impact on my particular nervous system, that possessed the most power to harrow up my soul and freeze my aging blood?

I guessed that he – like most people – probably intended the second option, so I answered, *"The Texas Chain Saw Massacre"* [Fig. 70].

Even on a more analytic level, such questions inevitably influence one's perception of what is or is not thrilling – and, by extension, a

Figure 70. *The Texas Chain Saw Massacre:* Leatherface tops my Thrill Parade.

thriller. In Chapter 2, I cite the case of film theorist Noël Carroll, who found a particular scene in Hitchcock's *Frenzy* (1972) amusing rather than agonizing, a response at variance with (though not less valid than) that of other viewers (including myself). In the section on anti-Bond spy thrillers in Chapter 5, I discuss the 1965 film version of *The Spy Who Came in from the Cold,* which contains many of the objective criteria of a spy thriller and would probably be considered one by many observers, but my subjective, visceral response (it didn't *feel* thrilling) induced me to seek more concrete reasons why the film is more a spy drama than a spy thriller.

Contextualization

Because the thriller has grown out of a certain context, the question arises: To what extent is it limited by that context? The originating matrix of the thriller is both historical and cultural. The cultural perspective is essentially (though not exclusively) bourgeois and Western (i.e.,

Euro-American). In the thriller, the disruptive, transformative force is therefore characteristically identified with an Other that is exotic (traditionally from the East) and non–middle class (e.g., the aristocratic and filthy-rich villains of much early spy fiction and hard-boiled detective fiction, or, more frequently and durably, a swarm of underclass antagonists, from the tramps who besiege the plucky heroine in 1912's *The Girl and Her Trust* to the rednecks who bedevil the yuppie protagonists of 1997's *Breakdown*). A highly Westernized, urbanized, and capitalized non-Western society such as Hong Kong, with its spate of influential action thrillers in the 1980s and 1990s, has proven more receptive to the production and consumption of thrillers than have substantially agrarian societies like China, India, and Iran, whose active film industries are more closely tied to other, non-Western traditions of entertainment. As the dollar-dominated, media-saturated global village becomes ever more inclusive and homogenized, it seems likely that the thriller will extend its reach and follow the blanketing flag of post-cold-war, multinational capitalism.

As noted in Chapter 3 (see "Precinematic Forerunners"), the thriller is an essentially modern form, germinating toward the end of the eighteenth century (in the Gothic novel), developing during the nineteenth (in such forms as the Victorian sensation novel, early detective story, and melodrama), and crystallizing in the early twentieth, when such central thriller forms as the detective novel, the spy story, and the post-Gothic horror tale came to maturity.

Yet the thriller is also anachronistic: Although allied to a context of modern, everyday, predominantly urban life, it preserves earlier storytelling traditions – notably, the heroic romance, associated with the Age of Chivalry, and the adventure tale, associated with the age of colonial exploration and imperialism. In this sense, the thriller resembles other genres that perform a similar curatorial function, serving to keep alive a receding piece of the past. These include the western, which preserves the myth of the American frontier, and the musical, which preserves a certain theatrical tradition of the nineteenth and early twentieth centuries (exemplified by such spectacle-oriented, heterogeneous forms as the minstrel show, vaudeville, the revue, and the musical itself).

Both the western and the musical are currently moribund movie genres, well past their prime, although fitful stirrings are occasionally observed (e.g., *Unforgiven* [1992] and *Wild Bill* [1995] in the western; *Evita* [1996] and *Everyone Says I Love You* [1996] in the musical). Does a similar antiquation await the thriller? At the moment, such a grim prognosis seems premature. Of the twenty top-grossing U.S. releases of 1997, seven fell generally within the domain of the thriller (*Air Force One, Tomorrow Never Dies, Face/Off, Con Air, Scream 2, Conspiracy Theory, I Know What You Did Last Summer*), compared to three science-fiction films, three comedies, three children's pictures, two adventure movies, one melodrama, and one romantic disaster film.[5]

The very breadth and semantic/iconographic indeterminacy of the thriller work to extend its life span: When certain constituent genres decline, the baton is easily passed to other, healthier ones – as when the spy film yielded to the cop film in the 1970s, and the cop film shaded into the serial-killer film in the 1990s. In addition, the idea of pastness invoked by the thriller seems more abstract, less specific than those found in the western and the musical. The myth of a more heroic and adventurous past that is yearned for by a humdrum and diminished present seems extensively if not endlessly renewable. In this sense, the thriller resembles science fiction, which evolved around the same time and now seems in comparably good health, in part because it, too, is based upon a flexible concept of historical time, though one that is conceived more in terms of a continually looming future than of a continually beckoning past.

It seems unlikely that a time will come in the foreseeable future when everyday life is not viewed as bland and oppressive, generating a desire for an adventurous alternative that is sought within the confines of our familiar modern world rather than in other worlds or other times (as in adventure, science fiction, and westerns). The thriller indulges the mingled daydreams and nightmares of the housewife chopping vegetables in her kitchen (and imagining her lover beside her, as they plot the murder of her husband), the white-collar worker clicking away at his computer terminal (and imagining himself a double agent, receiving top-secret messages from a foreign power), the commuter slogging his way home through a bumper-to-bumper traffic jam (and imagining those bumpers crumpled like tin foil in the wake of a death-defying car chase), the student in her dorm dozing through a film-studies textbook (and imagining how she will defend herself against the masked prowler who creeps up behind her).

Some daydreams turn inward from the everyday world toward the intimacy of erotic fantasy. Others, Walter Mitty–like, turn outward from the everyday world toward distant times and places: jungles, battlefields, bounding mains. The particular kick of the thrilleresque daydream is that it does not require us to leave that context of the quotidian world in order to find adventure or experience intense sensations. We can "order in," so to speak – such delicacies will be delivered direct to our doorsteps, our desktops, our dashboards.

All genres are problematic. They are driven by bundles of unresolved tensions, suspensions, and contradictions – for example, between lamented wilderness and triumphant settlement in the western, between narrative progression and show-stopping spectacle in the musical, between scientific credibility and fabulous speculation in the oxymoronically named science fiction, between familiar routine and exotic adventure in the thriller. As the twenty-first century looms, this essentially twentieth-century form shows no sign of releasing its grip upon our ambivalent desires both to escape from and to remain within the uneasy security of our increasingly downsized world.

Notes

N.B.: Where both an earlier and a later edition of a work are cited in the same note (e.g., hardcover and paperback), the page numbers given are for the later, more readily available edition.

PART I. APPROACHES

1. Introduction

1. Rick Altman, "A Semantic/Syntactic Approach to Film Genre," in *Film Genre Reader II*, ed. Barry Keith Grant (Austin: University of Texas Press, 1995), pp. 26–40; Fredric Jameson, *The Political Unconscious: Narrative as a Socially Symbolic Act* (Ithaca, N.Y.: Cornell University Press, 1981), pp. 107–10; Tzvetan Todorov, *The Fantastic: A Structural Approach to a Literary Genre,* trans. Richard Howard (Ithaca, N.Y.: Cornell University Press, 1975), p. 20.
2. Quoted in Tony Bennett and Janet Woollacott, *Bond and Beyond: The Political Career of a Popular Hero* (New York: Methuen, 1987), p. 88.

2. Critical Overview

1. Charles Derry, *The Suspense Thriller: Films in the Shadow of Alfred Hitchcock* (Jefferson, N.C.: McFarland, 1988), p. 68.
2. Ibid., p. 63.
3. Jean-Paul Sartre, *Existentialism,* trans. Bernard Frechtman (New York: Philosophical Library, 1947), p. 27.
4. Ralph Harper, *The World of the Thriller* (Cleveland: Press of Case Western Reserve University, 1969), pp. 8–11.
5. Jerry Palmer, *Thrillers: Genesis and Structure of a Popular Genre* (New York: St. Martin's Press, 1979), pp. 53, 82.
6. Ibid., pp. 9–15, 24–40, 52, 82–3, 125.
7. Ibid., pp. 42, 51–2, 58–67, 95–6, 105, 134, 209, 212–20.
8. Ibid., pp. 53, 59, 212–15.
9. Ibid., pp. 40–52, 62.
10. G. K. Chesterton, *The Defendant* (London: R. B. Johnson, 1901), p. 158; Robin Wood, *Hitchcock's Films,* rev. ed. (London: A. Zwemmer, 1969), pp. 9–12.
11. Chesterton, *Defendant,* p. 158.
12. Ibid., p. 161.

13. Ibid., p. 158.
14. Ibid., pp. 158–9.
15. Alfred Hitchcock, "Why 'Thrillers' Thrive," *Picturegoer* (18 January 1936); reprinted in Sidney Gottlieb, ed., *Hitchcock on Hitchcock* (Berkeley: University of California Press, 1995), pp. 109–12, at p. 109.
16. Martin Green, *Dreams of Adventure, Deeds of Empire* (New York: Basic Books, 1979), pp. 1–36.
17. Northrop Frye, *Anatomy of Criticism: Four Essays* (Princeton: Princeton University Press, 1957; Princeton Paperback, 1971), pp. 139–40, 162.
18. Ibid., pp. 33–4.
19. Ibid., pp. 34, 36, 57–8, 186–7, 190, 193.
20. Ibid., p. 34.
21. Ibid., pp. 33–4, 41–2, 139–40.
22. Ibid., p. 46.
23. Ibid., p. 155.
24. Ibid., pp. 162, 177.
25. Ibid., p. 185.
26. John G. Cawelti, *Adventure, Mystery, and Romance: Formula Stories as Art and Popular Culture* (Chicago: University of Chicago Press, 1976), p. 141.
27. Ibid.
28. Ibid., pp. 141–2.
29. Edward W. Said, *Orientalism* (New York: Random House, 1978; paperback ed., New York: Vintage Books, 1979), pp. 49–73.
30. H. A. Guerber, *The Myths of Greece and Rome,* ed. and rev. Dorothy Margaret Stuart, 2d ed. (London: George G. Harrap, 1938), p. 150.
31. W. H. Matthews, *Mazes and Labyrinths: A General Account of Their History and Development* (London: Longmans, Green, 1922; reprint ed., New York: Dover Publications, 1970), p. 183.
32. Ibid., pp. 188–9.
33. Ibid., p. 185.
34. Jorge Luis Borges, *Ficciones,* ed. Anthony Kerrigan (New York: Grove Press, 1962), pp. 89–101, at p. 96.
35. André Bazin, *What Is Cinema?,* vol. 1, ed. and trans. Hugh Gray (Berkeley: University of California Press, 1967), pp. 102–7.
36. Pascal Bonitzer, "Partial Vision: Film and the Labyrinth," trans. Fabrice Ziolkowski, *Wide Angle 4,* no. 4 (1982): 56–63, at p. 63.
37. Ibid., p. 62.
38. François Truffaut, *Hitchcock* (New York: Simon & Schuster, 1967), p. 9.
39. Lars Ole Sauerberg, *Secret Agents in Fiction: Ian Fleming, John le Carré, and Len Deighton* (New York: St. Martin's Press, 1984), p. 83.
40. Ibid.
41. Ibid.
42. Noël Carroll, "Toward a Theory of Film Suspense," *Persistence of Vision 1,* no. 1 (Summer 1984): 65–89, at pp. 66–7.
43. Ibid., pp. 67, 81–2.
44. Ibid., pp. 71–2, 75–6, 83.
45. Ibid., pp. 82–3.
46. Ibid., p. 89.

PART II. HISTORICAL OVERVIEW

3. Formative Period

1. William Patrick Day, *In the Circles of Fear and Desire: A Study of Gothic Fantasy* (Chicago: University of Chicago Press, 1985), pp. 16–27.
2. Robert D. Hume, "Gothic versus Romantic: A Revaluation of the Gothic Novel," *PMLA 84*, no. 2 (March 1969): 282–90, at p. 284.
3. Frederick S. Frank, "The Gothic Romance 1762–1820," in *Horror Literature: A Core Collection and Reference Guide*, ed. Marshall B. Tymn (New York: R. R. Bowker, 1981), pp. 3–34, at p. 8.
4. Walter C. Phillips, *Dickens, Reade, and Collins: Sensation Novelists* (New York: Columbia University Press, 1919), p. 27.
5. Wilkie Collins, *The Woman in White* (London: Sampson Low, 1860; paperback ed., Toronto: Bantam Books, 1985), chap. 1, pt. iii, p. 14.
6. Norman Page, ed., *Wilkie Collins: The Critical Heritage* (London: Routledge & Kegan Paul, 1974), p. 118.
7. Collins, *Woman in White*, chap. 1, pt. iii, p. 17.
8. Phillips, *Dickens, Reade, and Collins*, pp. 85–9.
9. John G. Cawelti, *Adventure, Mystery, and Romance: Formula Stories as Art and Popular Culture* (Chicago: University of Chicago Press, 1976), pp. 94–105; Day, *Circles of Fear and Desire*, pp. 50–9.
10. Harlowe R. Hoyt, *Town Hall Tonight* (Englewood Cliffs, N.J.: Prentice–Hall, 1955), p. 97.
11. John F. Kasson, *Amusing the Million: Coney Island at the Turn of the Century* (New York: Hill & Wang, 1978), p. 100.
12. Tom Gunning, "The Cinema of Attraction: Early Film, Its Spectator and the Avant-Garde," *Wide Angle 8*, nos. 3–4 (1986), 63–70.
13. Stuart M. Kaminsky, *American Film Genres: Approaches to a Critical Theory of Popular Film* (Dayton, Ohio: Pflaum, 1974), p. 75.
14. Barry Salt, "The Early Development of Film Form," in *Film before Griffith*, ed. John L. Fell (Berkeley: University of California Press, 1983), pp. 284–98, at p. 287.
15. John Buchan, *The Thirty-Nine Steps* (London: Hodder & Stoughton, 1915; paperback ed., Ware, England: Wordsworth Classics, 1993), chap. 1, p. 2.
16. Kalton C. Lahue, *Continued Next Week: A History of the Motion Picture Serial* (Norman: University of Oklahoma Press, 1964), pp. 7–8; Terry Ramsaye, *A Million and One Nights: A History of the Motion Picture* (New York: Simon & Schuster, 1926; paperback ed., New York: Essandess, 1964), pp. 657–60; Raymond William Stedman, *The Serials: Suspense and Drama by Installment*, 2d ed. (Norman: University of Oklahoma Press, 1977), pp. 8–9.
17. Lahue, *Continued Next Week*, pp. 60, 126; Stedman, *Serials*, p. 51.
18. Peter Bogdanovich, *Who the Devil Made It* (New York: Alfred A. Knopf, 1997), p. 501.
19. Lahue, *Continued Next Week*, pp. 76, 91–3, 112.
20. Eric Rhode, *Tower of Babel: Speculations on the Cinema* (Philadelphia: Chilton Books, 1967), p. 93.
21. Richard Abel, *French Cinema: The First Wave, 1915–1929* (Princeton: Princeton University Press, 1984), p. 76.

22. Ibid., pp. 73–4; Richard Abel, "The Thrills of *Grande Peur:* Crime Series and Serials in the Belle Époque," *Velvet Light Trap,* no. 37 (Spring 1996): 3–9.

23. Siegfried Kracauer, *From Caligari to Hitler: A Psychological History of the German Film* (Princeton: Princeton University Press, 1947; Princeton Paperback, 1969), pp. 83–4.

24. William Cahn, *Harold Lloyd's World of Comedy* (New York: Duell, Sloan & Pearce, 1964), p. 99.

25. James Agee, "Comedy's Greatest Era," *Life 27,* no. 10 (5 September 1949): 70–88; reprinted in *Agee on Film: Reviews and Comments* (New York: McDowell, 1958; paperback ed., Boston: Beacon Press, 1964), pp. 1–19, at p. 11.

26. Harold Lloyd, *An American Comedy: Acted by Harold Lloyd, Directed by Wesley W. Stout* (New York: Longmans, Green, 1928; reprint ed., New York: Dover Publications, 1971), p. 84.

27. Walter Kerr, *The Silent Clowns* (New York: Alfred Knopf, 1979), pp. 197–8; Gerald Mast, *The Comic Mind: Comedy and the Movies,* 2d ed. (Chicago: University of Chicago Press, 1979), p. 157; Richard Schickel, *Harold Lloyd: The Shape of Laughter* (Boston: New York Graphic Society, 1974), p. 71.

28. *Film Daily* review of *Safety Last* (8 April 1923), excerpted in *Harold Lloyd: The King of Daredevil Comedy,* ed. Adam Reilly (New York: Macmillan, 1977), p. 60; Robert Sherwood, "Silent Drama," *Life 81* (26 April 1923), excerpted in Donald W. McCaffrey, *Three Classic Silent Screen Comedies Starring Harold Lloyd* (Rutherford, N.J.: Associated University Presses, 1976), p. 178.

29. As detailed in Kevin Brownlow and David Gill's documentary film *Harold Lloyd: The Third Genius* (1989).

30. Raymond Durgnat, *The Crazy Mirror: Hollywood Comedy and the American Image* (Plymouth, England: Latimer Trend, 1969; paperback ed., New York: Delta Books, 1970), p. 87; William K. Everson, "Harold Lloyd: The Climb to Success," in Reilly, ed., *Harold Lloyd,* pp. 168–75, at p. 169; Mast, *Comic Mind,* p. 180; *New York Times* review of *Grandma's Boy* (4 September 1922), excerpted in Reilly, ed., *Harold Lloyd,* p. 49.

31. Everson, "Harold Lloyd," in Reilly, ed., *Harold Lloyd,* p. 174; Andrew Sarris, "Harold Lloyd: A Rediscovery," in Reilly, ed., *Harold Lloyd,* pp. 159–67, at p. 165.

32. Robert Warshow, "The Gangster as Tragic Hero," *Partisan Review* (February 1948), reprinted in Warshow, *The Immediate Experience* (Garden City, N.Y.: Doubleday, 1962; paperback ed., New York: Atheneum, 1979), pp. 127–33, at p. 131.

4. Classical Period

1. Arthur A. Ekirch Jr., *Ideologies and Utopias: The Impact of the New Deal on American Thought* (Chicago: Quadrangle Books, 1969), pp. 208, 216; Frederick Lewis Allen, *Since Yesterday: The Nineteen-Thirties in America* (New York: Harper & Row, 1940; paperback ed., New York: Bantam Books, 1965), p. 257.

2. Andrew Sarris, *The American Cinema: Directors and Directions 1929–1968* (New York: E. P. Dutton, 1968), p. 64.
3. Michael Denning, *Cover Stories: Narrative and Ideology in the British Spy Thriller* (London: Routledge & Kegan Paul, 1987), pp. 100–7.
4. William K. Everson, *The Detective in Film* (Secaucus, N.J.: Citadel Press, 1972), pp. 38–9; Nick Roddick, *A New Deal in Entertainment: Warner Brothers in the 1930s* (London: BFI, 1983), p. 282.
5. Raymond Chandler, *The Big Sleep* (New York: Knopf, 1939; paperback ed., New York: Vintage Books, 1976), chap. 1, p. 1; Chandler, *The High Window* (New York: Knopf, 1942; paperback ed., New York: Ballantine Books, 1971), chap. 28, p. 161; Chandler, *The Little Sister* (Boston: Houghton Mifflin, 1949; paperback ed., New York: Ballantine Books, 1971), chap. 27, p. 214.
6. David Caute, *The Great Fear: The Anti-Communist Purge under Truman and Eisenhower* (New York: Simon & Schuster, 1978), p. 43.
7. Daniel Bell, "Crime as an American Way of Life," *Antioch Review 13* (June 1953), reprinted in *The End of Ideology: On the Exhaustion of Political Ideas in the Fifties*, rev. ed. (New York: Free Press, 1965), pp. 127–50, at pp. 138–41; Lawrence M. Friedman, *Crime and Punishment in American History* (New York: Basic Books, 1993), pp. 272–3; David L. Herbert and Howard Tritt, *Corporations of Corruption: A Systematic Study of Organized Crime* (Springfield, Ill.: Charles C. Thomas, 1984), p. 6; Geoffrey Perrett, *A Dream of Greatness: The American People 1945–1963* (New York: Coward, McCann & Geoghegan, 1979), pp. 245–6, 341–2; Dwight C. Smith Jr., *The Mafia Mystique* (New York: Basic Books, 1975), pp. 149–51.
8. Vivian Sobchack, *Screening Space: The American Science Fiction Film*, 2d ed. (New York: Ungar, 1987), pp. 110–20; Darko Suvin, *Metamorphoses of Science Fiction: On the Poetics and History of a Literary Genre* (New Haven: Yale University Press, 1979), pp. 3–15, 63–84.
9. Barry Keith Grant, "Rich and Strange: The Yuppie Horror Film," *Journal of Film and Video 48*, nos. 1–2 (Spring–Summer 1996): 4–16, at pp. 8–9, 13.
10. Robert E. Kapsis, *Hitchcock: The Making of a Reputation* (Chicago: University of Chicago Press, 1992), p. 58.

5. Modern Period

1. "The Wages of Fear," *Time* (21 February 1955): 84.
2. John Brosnan, *James Bond in the Cinema*, 2d ed. (San Diego: A. S. Barnes, 1981), pp. 11–12.
3. Tony Bennett and Janet Woollacott, *Bond and Beyond: The Political Career of a Popular Hero* (New York: Methuen, 1987), p. 37.
4. Michael Denning, *Cover Stories: Narrative and Ideology in the British Spy Thriller* (London: Routledge & Kegan Paul, 1987), p. 35.
5. Nick Roddick, "Only the Stars Survive: Disaster Movies in the Seventies," in *Performance and Politics in Popular Drama*, eds. David Bradby, Louis James, and Benjamin Sharratt (Cambridge: Cambridge University Press, 1980), pp. 243–69, at pp. 250, 254.

6. Dennis Giles, "Conditions of Pleasure in Horror Cinema," in *Planks of Reason: Essays on the Horror Film,* ed. Barry Keith Grant (Metuchen, N.J.: Scarecrow Press, 1984), pp. 38–52, at p. 47.

7. Roger Ebert, "Why Movie Audiences Aren't Safe Anymore," *American Film 6,* no. 5 (March 1981): 54–6, at pp. 55–6.

8. Foster Hirsch, *The Dark Side of the Screen: Film Noir* (New York: A. S. Barnes, 1981), p. 57; Robin Wood, *Howard Hawks* (Garden City, N.Y.: Doubleday, 1968), p. 169.

9. Carol J. Clover, *Men, Women, and Chain Saws: Gender in the Modern Horror Film* (Princeton: Princeton University Press, 1992), pp. 45–6; Vera Dika, "The Stalker Film, 1978–81," in *American Horrors: Essays on the Modern American Horror Film,* ed. Gregory A. Waller (Urbana: University of Illinois Press, 1987), pp. 86–101, at pp. 88–9.

10. Todd Erickson, "Kill Me Again: Movement Becomes Genre," in *Film Noir Reader,* eds. Alain Silver and James Ursini (New York: Limelight Editions, 1996), pp. 306–29, at pp. 312–13.

PART III. FILM ANALYSES

6. The Detective Thriller

1. Raymond Chandler, "The Simple Art of Murder," *Atlantic Monthly* (December 1944), reprinted in Chandler, *The Simple Art of Murder* (Boston: Houghton Mifflin, 1950; paperback ed., New York: Pocket Books, 1952), pp. 177–94, at pp. 188–92.

2. Peter Bogdanovich, *Who the Devil Made It* (New York: Alfred A. Knopf, 1997), p. 497; Alfred Hitchcock, "Let 'Em Play God," *Hollywood Reporter 100,* no. 47 (11 October 1948), reprinted in *Hitchcock on Hitchcock: Selected Writings and Interviews,* ed. Sidney Gottlieb (Berkeley: University of California Press, 1995), pp. 113–15, at pp. 113–14; François Truffaut, *Hitchcock* (New York: Simon & Schuster, 1967), pp. 51–2.

3. S. S. Van Dine, *The Kennel Murder Case* (New York: Charles Scribner's Sons, 1933; reprint ed., Boston: Gregg Press, 1980), p. 22.

4. John G. Cawelti, *Adventure, Mystery, and Romance: Formula Stories as Art and Popular Culture* (Chicago: University of Chicago Press, 1976), pp. 81, 91–2.

5. Joseph Wood Krutch, "'Only a Detective Story,'" *The Nation* (25 November 1944), reprinted in *Detective Fiction,* ed. Robin W. Winks, rev. ed. (Englewood Cliffs, N.J.: Prentice–Hall, 1988), pp. 41–6, at p. 43.

6. Dorothy L. Sayers, "Introduction" to *Great Short Stories of Detection, Mystery, and Horror,* ed. Sayers (London: Gollancz, 1928); excerpted as "The Omnibus of Crime" in Winks, ed., *Detective Fiction,* pp. 53–83, at p. 77.

7. Cawelti, *Adventure, Mystery, and Romance,* pp. 81, 92–3.

8. Walter Benjamin, *Reflections: Essays, Aphorisms, Autobiographical Writings,* ed. Peter Demetz (New York: Schocken Books, 1978), pp. 64–5.

9. Cawelti, *Adventure, Mystery, and Romance,* pp. 96–7.

10. Ogden Nash, "Literary Reflection," *Verses from 1929 On* (Boston: Little Brown, 1952), p. 64.

11. William F. Nolan, *The Black Mask Boys* (New York: William Morrow, 1985), pp. 20–6.
12. Cawelti, *Adventure, Mystery, and Romance*, pp. 139–40.
13. Todd McCarthy, *Howard Hawks: The Grey Fox of Hollywood* (New York: Grove Press, 1997), pp. 393–4.
14. Tzvetan Todorov, "The Typology of Detective Fiction," in *The Poetics of Prose*, trans. Richard Howard (Ithaca, N.Y.: Cornell University Press, 1977), pp. 42–52, at pp. 44–5.
15. Ibid., p. 44.
16. Ibid., p. 47.
17. Cawelti, *Adventure, Mystery, and Romance*, p. 153.
18. S. S. Van Dine, "I Used to Be a Highbrow but Look at Me Now," *American Magazine 106* (September 1928); reprinted as "Twenty Rules for Writing Detective Stories" in *The Art of the Mystery Story*, ed. Howard Haycraft (New York: Simon & Schuster, 1946), pp. 189–93, at p. 189.
19. Sayers, "Introduction," p. 79.
20. Cawelti, *Adventure, Mystery, and Romance*, p. 151.
21. Ibid., p. 99; George Grella, "The Formal Detective Novel," in Winks, ed., *Detective Fiction*, pp. 84–102, at pp. 84, 94, 101.
22. Chandler, "Simple Art of Murder," pp. 181–4.
23. Cawelti, *Adventure, Mystery, and Romance*, pp. 146–8.
24. Frank MacShane, ed., *Selected Letters of Raymond Chandler* (New York: Columbia University Press, 1981), pp. 155–6; Joseph McBride, *Hawks on Hawks* (Berkeley: University of California Press, 1982), p. 104.
25. Raymond Chandler, *The Big Sleep* (New York: Knopf, 1939; paperback ed., New York: Vintage Books, 1976), chap. 9, p. 43.
26. McBride, *Hawks on Hawks*, p. 104.
27. Van Dine, "I Used to Be a Highbrow," pp. 191–2.
28. Cawelti, *Adventure, Mystery, and Romance*, p. 154.

7. The Psychological Crime Thriller

1. Julian Symons, *Bloody Murder: From the Detective Story to the Crime Novel: A History*, rev. ed. (New York: Viking, 1985), pp. 162–5.
2. Frank MacShane, ed., *Selected Letters of Raymond Chandler* (New York: Columbia University Press, 1981), p. 17.
3. G. K. Chesterton, "On Detective Novels," in *Generally Speaking* (London: Methuen, 1928); reprinted in *The Man Who Was Chesterton: The Best Essays, Stories, Poems and Other Writings of G. K. Chesterton*, ed. Raymond T. Bond (New York: Dodd, Mead, 1937), pp. 79–83, at p. 82.
4. Symons, *Bloody Murder*, p. 163.
5. Ibid.
6. Ibid., p. 162.
7. Ibid.
8. Ibid., p. 166.
9. Donald Spoto, *The Dark Side of Genius: The Life of Alfred Hitchcock* (Boston: Little, Brown, 1983), pp. 321–2.

10. François Truffaut, *Hitchcock* (New York: Simon & Schuster, 1967), p. 146.
11. Morris Dickstein, "Beyond Good and Evil: The Morality of Thrillers," *American Film 6*, no. 9 (July–August 1981): 49–52, 67–9, at p. 52.
12. Spoto, *Dark Side of Genius,* pp. 67–8.
13. Gene D. Phillips, *Alfred Hitchcock* (Boston: Twayne Publishers, 1984), p. 125; Spoto, *Dark Side of Genius,* p. 331.
14. Noël Carroll, "Toward a Theory of Film Suspense," *Persistence of Vision 1,* no. 1 (Summer 1984): 65–89, at pp. 68–9.
15. Truffaut, *Hitchcock,* pp. 144–5.
16. Carroll, "Toward a Theory of Film Suspense," p. 71.
17. Truffaut, *Hitchcock,* p. 50.
18. Ibid., p. 145.
19. Carroll, "Toward a Theory of Film Suspense," pp. 76–7.
20. Truffaut, *Hitchcock,* p. 52.
21. Carroll, "Toward a Theory of Film Suspense," pp. 87–8.
22. Truffaut, *Hitchcock,* p. 51.
23. Ibid., p. 144.

8. The Spy Thriller

1. Ralph Harper, *The World of the Thriller* (Cleveland: Press of Case Western Reserve University, 1969), p. 46.
2. John G. Cawelti and Bruce A. Rosenberg, *The Spy Story* (Chicago: University of Chicago Press, 1987), pp. 153–4, 3, 11.
3. Michael Denning, *Cover Stories: Narrative and Ideology in the British Spy Thriller* (London: Routledge & Kegan Paul, 1987), p. 14.
4. LeRoy L. Panek, *The Special Branch: The British Spy Novel, 1890–1980* (Bowling Green, Ohio: Bowling Green University Popular Press, 1981), p. 42.
5. Cawelti and Rosenberg, *Spy Story,* p. 47.
6. Clayton R. Koppes and Gregory D. Black, *Hollywood Goes to War* (Berkeley: University of California Press, 1987), p. 35.
7. Morris Dickstein, "Beyond Good and Evil: The Morality of Thrillers," *American Film 6,* no. 9 (July–August 1981): 49–52, 67–9, at p. 51.

9. The Police Thriller

1. Stephen Knight, *Form and Ideology in Crime Fiction* (Bloomington: Indiana University Press, 1980), pp. 168–9.
2. Hillary Waugh, "The Police Procedural," in *The Mystery Story,* ed. John Ball (San Diego: University Extension of the University of California, 1976), pp. 163–87, at p. 167.
3. Thomas D. Clagett, *William Friedkin: Films of Aberration, Obsession and Reality* (Jefferson, N.C.: McFarland, 1990), p. 87; Nat Segaloff, *Hurricane Billy: The Stormy Life and Films of William Friedkin* (New York: William Morrow, 1990), p. 104.
4. Clagett, *William Friedkin,* p. 87.
5. Ibid., p. 95.

6. Ibid.
7. Ibid., p. 91.
8. William Park, "The Police State," *Journal of Popular Film and Television 6,* no. 3 (Fall 1978): 229–37, at p. 237.

10. Conclusion

1. Charles Derry, *The Suspense Thriller: Films in the Shadow of Alfred Hitchcock* (Jefferson, N.C.: McFarland, 1988), p. 63.
2. Alan Williams, "Is a Radical Genre Criticism Possible?" *Quarterly Review of Film Studies 9,* no. 2 (Spring 1984): 121–5, at p. 121.
3. Todd Erickson, "Kill Me Again: Movement Becomes Genre," in *Film Noir Reader,* eds. Alain Silver and James Ursini (New York: Limelight Editions, 1996), pp. 306–29, at p. 308.
4. Janet Staiger, "Hybrid or Inbred: The Purity Hypothesis and Hollywood Genre History," *Film Criticism 22,* no. 1 (Fall 1997): 5–20, at pp. 6, 11.
5. Gregg Kilday, "For Richer or Poorer: 1997 Box Office Report," *Entertainment Weekly* (30 January 1998): 34–7, at p. 36.

Selected Bibliography

For an introductory overview of the subject, the following compact bookshelf is recommended: Cawelti, *Adventure, Mystery, and Romance;* Denning, *Cover Stories;* Day, *In the Circles of Fear and Desire;* Derry, *The Suspense Thriller;* Grant, *Planks of Reason;* Haycraft, *The Art of the Mystery Story;* Shadoian, *Dreams and Dead Ends;* Silver and Ursini, *Film Noir Reader;* Truffaut, *Hitchcock;* Waller, *American Horrors.*

Abel, Richard. *French Cinema: The First Wave, 1915–1929.* Princeton: Princeton University Press, 1984.
  "The Thrills of *Grande Peur:* Crime Series and Serials in the Belle Époque." *Velvet Light Trap,* no. 37 (Spring 1996): 3–9.
Agee, James. "Comedy's Greatest Era." *Life 27,* no. 10 (5 September 1949): 70–88. Reprinted in Agee, *Agee on Film: Reviews and Comments.* New York: McDowell, 1958; paperback ed., Boston: Beacon Press, 1964, pp. 1–19.
Altman, Rick. "A Semantic/Syntactic Approach to Film Genre." In Grant, ed., *Film Genre Reader II,* pp. 26–40.
Balint, Michael. *Thrills and Regressions.* London: Hogarth Press, 1959.
Ball, John, ed. *The Mystery Story.* San Diego: University Extension of the University of California, 1976.
Bazin, André. *What Is Cinema?,* vol. 1. Ed. and trans. Hugh Gray. Berkeley: University of California Press, 1967.
Benjamin, Walter. *Reflections: Essays, Aphorisms, Autobiographical Writings.* Ed. Peter Demetz. New York: Schocken Books, 1978.
Bennett, Tony, and Janet Woollacott. *Bond and Beyond: The Political Career of a Popular Hero.* New York: Methuen, 1987.
Binyon, T. J. *'Murder Will Out': The Detective in Fiction.* Oxford: Oxford University Press, 1989.
Bogdanovich, Peter. *Who the Devil Made It.* New York: Alfred A. Knopf, 1997.
Bonitzer, Pascal. "Partial Vision: Film and the Labyrinth." Trans. Fabrice Ziolkowski. *Wide Angle 4,* no. 4 (1982): 56–63.
Borde, Raymond, and Étienne Chaumeton. *Panorama du film noir américain.* Paris: Les Éditions de Minuit, 1955. Excerpted as "The Sources of Film Noir" in *Film Reader,* no. 3 (February 1978): 58–66. Excerpted as "Towards a Definition of Film Noir" in Silver and Ursini, eds., *Film Noir Reader,* pp. 16–25.
Borges, Jorge Luis. *Ficciones.* Ed. Anthony Kerrigan. New York: Grove Press, 1962.
Brosnan, John. *James Bond in the Cinema.* 2d ed. San Diego: A. S. Barnes, 1981.

Buchan, John. *The Thirty-Nine Steps.* London: Hodder & Stoughton, 1915; paperback ed., Ware, England: Wordsworth Classics, 1993.

Cahn, William. *Harold Lloyd's World of Comedy.* New York: Duell, Sloan & Pearce, 1964.

Cameron, Ian, ed. *The Book of Film Noir.* New York: Continuum, 1992.

Carroll, Noël. *The Philosophy of Horror; or, Paradoxes of the Heart.* New York: Routledge, 1990.

"Toward a Theory of Film Suspense." *Persistence of Vision 1,* no. 1 (Summer 1984): 65–89.

Cawelti, John G. *Adventure, Mystery, and Romance: Formula Stories as Art and Popular Culture.* Chicago: University of Chicago Press, 1976.

Cawelti, John G., and Bruce A. Rosenberg. *The Spy Story.* Chicago: University of Chicago Press, 1987.

Chandler, Raymond. *The Big Sleep.* New York: Knopf, 1939; paperback ed., New York: Vintage Books, 1976.

"The Simple Art of Murder." *Atlantic Monthly* (December 1944). Reprinted in Chandler, *The Simple Art of Murder.* Boston: Houghton Mifflin, 1950; paperback ed., New York: Pocket Books, 1952, pp. 177–94. Reprinted in Haycraft, ed., *Art of the Mystery Story,* pp. 222–37.

Chesterton, G. K. "A Defence of Detective Stories." In Chesterton, *The Defendant.* London: R. B. Johnson, 1901, pp. 157–62. Reprinted in Haycraft, ed., *Art of the Mystery Story,* pp. 3–6.

"On Detective Novels." In Chesterton, *Generally Speaking.* London: Methuen, 1928. Reprinted in Chesterton, *The Man Who Was Chesterton: The Best Essays, Stories, Poems and Other Writings of G. K. Chesterton.* Ed. Raymond T. Bond. New York: Dodd, Mead, 1937, pp. 79–83.

Clagett, Thomas D. *William Friedkin: Films of Aberration, Obsession and Reality.* Jefferson, N.C.: McFarland, 1990.

Clarens, Carlos. *Crime Movies: An Illustrated History.* New York: W. W. Norton, 1980.

An Illustrated History of the Horror Film. New York: Capricorn Books, 1968.

Clover, Carol J. *Men, Women, and Chain Saws: Gender in the Modern Horror Film.* Princeton: Princeton University Press, 1992.

Collins, Wilkie. *The Woman in White.* London: Sampson Low, 1860; paperback ed., Toronto: Bantam Books, 1985.

Davis, Brian. *The Thriller: The Suspense Film from 1946.* London: Studio Vista, 1973.

Day, William Patrick. *In the Circles of Fear and Desire: A Study of Gothic Fantasy.* Chicago: University of Chicago Press, 1985.

Denning, Michael. *Cover Stories: Narrative and Ideology in the British Spy Thriller.* London: Routledge & Kegan Paul, 1987.

Derry, Charles. *Dark Dreams: A Psychological History of the Modern Horror Film.* Cranbury, N.J.: A. S. Barnes, 1977.

The Suspense Thriller: Films in the Shadow of Alfred Hitchcock. Jefferson, N.C.: McFarland, 1988.

Dickstein, Morris. "Beyond Good and Evil: The Morality of Thrillers." *American Film 6,* no. 9 (July–August 1981): 49–52, 67–9.

Dika, Vera. "The Stalker Film, 1978–81." In Waller, ed., *American Horrors,* pp. 86–101.

Dove, George N. *The Police Procedural.* Bowling Green, Ohio: Bowling Green University Popular Press, 1982.

Dubrow, Heather. *Genre.* The Critical Idiom, no. 42. London: Methuen, 1982.

Durgnat, Raymond. *The Crazy Mirror: Hollywood Comedy and the American Image.* Plymouth, England: Latimer Trend, 1969; paperback ed., New York: Delta Books, 1970.

Ebert, Roger. "Why Movie Audiences Aren't Safe Anymore." *American Film 6,* no. 5 (March 1981): 54–6.

Eisner, Lotte. *Fritz Lang.* London: Secker & Warburg, 1976; paperback ed., New York: Da Capo, 1986.

Erickson, Todd. "Kill Me Again: Movement Becomes Genre." In Silver and Ursini, eds., *Film Noir Reader,* pp. 306–29.

Everson, William K. *The Detective in Film.* Secaucus, N.J.: Citadel Press, 1972. "Harold Lloyd: The Climb to Success." In Reilly, ed., *Harold Lloyd,* pp. 168–75.

Frank, Frederick S. "The Gothic Romance 1762–1820." In *Horror Literature: A Core Collection and Reference Guide.* Ed. Marshall B. Tymn. New York: R. R. Bowker, 1981, pp. 3–34.

Friedkin, William. "The Chase." In *Directors in Action.* Ed. Bob Thomas. Indianapolis: Bobbs Merrill, 1973, pp. 175–87.

Frye, Northrop. *Anatomy of Criticism: Four Essays.* Princeton: Princeton University Press, 1957; Princeton Paperback, 1971.

Giles, Dennis. "Conditions of Pleasure in Horror Cinema." In Grant, ed., *Planks of Reason,* pp. 38–52.

Gottlieb, Sidney, ed. *Hitchcock on Hitchcock: Selected Writings and Interviews.* Berkeley: University of California Press, 1995.

Grant, Barry Keith, "Rich and Strange: The Yuppie Horror Film," *Journal of Film and Video 48,* nos. 1–2 (Spring–Summer 1996): 4–16.

    ed. *The Dread of Difference: Gender and the Horror Film.* Austin: University of Texas Press, 1996.

    ed. *Film Genre: Theory and Criticism.* Metuchen, N.J.: Scarecrow Press, 1977.

    ed. *Film Genre Reader.* Austin: University of Texas Press, 1986.

    ed. *Film Genre Reader II.* Austin: University of Texas Press, 1995.

    ed. *Planks of Reason: Essays on the Horror Film.* Metuchen, N.J.: Scarecrow Press, 1984.

Green, Martin. *Dreams of Adventure, Deeds of Empire.* New York: Basic Books, 1979.

Grella, George. "Murder and Manners: The Formal Detective Novel." In *Dimensions of Detective Fiction.* Eds. Larry Landrum, Pat Browne, and Ray B. Browne. Bowling Green, Ohio: Bowling Green University Popular Press, 1976, pp. 37–57. Reprinted as "The Formal Detective Novel," in Winks, ed., *Detective Fiction,* pp. 84–102.

    "Murder and the Mean Streets: The Hard-Boiled Detective Novel." In *Detective Fiction: Crime and Compromise.* Eds. Dick Allen and David Chacko. New York: Harcourt Brace Jovanovich, 1974, pp. 411–28. Reprinted as "The Hard-Boiled Detective Novel," in Winks, ed., *Detective Fiction,* pp. 103–20.

Guerber, H. A. *The Myths of Greece and Rome.* Ed. and rev. Dorothy Margaret Stuart. 2d ed. London: George G. Harrap, 1938.

Gunning, Tom. "The Cinema of Attraction: Early Film, Its Spectator and the Avant-Garde." *Wide Angle 8,* nos. 3–4 (1986): 63–70.

Hammond, Lawrence. *Thriller Movies: Classic Films of Suspense and Mystery.* London: Octopus Books, 1974.

Harper, Ralph. *The World of the Thriller.* Cleveland: Press of Case Western Reserve University, 1969.

Haycraft, Howard. *Murder for Pleasure: The Life and Times of the Detective Story.* Rev. ed. New York: Biblo and Tannen, 1968.

—— ed. *The Art of the Mystery Story: A Collection of Critical Essays.* New York: Simon & Schuster, 1946.

Highsmith, Patricia. *Strangers on a Train.* New York: Harper, 1950; paperback ed., London: Penguin Books, 1974.

Hirsch, Foster. *The Dark Side of the Screen: Film Noir.* New York: A. S. Barnes, 1981.

Household, Geoffrey. *Rogue Male.* London: Chatto & Windus, 1939; paperback ed., New York: Pyramid Books, 1963.

Hoyt, Harlowe R. *Town Hall Tonight.* Englewood Cliffs, N.J.: Prentice–Hall, 1955.

Hume, Robert D. "Gothic versus Romantic: A Revaluation of the Gothic Novel." *PMLA 84,* no. 2 (March 1969): 282–90.

Jameson, Fredric. *The Political Unconscious: Narrative as a Socially Symbolic Act.* Ithaca, N.Y.: Cornell University Press, 1981.

Jensen, Paul M. *The Cinema of Fritz Lang.* New York: A. S. Barnes, 1969.

Jowett, Garth. *Film: The Democratic Art.* Boston: Little, Brown, 1976.

Kaminsky, Stuart M. *American Film Genres: Approaches to a Critical Theory of Popular Film.* Dayton, Ohio: Pflaum, 1974.

Kapsis, Robert E. *Hitchcock: The Making of a Reputation.* Chicago: University of Chicago Press, 1992.

Kasson, John F. *Amusing the Million: Coney Island at the Turn of the Century.* New York: Hill & Wang, 1978.

Kayman, Martin A. *From Bow Street to Baker Street: Mystery, Detection and Narrative.* New York: St. Martin's Press, 1992.

Kendrick, Walter. *The Thrill of Fear: 250 Years of Scary Entertainment.* New York: Grove Press, 1991.

Kerr, Walter. *The Silent Clowns.* New York: Alfred Knopf, 1979.

Knight, Stephen. *Form and Ideology in Crime Fiction.* Bloomington: Indiana University Press, 1980.

Koppes, Clayton R., and Gregory D. Black. *Hollywood Goes to War.* Berkeley: University of California Press, 1987.

Kracauer, Siegfried. *From Caligari to Hitler: A Psychological History of the German Film.* Princeton: Princeton University Press, 1947; Princeton Paperback, 1969.

Krutch, Joseph Wood. "'Only a Detective Story.'" *The Nation* (25 November 1944). Reprinted in Haycraft, ed., *Art of the Mystery Story,* pp. 178–85; also reprinted in Winks, ed., *Detective Fiction,* pp. 41–6.

Krutnik, Frank. *In A Lonely Street: Film Noir, Genre, Masculinity.* London: Routledge, 1991.

Lahue, Kalton C. *Bound and Gagged: The Story of the Silent Serials.* New York: A. S. Barnes, 1968.

Continued Next Week: A History of the Motion Picture Serial. Norman: University of Oklahoma Press, 1964.

Lambert, Gavin. *The Dangerous Edge.* New York: Viking, 1976.

Lloyd, Harold. *An American Comedy: Acted by Harold Lloyd, Directed by Wesley W. Stout.* New York: Longmans, Green, 1928; reprint ed., New York: Dover Publications, 1971.

Löker, Altan. *Film and Suspense.* Istanbul: Altan Löker, 1976.

Loughery, John. *Alias S. S. Van Dine: The Man Who Created Philo Vance.* New York: Scribner's, 1992.

Luhr, William. *Raymond Chandler and Film.* New York: Frederick Ungar, 1982.

McBride, Joseph. *Hawks on Hawks.* Berkeley: University of California Press, 1982.

ed. *Focus on Howard Hawks.* Englewood Cliffs, N.J.: Prentice–Hall, 1972.

McCaffrey, Donald W. *Three Classic Silent Screen Comedies Starring Harold Lloyd.* Rutherford, N.J.: Associated University Presses, 1976.

McCarthy, Todd. *Howard Hawks: The Grey Fox of Hollywood.* New York: Grove Press, 1997.

McCarty, John. *Splatter Movies: Breaking the Last Taboo of the Screen.* New York: St. Martin's Press, 1984.

Thrillers: Seven Decades of Classic Film Suspense. New York: Citadel Press, 1992.

McGilligan, Patrick. *Fritz Lang: The Nature of the Beast.* New York: St. Martin's Press, 1997.

MacShane, Frank, ed. *Selected Letters of Raymond Chandler.* New York: Columbia University Press, 1981.

Mast, Gerald. *The Comic Mind: Comedy and the Movies.* 2d ed. Chicago: University of Chicago Press, 1979.

Howard Hawks: Storyteller. Oxford: Oxford University Press, 1982.

Matthews, W. H. *Mazes and Labyrinths: A General Account of Their History and Development.* London: Longmans, Green, 1922; reprint ed., New York: Dover Publications, 1970.

Moore, Robin. *The French Connection: The World's Most Crucial Narcotics Investigation.* Boston: Little, Brown, 1969.

Murphy, Robert. *Sixties British Cinema.* London: BFI Publishing, 1992.

Newman, Kim. *Nightmare Movies: A Critical Guide to Contemporary Horror Films.* New York: Harmony Books, 1988.

Nolan, William F. *The Black Mask Boys.* New York: William Morrow, 1985.

Ott, Frederick W. *The Films of Fritz Lang.* Secaucus, N.J.: Citadel Press, 1979.

Page, Norman, ed. *Wilkie Collins: The Critical Heritage.* London: Routledge & Kegan Paul, 1974.

Palmer, Jerry. *Thrillers: Genesis and Structure of a Popular Genre.* New York: St. Martin's Press, 1979.

Panek, LeRoy Lad. *An Introduction to the Detective Story.* Bowling Green, Ohio: Bowling Green University Popular Press, 1987.

The Special Branch: The British Spy Novel, 1890–1980. Bowling Green, Ohio: Bowling Green University Popular Press, 1981.

Parish, James Robert, and George H. Hill. *Black Action Films.* Jefferson, N.C.: McFarland, 1989.

Park, William. "The Police State." *Journal of Popular Film and Television 6,* no. 3 (Fall 1978): 229–37.

Paul, William. *Laughing Screaming: Modern Hollywood Horror and Comedy.* New York: Columbia University Press, 1994.

Pendo, Stephen. *Raymond Chandler on Screen: His Novels into Film.* Metuchen, N.J.: Scarecrow Press, 1976.

Phillips, Gene D. *Alfred Hitchcock.* Boston: Twayne Publishers, 1984.

Phillips, Walter C. *Dickens, Reade, and Collins: Sensation Novelists.* New York: Columbia University Press, 1919.

Place, J. A., and L. S. Peterson. "Some Visual Motifs of Film Noir." *Film Comment 10,* no. 1 (January–February 1974): 30–5. Reprinted in Silver and Ursini, eds., *Film Noir Reader,* pp. 64–75.

Propp, Vladimir. *Morphology of the Folktale.* 2d ed. Texas: University of Texas Press, 1968.

Punter, David. *The Literature of Terror: A History of Gothic Fictions from 1765 to the Present Day.* London: Longman, 1980.

Ramsaye, Terry. *A Million and One Nights: A History of the Motion Picture.* New York: Simon & Schuster, 1926; paperback ed., New York: Essandess, 1964.

Reilly, Adam, ed. *Harold Lloyd: The King of Daredevil Comedy.* New York: Macmillan, 1977.

Rhode, Eric. *Tower of Babel: Speculations on the Cinema.* Philadelphia: Chilton Books, 1967.

Roddick, Nick. *A New Deal in Entertainment: Warner Brothers in the 1930s.* London: BFI, 1983.

"Only the Stars Survive: Disaster Movies in the Seventies." In *Performance and Politics in Popular Drama.* Eds. David Bradby, Louis James, and Benjamin Sharratt. Cambridge: Cambridge University Press, 1980, pp. 243–69.

Rohmer, Eric, and Claude Chabrol. *Hitchcock: The First Forty-four Films.* Trans. Stanley Hochman. New York: Frederick Ungar, 1979.

Said, Edward W. *Orientalism.* New York: Random House, 1978; paperback ed., New York: Vintage Books, 1979.

Salt, Barry. "The Early Development of Film Form." In *Film before Griffith.* Ed. John L. Fell. Berkeley: University of California Press, 1983, pp. 284–98.

Sarris, Andrew. *The American Cinema: Directors and Directions 1929–1968.* New York: E. P. Dutton, 1968.

"Harold Lloyd: A Rediscovery." In Reilly, ed., *Harold Lloyd,* pp. 159–67.

Sauerberg, Lars Ole. *Secret Agents in Fiction: Ian Fleming, John le Carré, and Len Deighton.* New York: St. Martin's Press, 1984.

Sayers, Dorothy L. "Introduction" to *Great Short Stories of Detection, Mystery, and Horror.* Ed. Dorothy L. Sayers. London: Gollancz, 1928. Reprinted as "The Omnibus of Crime" in Haycraft, ed., *Art of the Mystery Story,* pp. 71–109. Excerpted as "The Omnibus of Crime" in Winks, ed., *Detective Fiction,* pp. 53–83.

Schatz, Thomas. *Hollywood Genres: Formulas, Filmmaking, and the Studio System.* New York: Random House, 1981.

Schickel, Richard. *Harold Lloyd: The Shape of Laughter.* Boston: New York Graphic Society, 1974.

Schrader, Paul. "Notes on Film Noir." *Film Comment 8,* no. 1 (Spring 1972): 8–13. Reprinted in Grant, ed., *Film Genre Reader II,* pp. 213–26; also reprinted in Silver and Ursini, eds., *Film Noir Reader,* pp. 52–63.

Segaloff, Nat. *Hurricane Billy: The Stormy Life and Films of William Friedkin.* New York: William Morrow, 1990.

Shadoian, Jack. *Dreams and Dead Ends: The American Gangster/Crime Film.* Cambridge: MIT Press, 1977.

Silver, Alain, and James Ursini, eds. *Film Noir Reader.* New York: Limelight Editions, 1996.

Silver, Alain, and Elizabeth Ward, eds. *Film Noir: An Encyclopedic Reference to the American Style.* 3d ed. Woodstock, N.Y.: Overlook Press, 1992.

Skal, David J. *The Monster Show: A Cultural History of Horror.* New York: W. W. Norton, 1993; paperback ed., New York: Penguin Books, 1994.

Sobchack, Vivian. *Screening Space: The American Science Fiction Film.* 2d ed. New York: Ungar, 1987.

Spoto, Donald. *The Art of Alfred Hitchcock: Fifty Years of His Motion Pictures.* New York: Hopkinson and Blake, 1976.

The Dark Side of Genius: The Life of Alfred Hitchcock. Boston: Little, Brown, 1983.

Staiger, Janet. "Hybrid or Inbred: The Purity Hypothesis and Hollywood Genre History." *Film Criticism 22,* no. 1 (Fall 1997): 5–20.

Stedman, Raymond William. *The Serials: Suspense and Drama by Installment.* 2d ed. Norman: University of Oklahoma Press, 1977.

Suvin, Darko. *Metamorphoses of Science Fiction: On the Poetics and History of a Literary Genre.* New Haven: Yale University Press, 1979.

Symons, Julian. *Bloody Murder: From the Detective Story to the Crime Novel: A History.* Rev. ed. New York: Viking, 1985.

Taylor, John Russell. *Hitch: The Life and Times of Alfred Hitchcock.* New York: Pantheon, 1978.

Todorov, Tzvetan. *The Fantastic: A Structural Approach to a Literary Genre.* Trans. Richard Howard. Ithaca, N.Y.: Cornell University Press, 1975.

"The Typology of Detective Fiction." In Todorov, *The Poetics of Prose.* Trans. Richard Howard. Ithaca, N.Y.: Cornell University Press, 1977, pp. 42–52.

Truffaut, François. *Hitchcock.* New York: Simon & Schuster, 1967.

Tuska, Jon. *The Detective in Hollywood.* Garden City, N.Y.: Doubleday, 1978.

Twitchell, James B. *Dreadful Pleasures: An Anatomy of Modern Horror.* New York: Oxford University Press, 1985.

Van Dine, S. S. "I Used to Be a Highbrow but Look at Me Now." *American Magazine 106* (September 1928). Reprinted as "Twenty Rules for Writing Detective Stories" in Haycraft, ed., *Art of the Mystery Story,* pp. 189–93.

The Kennel Murder Case. New York: Charles Scribner's Sons, 1933; reprint ed., Boston: Gregg Press, 1980.

Waller, Gregory A. *The Living and the Undead: From Stoker's Dracula to Romero's Dawn of the Dead.* Urbana: University of Illinois Press, 1986.

ed. *American Horrors: Essays on the Modern American Horror Film.* Urbana: University of Illinois Press, 1987.

Warshow, Robert. "The Gangster as Tragic Hero." *Partisan Review* (February 1948). Reprinted in Warshow, *The Immediate Experience.* Garden City, New York: Doubleday, 1962; paperback ed., New York: Atheneum, 1979, pp. 127–33.

Waugh, Hillary. "The Police Procedural." In Ball, ed., *Mystery Story,* pp. 163–87.

Williams, Alan. "Is a Radical Genre Criticism Possible?" *Quarterly Review of Film Studies 9,* no. 2 (Spring 1984): 121–5.

Winks, Robin W., ed. *Detective Fiction: A Collection of Critical Essays.* Rev. ed. Englewood Cliffs, N.J.: Prentice–Hall, 1988.

Wood, Robin. *Hitchcock's Films.* Rev. ed. London: A. Zwemmer, 1969.

Hitchcock's Films Revisited. New York: Columbia University Press, 1989.

Hollywood from Vietnam to Reagan. New York: Columbia University Press, 1986.

Howard Hawks. Garden City, N.Y.: Doubleday, 1968.

"An Introduction to the American Horror Film." In *The American Nightmare: Essays on the Horror Film.* Eds. Robin Wood and Richard Lippe. Toronto: Festival of Festivals, 1979. Reprinted in Grant, ed., *Planks of Reason,* pp. 164–200. Excerpted as "Return of the Repressed," *Film Comment 14,* no. 4 (July–August 1978): 24–32.

Filmography/Videography

This stringent, chronological selection concentrates on (1) films discussed in detail or otherwise highlighted in the text and (2) films of special significance and influence in the history of the thriller. It is not intended to represent "The 100 Greatest Thrillers of All Time," "My Favorite Thrillers," or anything of the sort. Films made in widescreen processes (as indicated) will suffer even more degradation than usual in video, unless they are available in letterboxed format (common in laserdisc, uncommon but increasing in VHS). The customer should proceed cautiously when ordering public-domain titles that are available from numerous distributors, often in inferior dupe versions. Much of this information is likely to be outdated by the time it reaches the reader:

The Great Train Robbery (dir. Edwin S. Porter, 1903) Chase; Heist; Melodrama; Western
VHS: KINO (in "The Movies Begin: Vol. 1"), MOVIES (in "*The Great Train Robbery:* The Cinema Begins"), PYRAMID (in "The First Twenty Years: Part 2"), VIDEO (in "Cinema Begins")
Laser: n/a

The Girl and Her Trust (dir. D. W. Griffith, 1912) Chase; Melodrama; Western
VHS: KINO (in "The Movies Begin: Vol. 5")
Laser: FACETS (in "D. W. Griffith's Years of Discovery")

Juve contre Fantômas (episode 2 of *Fantômas*) (dir. Louis Feuillade, 1913) Melodrama; Serial
VHS: GLENN, HALF, NOSTALGIA
Laser: n/a

The Perils of Pauline (dir. Louis Gasnier and Donald MacKenzie, 1914) Adventure; Melodrama; Serial
VHS: GRAPEVINE, MOVIES, NOSTALGIA
Laser: n/a
Beware of inauthentic reedited versions and 1934 serial of the same name.

Les Vampires (dir. Louis Feuillade, 1915–16) Melodrama; Serial
VHS: FACETS
Laser: n/a

Dr. Mabuse, the Gambler (*Dr. Mabuse, der Spieler*) (dir. Fritz Lang, 1922) Gangster; Melodrama; Serial
VHS: FACETS, GERMAN, GRAPEVINE, MOORE, MOVIES, NOSTALGIA, SINISTER
Laser: n/a
  Distributed in two parts – 1: The Great Gambler, 2: Inferno.

Safety Last (dir. Fred Newmeyer and Sam Taylor, 1923) Thrill Comedy
VHS: FACETS, MOVIES
Laser: n/a

Girl Shy (dir. Fred Newmeyer and Sam Taylor, 1924) Thrill Comedy
VHS: FACETS, TIME–LIFE
Laser: n/a

Spies (*Spione*) (dir. Fritz Lang, 1928) Spy
VHS: FACETS, FESTIVAL, GERMAN, GRAPEVINE, KINO, NOSTALGIA, REPUBLIC, SINISTER, VIDEO
Laser: FACETS, FESTIVAL, IMAGE

Little Caesar (dir. Mervyn LeRoy, 1930) Gangster
VHS: CBS, FACETS, MGM, MOVIES, REPUBLIC
Laser: n/a

Dracula (dir. Tod Browning, 1931) Gothic; Horror
VHS: ADMIT, BARR, FACETS, HALF, HOLLYWOOD, MOORE, MOVIES, NOSTALGIA, SINISTER, TIMELESS, VIDEO
Laser: IMAGE

Frankenstein (dir. James Whale, 1931) Gothic; Horror
VHS: FACETS, HOME, MCA, MOVIES, REPUBLIC, TIME–LIFE
Laser: MCA

M (dir. Fritz Lang, 1931) Police; Psychological Crime
VHS: ADMIT, BARR, COLUMBIA, FACETS, FESTIVAL, HOLLYWOOD, MOVIES, NEW LINE, NOSTALGIA, SINISTER, TIMELESS, VIDEO
Laser: FACETS
  Restored version contains additional footage.

The Public Enemy (dir. William A. Wellman, 1931) Gangster
VHS: CBS, MGM, MOVIES, REPUBLIC
Laser: CBS

The Star Witness (dir. William A. Wellman, 1931) Gangster
VHS: n/a
Laser: n/a

Scarface (dir. Howard Hawks, 1932) Gangster
VHS: FACETS, MCA, MOVIES
Laser: FACETS, MCA

The Kennel Murder Case (dir. Michael Curtiz, 1933) Whodunit Detective
VHS: ALLIED, CABLE, CONGRESS, HOLLYWOOD, NOSTALGIA, SINISTER, VIDEO
Laser: n/a

Mystery of the Wax Museum (dir. Michael Curtiz, 1933) Gothic; Horror
VHS: FACETS, MGM, MIKE, MOVIES
Laser: n/a

The Man Who Knew Too Much (dir. Alfred Hitchcock, 1934) Spy
VHS: BARR, CABLE, CONGRESS, FACETS, HALF, HOLLYWOOD, MOORE, NOSTALGIA, REPUBLIC, SINISTER, VIDEO
Laser: IMAGE

Bride of Frankenstein (dir. James Whale, 1935) Gothic; Horror
VHS: FACETS, FESTIVAL, MCA, MIKE, MOVIES
Laser: FACETS, MCA

The 39 Steps (dir. Alfred Hitchcock, 1935) Spy
VHS: ALLIED, CONGRESS, FACETS, FESTIVAL, HALF, HOLLYWOOD, MOVIES, NEW LINE, NOSTALGIA, SINISTER, SULTAN, TIMELESS, VIDEO, WARNER
Laser: CRITERION, FACETS, FESTIVAL

Sabotage (dir. Alfred Hitchcock, 1936) Spy
VHS: BARR, CABLE, FACETS, HOLLYWOOD, MOVIES, NOSTALGIA, SINISTER, VIDEO
Laser: CRITERION, FACETS, IMAGE

Secret Agent (dir. Alfred Hitchcock, 1936) Spy
VHS: ALLIED, BARR, CABLE, CONGRESS, FACETS, HALF, HOLLYWOOD, MOVIES, NOSTALGIA, SINISTER, TIMELESS, VIDEO
Laser: FACETS

The Lady Vanishes (dir. Alfred Hitchcock, 1938) Spy
VHS: ALLIED, FACETS, FESTIVAL, HALF, HOLLYWOOD, MOVIES, NEW LINE, NOSTALGIA, SINISTER, SULTAN, VIDEO, WARNER
Laser: CRITERION, FACETS, FESTIVAL

The Maltese Falcon (dir. John Huston, 1941) Hard-boiled Detective
VHS: CBS, FACETS, FESTIVAL, MGM, MOVIES, REPUBLIC, TIME–LIFE
Laser: CBS, FACETS, FESTIVAL
  Beware colorized version.

Man Hunt (dir. Fritz Lang, 1941) Adventure; Spy
VHS: n/a
Laser: n/a

Saboteur (dir. Alfred Hitchcock, 1942) Spy
VHS: MCA, MOVIES
Laser: MCA

Double Indemnity (dir. Billy Wilder, 1944) Film Noir
VHS: FACETS, FESTIVAL, MCA, MOVIES
Laser: FACETS, FESTIVAL, MCA

Murder, My Sweet (dir. Edward Dmytryk, 1944) Film Noir; Hard-boiled Detective
VHS: FACETS, MEDIA, MOVIES, TIMELESS
Laser: IMAGE

The House on 92nd Street (dir. Henry Hathaway, 1945) Police; Semidocumentary; Spy
VHS: FOX, FUSION, MOVIES
Laser: n/a

Scarlet Street (dir. Fritz Lang, 1945) Film Noir
VHS: BARR, CABLE, CONGRESS, FACETS, HOLLYWOOD, MOVIES, NOSTALGIA, SINISTER, TIMELESS, TURNER, VIDEO
Laser: n/a
Beware colorized version.

The Big Sleep (dir. Howard Hawks, 1946) Hard-boiled Detective
VHS: COLUMBIA, CBS, FACETS, FESTIVAL, MGM, MOVIES, REPUBLIC
Laser: CBS, FACETS, MGM

The Killers (dir. Robert Siodmak, 1946) Detective; Film Noir; Heist
VHS: MOVIES
Laser: n/a

The Postman Always Rings Twice (dir. Tay Garnett, 1946) Film Noir
VHS: FACETS, FESTIVAL, MGM, MOVIES, REPUBLIC
Laser: FESTIVAL, MGM
Beware colorized version.

Call Northside 777 (dir. Henry Hathaway, 1947) Police; Semidocumentary
VHS: FACETS, FOX, MOVIES
Laser: n/a

Out of the Past (dir. Jacques Tourneur, 1947) Film Noir; Hard-boiled Detective
VHS: FACETS, MEDIA, TURNER
Laser: IMAGE

The Lady from Shanghai (dir. Orson Welles, 1948) Film Noir
VHS: COLUMBIA, FACETS, MIKE, MOVIES, REPUBLIC
Laser: COLUMBIA

The Naked City (dir. Jules Dassin, 1948) Police; Semidocumentary
VHS: FACETS, IVY, MOVIES
Laser: n/a

He Walked By Night (dir. Alfred Werker [and Anthony Mann], 1949)
Film Noir; Police; Semidocumentary
VHS: BARR, CONGRESS, FACETS, HALF, KINO, MOVIES, NOSTALGIA,
SINISTER, TIMELESS, VIDEO
Laser: n/a

The Third Man (dir. Carol Reed, 1949) Film Noir; Police; Spy
VHS: ANCHOR, FACETS, FESTIVAL, HALF, HOLLYWOOD, HOME, MEDIA,
MOVIES, NOSTALGIA, REPUBLIC, SINISTER, VIDEO, WARNER
Laser: CRITERION, FACETS, FESTIVAL

The Asphalt Jungle (dir. John Huston, 1950) Film Noir; Heist
VHS: FACETS, MGM, MOVIES
Laser: CRITERION, FACETS, MGM, PIONEER

Where the Sidewalk Ends (dir. Otto Preminger, 1950) Film Noir; Police;
Psychological Crime
VHS: n/a
Laser: n/a

The Enforcer (dir. Bretaigne Windust [and Raoul Walsh], 1951) Film
Noir; Gangster; Police
VHS: FACETS, MOVIES, REPUBLIC
Laser: PIONEER, REPUBLIC

Strangers on a Train (dir. Alfred Hitchcock, 1951) Film Noir;
Psychological Crime
VHS: FACETS, FESTIVAL, MIKE, MOVIES, WARNER
Laser: FACETS, FESTIVAL, WARNER
   "Restored" (i.e., British-release) version is not recommended (see
   Chapter 7).

On Dangerous Ground (dir. Nicholas Ray, 1952) Film Noir; Police
VHS: FACETS, TURNER
Laser: IMAGE

The Big Heat (dir. Fritz Lang, 1953) Gangster; Police
VHS: COLUMBIA, FACETS
Laser: IMAGE

Invaders from Mars (dir. William Cameron Menzies, 1953) Science
Fiction
VHS: ANCHOR, MEDIA, MIKE, MOVIES
Laser: IMAGE

Pickup on South Street (dir. Samuel Fuller, 1953) Anticommunist; Spy
VHS: CBS, FACETS, FOX, MOVIES
Laser: n/a

The Wages of Fear (*Le Salaire de la peur*) (dir. Henri-Georges Clouzot, 1953) Adventure; Film Noir
VHS: FACETS, FESTIVAL, HOLLYWOOD, HOME, MOVIES, NOSTALGIA, SINISTER, TIMELESS, VIDEO
Laser: CRITERION, FACETS, FESTIVAL
Restored (148-min.), subtitled version is strongly recommended.

Rear Window (dir. Alfred Hitchcock, 1954) Mystery
VHS: FACETS, FESTIVAL, HOME, MCA, TIME–LIFE
Laser: FACETS, MCA

Kiss Me Deadly (dir. Robert Aldrich, 1955) Film Noir; Hard-boiled Detective; Spy
VHS: FACETS, MGM, MOVIES, REPUBLIC
Laser: FACETS, MGM
"Special edition" includes alternative ending.

The Phenix City Story (dir. Phil Karlson, 1955) Gangster
VHS: n/a
Laser: n/a

Rififi (*Du Rififi chez les hommes*) (dir. Jules Dassin, 1955) Film Noir; Heist
VHS: FACETS, HOLLYWOOD, MOVIES, NOSTALGIA, VIDEO
Laser: n/a

Invasion of the Body Snatchers (dir. Don Siegel, 1956) Film Noir; Horror; Science Fiction
VHS: FACETS, MIKE, MOVIES, REPUBLIC
Laser: CRITERION, FACETS
Widescreen. Beware colorized version.

The Brothers Rico (dir. Phil Karlson, 1957) Gangster
VHS: n/a
Laser: n/a

The Incredible Shrinking Man (dir. Jack Arnold, 1957) Science Fiction
VHS: MCA, FACETS, MIKE, MOVIES
Laser: MCA

Touch of Evil (dir. Orson Welles, 1958) Film Noir; Police
VHS: FACETS, FESTIVAL, MCA, MOVIES
Laser: FACETS, FESTIVAL, MCA
108-min. restored version has largely supplanted 95-min. original-release version; reedited 111-min. 1998 version will likely supersede both.

Vertigo (dir. Alfred Hitchcock, 1958) Detective; Film Noir;
Psychological Crime
VHS: FACETS, FESTIVAL, MCA, MOVIES, TIME–LIFE
Laser: FACETS, FESTIVAL, MCA
*Widescreen. Restored version concerns image and sound quality rather
than length.*

Breathless (*À bout de souffle*) (dir. Jean-Luc Godard, 1959) Film Noir;
Gangster
VHS: CONNOISSEUR, FACETS, FESTIVAL, NOSTALGIA, MOORE, MOVIES,
TIMELESS
Laser: FACETS, FESTIVAL

Web of Passion (*À double tour;* a.k.a. *Leda*) (dir. Claude Chabrol, 1959)
Mystery
VHS: n/a
Laser: n/a

North by Northwest (dir. Alfred Hitchcock, 1959) Spy
VHS: FACETS, FESTIVAL, FUSION, MGM, MOVIES, TIME–LIFE
Laser: CRITERION, FACETS, FESTIVAL, MGM
Widescreen.

Peeping Tom (dir. Michael Powell, 1960) Psychological Crime
VHS: ADMIT, FACETS, FESTIVAL, HOME, MOVIES
Laser: FACETS

Psycho (dir. Alfred Hitchcock, 1960) Horror; Psychological Crime
VHS: FACETS, FESTIVAL, MCA, MOVIES, TIME–LIFE
Laser: FACETS, FESTIVAL, MCA

Shoot the Piano Player (*Tirez sur le pianiste*) (dir. François Truffaut,
1960) Film Noir; Gangster
VHS: CABLE, CONNOISSEUR, FACETS, FESTIVAL, HOLLYWOOD, HOME,
MOVIES, NOSTALGIA
Laser: CRITERION, FACETS, FESTIVAL
Widescreen.

Dr. No (dir. Terence Young, 1962) Adventure; Spy
VHS: FACETS, FOX, MGM, MOVIES, REPUBLIC, TIME–LIFE
Laser: CRITERION, FACETS, MGM

The Birds (dir. Alfred Hitchcock, 1963) Horror; Science Fiction
VHS: FACETS, MCA, MOVIES
Laser: FACETS, MCA

The Ipcress File (dir. Sidney J. Furie, 1965) Spy
VHS: FACETS, MCA
Laser: n/a
Widescreen

The Quiller Memorandum (dir. Michael Anderson, 1966) Spy
VHS: CBS, FOX, MOVIES
Laser: n/a
Widescreen.

Bullitt (dir. Peter Yates, 1968) Police
VHS: MOVIES, WARNER
Laser: WARNER
Widescreen.

Coogan's Bluff (dir. Don Siegel, 1968) Police
VHS: MOVIES, MCA
Laser: MCA

Night of the Living Dead (dir. George A. Romero, 1968) Horror;
Science Fiction
VHS: ADMIT, ALLIED, CABLE, FACETS, FUSION, HOLLYWOOD, MOORE,
MOVIES, NOSTALGIA, REPUBLIC, SINISTER, VIDEO
Laser: IMAGE, LANDMARK
Beware colorized version.

Rosemary's Baby (dir. Roman Polanski, 1968) Horror
VHS: FACETS, FESTIVAL, MIKE, MOVIES, PARAMOUNT
Laser: PARAMOUNT

On Her Majesty's Secret Service (dir. Peter Hunt, 1969) Spy
VHS: CBS, FACETS, MGM, MOVIES, TIME–LIFE
Laser: FACETS, MGM
Widescreen.

Dirty Harry (dir. Don Siegel, 1971) Police
VHS: FACETS, MOVIES, TIME–LIFE, WARNER
Laser: CRITERION, WARNER
Widescreen.

The French Connection (dir. William Friedkin, 1971) Police
VHS: CBS, FOX, FUSION, MOVIES
Laser: FOX

Shaft (dir. Gordon Parks, 1971) Black Action; Hard-boiled Detective
VHS: FACETS, MGM, MOVIES
Laser: n/a

Sweet Sweetback's Baad Asssss Song (dir. Melvin Van Peebles, 1971)
Black Action
VHS: MAGNUM, MOVIES, SUN
Laser: n/a

The Poseidon Adventure (dir. Ronald Neame, 1972) Adventure;
Disaster
VHS: CBS, FACETS, FOX, MOVIES
Laser: FOX
Widescreen.

The Exorcist (dir. William Friedkin, 1973) Horror
VHS: MOVIES, WARNER
Laser: WARNER

The Long Goodbye (dir. Robert Altman, 1973) Hard-boiled Detective
VHS: FACETS, MGM, MOVIES
Laser: FACETS, MGM
Widescreen.

Chinatown (dir. Roman Polanski, 1974) Hard-boiled Detective
VHS: FACETS, FESTIVAL, FUSION, MOVIES, PARAMOUNT
Laser: PARAMOUNT
Widescreen.

The Parallax View (dir. Alan J. Pakula, 1974) Conspiracy
VHS: MOVIES, PARAMOUNT
Laser: n/a
Widescreen.

The Texas Chain Saw Massacre (dir. Tobe Hooper, 1974) Horror
VHS: ANCHOR, FACETS, FUSION, MEDIA, MOVIES, MPI
Laser: FACETS, MPI

The Towering Inferno (dir. John Guillermin and Irwin Allen, 1974)
Disaster
VHS: CBS, FOX, MOVIES
Laser: FOX
Widescreen.

Black Christmas (dir. Bob Clark, 1975) Horror; Stalker
VHS: MOVIES, WARNER
Laser: n/a

Jaws (dir. Steven Spielberg, 1975) Adventure; Disaster; Horror; Stalker
VHS: FACETS, FESTIVAL, MCA, MOVIES
Laser: FESTIVAL, MCA
Widescreen.

Carrie (dir. Brian De Palma, 1978) Horror
VHS: CBS, MGM, MOVIES
Laser: CBS, CRITERION

Dawn of the Dead (dir. George A. Romero, 1978) Horror; Science Fiction
VHS: ANCHOR, FACETS, FUSION, MOVIES, REPUBLIC
Laser: FACETS, IMAGE, REPUBLIC
"Collector's Edition" contains additional footage.

Halloween (dir. John Carpenter, 1978) Horror; Stalker
VHS: ANCHOR, FACETS, MEDIA, MOVIES
Laser: IMAGE
Widescreen.

Martin (dir. George A. Romero, 1978) Horror
VHS: HBO, MOVIES
Laser: IMAGE

The Brood (dir. David Cronenberg, 1979) Horror
VHS: NEW LINE, SULTAN
Laser: n/a

Friday the 13th (dir. Sean S. Cunningham, 1980) Horror; Stalker
VHS: MOVIES, PARAMOUNT
Laser: PARAMOUNT

Body Heat (dir. Lawrence Kasdan, 1981) Neo-Noir
VHS: MOVIES, WARNER
Laser: WARNER
Widescreen.

Cutter's Way (dir. Ivan Passer, 1981) Mystery; Neo-Noir
VHS: FACETS, MGM, MOVIES
Laser: IMAGE

The Funhouse (dir. Tobe Hooper, 1981) Horror
VHS: MCA, MOVIES
Laser: MCA
Widescreen.

A Nightmare on Elm Street (dir. Wes Craven, 1984) Horror; Stalker
VHS: MEDIA, MOVIES, TIMELESS
Laser: IMAGE

Blue Velvet (dir. David Lynch, 1986) Neo-Noir
VHS: FACETS, FUSION, MOVIES, WARNER
Laser: FACETS, WARNER
Widescreen.

Basic Instinct (dir. Paul Verhoeven, 1992) Neo-Noir; Police; Sex Thriller
VHS: LIVE, MOVIES
Laser: PIONEER
Widescreen. Uncut, unrated version is recommended.

Pulp Fiction (dir. Quentin Tarantino, 1994) Gangster; Neo-Noir
VHS: BUENA, FACETS, MIRAMAX, MOVIES
Laser: BUENA, FACETS
Widescreen. "Special Collector's Edition" contains additional footage.

Heat (dir. Michael Mann, 1995) Heist; Police
VHS: MOVIES, WARNER
Laser: WARNER
Widescreen.

Distributors

Admit One Video Presentations
P.O. Box 66, Station O, Toronto, Ont., Canada M4A 2M8

Allied Artists Entertainment Group
3415 Sepulveda Blvd., Los Angeles CA 90034

Anchor Bay Entertainment/Video Treasures
500 Kirts Blvd., Troy MI 48084

Barr Films
12801 Schabarum, Irwindale CA 91706

Buena Vista Home Video c/o Walt Disney Home Video
500 South Buena Vista, Burbank CA 91521–7145

Cable Films
P.O. Box 7171, Country Club Station, Kansas City MO 64113

CBS/Fox Video (wholesale only; contact local video distributor)
P.O. Box 900, Beverly Hills CA 90213

Columbia Tristar Home Video (wholesale only; contact local video distributor)
Sony Pictures Plaza, 10202 W. Washington Blvd., Culver City CA 90232

Congress Entertainment/Congress Video Group
Learn Plaza, Suite 6, P.O. Box 845, Tannersville PA 18372–0845

Connoisseur Video Collection
1575 Westwood Blvd., Suite 305, Los Angeles CA 90024

Criterion Collection c/o The Voyager Company
1 Bridge Street, Irvington NY 10533–1543

Facets Multimedia
1517 W. Fullerton Ave., Chicago IL 60614

Festival Films
6115 Chestnut Terrace, Shorewood MN 55331

FoxVideo
2121 Avenue of the Stars, 25th Floor, Los Angeles CA 90067

Fusion Video
100 Fusion Way, Country Club Hills IL 60478

German Language Video Center
7625 Pendleton Pike, Indianapolis IN 46226–5298

Glenn Video Vistas
6924 Canby Ave., Suite 103, Reseda CA 91335

Grapevine Video
P.O. Box 46161, Phoenix AZ 85603

Half-Inch Heaven
4590 Santa Monica Blvd., Los Angeles CA 90029

HBO Video
1100 Avenue of the Americas, New York NY 10036

Hollywood Home Theatre
1540 N. Highland Ave., Suite 110, Hollywood CA 90028

Home Vision Cinema
5547 N. Ravenswood Ave., Chicago IL 60640–1199

Image Entertainment
9333 Oso Ave., Chatsworth CA 91311

Ivy Film/Video
P.O. Box 18376, Asheville NC 28814

Kino on Video
333 W. 39th St., Suite 503, New York NY 10018

Landmark Laservision
12636 Beatrice St., P.O. Box 66930, Los Angeles CA 90066

Live Entertainment/Vestron (wholesale only; contact local video distributor)
15400 Sherman Way, P.O. Box 10124, Van Nuys CA 91410–0124

MCA/Universal Home Video (wholesale only; contact local video distributor)
70 Universal City Plaza, Universal City CA 91608–9955

Magnum Entertainment
9650 De Soto Ave. #M, Chatsworth CA 91311–5012

Media Home Entertainment
510 W. 6th St., Suite 1032, Los Angeles CA 90014

MGM/UA Home Entertainment (wholesale only; contact local video distributor)
2500 Broadway, Santa Monica CA 90404–6061

Mike LeBell's Video
75 Freemont Pl., Los Angeles CA 90005

Miramax Pictures Home Video
500 S. Buena Vista St., Burbank CA 91521

Moore Video
P.O. Box 5703, Richmond VA 23220

Movies Unlimited
3015 Darnell Road, Philadelphia PA 19154–3295

MPI Home Video
16101 S. 108th Ave., Orland Park IL 60462

n/a
Not available, as far as could be determined at the time this list was compiled.

New Line Home Video
116 N. Robertson Blvd., Los Angeles CA 90048

Nostalgia Family Video
P.O. Box 606, Baker City OR 97814

Paramount Home Video (wholesale only; contact local video distributor)
Bludhorn Bldg., 5555 Melrose Ave., Los Angeles CA 90038

Pioneer Laser Entertainment c/o LDC America
2265 E. 220th St., P.O. Box 22782, Long Beach CA 90810

Pyramid Film and Video
2801 Colorado Ave., Santa Monica CA 90404

Republic Pictures Home Video (wholesale only; contact local video distributor)
5700 Wilshire Blvd., Suite 525, Los Angeles CA 90036

Sinister Cinema
P.O. Box 4369, Medford OR 97501–0168

Sultan Entertainment
116 N. Robertson Blvd., Los Angeles CA 90048

Sun Video
15 Donnybrook, Demarest NJ 07627

Time-Life Video and Television
1450 E. Parham Rd., Richmond VA 23280

Timeless Video
10010 Canoga Ave., #B-2, Chatsworth CA 91311

Turner Home Entertainment (wholesale only; contact local video distributor)
Box 105366, Atlanta GA 35366

Video Yesteryear
Box C, Sandy Hook CT 06482

Warner Home Video (wholesale only; contact local video distributor)
4000 Warner Blvd., Burbank CA 91522

Index

N.B.: Titles of works refer to films unless otherwise indicated. Movie titles are followed by release date and director. Boldface page numbers refer to illustrations.

Curtiz, Michael, 77, 183, 201; *see also*
    Kennel Murder Case, The; Mildred
    Pierce; Mystery of the Wax Museum
Cushing, Peter, 152
Cutter's Way (1981, Ivan Passer), 34, 171,
    172–4

Dall, John, 207
Daly, Carroll John, 189
Damien – Omen II (1978, Don Taylor), 156,
    160
Dandy in Aspic, A (1968, Anthony Mann
    [and Laurence Harvey]), 135, 136
Dannay, Frederic, 182
Dante's Peak (1997, Roger Donaldson), 150
D'Antoni, Philip, 138, 245
Dark Corner, The (1946, Henry Hathaway),
    88
Das Kabinett des Dr. Caligari, see Cabinet of
    Dr. Caligari, The
Dassin, Jules, 121, 122, 165; *see also Naked*
    City, The; Rififi; Topkapi
Davis, Brian, 9, 259
Dawn of the Dead (1978, George A.
    Romero), 156, 157–9, **159**
Day, William Patrick, 40, 43
Day of the Animals (1977, William Girdler),
    118
Day of the Jackal, The (1973, Fred Zinne-
    mann), 32, 34
    book (1971), 32
Day the Earth Stood Still, The (1951, Robert
    Wise), 110
Dead Heat on a Merry-Go-Round (1966,
    Bernard Girard), 123
Deadly Affair, The (1967, Sidney Lumet),
    135, 136
Death Wish (1974, Michael Winner), 144
de Corsia, Ted, **99**
Defector, The (1966, Raoul Levy), 134
"Defence of Detective Stories, A" (essay,
    1901), 13–16, 201; *see also* Chesterton,
    G. K.
Defendant, The (book, 1901), 13–14
Defiant Ones, The (1958, Stanley Kramer),
    146
de Havilland, Olivia, 53–4
Deighton, Len, 133, 134, 230
Demme, Jonathan, 12, 117; *see also Silence*
    of the Lambs, The
Demolition Man (1993, Marco Brambilla),
    144
De Niro, Robert, 34, 144
Denning, Michael, 85, 136, 226, 227–8
D'entre les morts (book, 1956), 206
De Palma, Brian, 117, 118, 127, 170; *see also*
    Carrie; Fury, The; Mission: Impossible
Depression, Great, 72, 79

Der letze Mann, see Last Laugh, The
Der müde Tod, see Destiny
de Rochemont, Louis, 97
Derry, Charles, 9–10, 259, 260
Desperate Hours, The (1955, William Wyler),
    77
Destination Moon (1950, Irving Pichel), 110
Destiny (*Der müde Tod*) (1921, Fritz Lang),
    236
Detective, The (1968, Gordon Douglas), 138
detective genre, 4, 9, 10, 13–16, 20, 54, 56,
    79, 92, 98, 100, 104, 118, 119, 164, 171,
    220, 226, 227, 242–4, 261, 262
    B-movie series, 87, 183, 190
    classical (or "whodunit") variety, 4, 6, 9,
    12, 25, 27, 32, 181–3, 185–8, 190, 193–
    202, 203–5, 212, 228
    early history, 42–3, 182, 266
    hard-boiled (or "thriller") variety, 4, 9,
    22, 25, 39, 53, 87–9, 92–4, 96, 116, 128,
    181–2, 186, 188–90, 193–202, 203, 205,
    206, 212, 263, 266
    inverted variety, 205
    locked-room variety, 183
    revisionist variety, 147–8, 170
    urban dimension, 14–15, 21, 73, 89, 187,
    201, 227, 255
Detour (1945, Edgar G. Ulmer), 92, 94–5
Diabolique (*Les Diaboliques*) (1955, Henri-
    Georges Clouzot), 120
Dial M for Murder (1954, Alfred Hitchcock),
    207
Diamonds Are Forever (1971, Guy Hamil-
    ton), 130, 132
Dickstein, Morris, 209, 240
Die Büchse der Pandora, see Pandora's Box
Die Hard (1988, John McTiernan), 255
    film series (1988–95), 144
Die Herrin der Welt, see Mistress of the
    World, The
Die Spinnen, see Spiders, The
Dika, Vera, 165
Dirty Harry (1971, Don Siegel), 60, 137, 140,
    142–4, **143**, 244, 245, 252–3, 255
Dirty Little Billy (1972, Stan Dragoti), 146
disaster movies, 4, 149–50, 156, 161, 263,
    267
Disclosure (1994, Barry Levinson), 176
Dix, Otto, 64
D.O.A. (1950, Rudolph Maté), 77, 172
D.O.A. (1988, Rocky Morton and Annabel
    Jankel), 172
Donat, Robert, 86
Donnie Brasco (1997, Mike Newell), 230
Dostoyevsky, Fyodor, 10, 186
Double Indemnity (1944, Billy Wilder), 91,
    102
Douglas, Michael, 177